CW00956445

The Cambridge Introduction to
British Romantic Poetry

The best way to learn about Romantic poetry is to plunge in and read a few Romantic poems. This book guides the new reader through this experience, focusing on canonical authors – Wordsworth, Coleridge, Byron, Keats, Blake, and Shelley – and including less familiar figures as well. Each chapter explains the history and development of a genre or sets out an important context for the poetry, with a wealth of practical examples. Michael Ferber emphasizes connections between poets as they responded to each other and to the great literary, social, and historical changes around them. A unique appendix resolves most difficulties new readers of works from this period might face: unfamiliar words, unusual word order, the subjunctive mood, and meter. This enjoyable and stimulating book is an ideal introduction to some of the most powerful and pleasing poems in the English language, written in one of the greatest periods in English poetry.

MICHAEL FERBER is Professor of English and Humanities at the University of New Hampshire.

The Cambridge Introduction to
British Romantic Poetry

MICHAEL FERBER

CAMBRIDGE
UNIVERSITY PRESS

CAMBRIDGE
UNIVERSITY PRESS

University Printing House, Cambridge CB2 8BS, United Kingdom

Cambridge University Press is part of the University of Cambridge.

It furthers the University's mission by disseminating knowledge in the pursuit of education, learning and research at the highest international levels of excellence.

www.cambridge.org
Information on this title: www.cambridge.org/9780521154376

© Michael Ferber 2012

This publication is in copyright. Subject to statutory exception and to the provisions of relevant collective licensing agreements, no reproduction of any part may take place without the written permission of Cambridge University Press.

First published 2012

A catalogue record for this publication is available from the British Library

Library of Congress Cataloguing in Publication data
Ferber, Michael.
    The Cambridge introduction to British romantic poetry / Michael Ferber.
        p. cm. – (Cambridge introductions to literature)
    Includes bibliographical references and index.
    ISBN 978-0-521-76906-8 (hardback) - ISBN 978-0-521-15437-6 (paperback)
    1. English poetry – 19th century – History and criticism   2. English poetry – 20th century – History and criticism   3. Romanticism – Great Britain.   I. Title.
    PR590.F48 2012
    821.709 – dc23   2012000286

ISBN 978-0-521-76906-8 Hardback
ISBN 978-0-521-15437-6 Paperback

Cambridge University Press has no responsibility for the persistence or accuracy of URLs for external or third-party internet websites referred to in this publication, and does not guarantee that any content on such websites is, or will remain, accurate or appropriate.

Contents

Preface

The texts of poems which I quote in their entirety are taken from facsimiles or older editions no longer in copyright, or from Literature Online, which also uses texts in the public domain. I have usually checked them against more recent editions and found only slight variations in spelling or punctuation. I have sometimes modified the source text in ways that agree with recent editorial practice, for example, changing "oh" to "O" several times in Shelley's "Ode to the West Wind" ("oh" seems more appropriate to an exclamation, "O" to a direct address, though they are arguably both at once). Occasionally I discuss variations in punctuation where they might bear on how we interpret a passage, for example, the final two lines of Keats's "Ode on a Grecian Urn," but by and large the variations seem of small importance in an introduction to the poems.

In the Further Reading section I recommend good (and affordable) recent editions of each poet. A few of these are the scholarly standard, but in some cases, such as Coleridge, the most exactingly edited editions are too cumbersome (and expensive) for most readers. That is not to deny that the different editorial philosophies invoked by different editors make for interesting debates: Use the earliest version of a poem or the latest, or something in between? Correct the final printed version with probably intended emendations in a notebook, or let it stand? Modernize punctuation and spelling or keep it in the original form? Indent lines to reflect the rhyme scheme or not? Readers of this book needn't worry about these issues, but if they find something ambiguous or puzzling in any of the texts, they might find something intriguing about it if they look it up in the modern scholarly editions.

Acknowledgments

For reading all or most of the chapters and making many helpful comments I am grateful to Susan Arnold, James Finley, and Martin McKinsey. For suggestions on the Appendix, my thanks go to Greg Olsen.

Introduction

This is a book about Romantic poetry written in Britain from the 1780s to the 1830s. By the middle of this period many readers of poetry, and many poets themselves, felt that theirs was a time when poetry had grown great again, comparable to the age of Shakespeare and Spenser two centuries earlier. As Keats stated it in the opening line of one of his sonnets (1817), "Great spirits now on earth are sojourning." Today, after two more centuries, most of those who care about poetry would agree. The most often anthologized poem in English, William Blake's "The Tyger," comes from this time (1794), and so do many of the most often quoted poetic passages: "Water, water, every where, / Nor any drop to drink"; "I wandered lonely as a cloud"; "O my luve's like a red, red rose"; "She walks in beauty, like the night / Of cloudless climes and starry skies"; "Hail to thee, blithe spirit"; "Beauty is truth, truth beauty." To some it feels as if poetry *is* Romantic poetry, while the prevalent caricature of "the poet" today is of someone impractical, bohemian, otherworldly, visionary, and young, that is, a "Romantic."

None of the poets we discuss in this book, however, called himself or herself "Romantic." None of them even denied being Romantic, as the word was unavailable until late in the period as a term for a literary school or movement. They would have been astonished to be lumped together under any label, for their differences from each other loomed larger in their minds than their similarities, which are easier for us to see at a distance. Various labels were pasted on various groups, sometimes by those who disliked them. Wordsworth, Coleridge, and Southey were called the "Lake School" because they were friends who lived in the Lake District of England. Keats, Hazlitt

1

(an essayist), and Leigh Hunt were called the "Cockney School" because they were friends who lived in London. Byron and Shelley were called the "Satanic School" because they were friends who lived in hell, or would live there soon. (It was Southey who came up with this last term; for his part, Byron reduced the "Lake School" to the "Pond School.") Apart from the labels themselves, some of those lumped together were displeased to be so lumped. Southey, for instance, when he learned in 1803 that an important reviewer had placed him in a "new school" (not yet dubbed "Lake School"), wrote that there is no "stronger proof of want of discernment or want of candour than in grouping together three men so different in style as Wordsworth, Coleridge and myself under one head." Coleridge made a similar claim many years later.[1] There was no overall "Romantic School."

"Romantic"

The word "romantic" had been in use in English for well over a century as an adjective based on "romance," the literary genre descended from the chivalric stories of the Middle Ages, such as the tales of King Arthur and his knights. That word comes from Old French *romaunt* or *romaunz*, among other spellings, which meant a work written in a "Romance" language (French, Provençal, or the others), that is, in the spoken vernacular language as distinct from Latin, which had been more or less frozen and confined to the learned members of church, court, and university. That seems odd at first, since "romance" goes back to an adverb meaning "in the Roman manner," and the Romans spoke Latin. In its earliest usage, however, "romance" referred to the daughter (or daughters) of Latin actually spoken in Gallia (Gaul), as opposed to Frankish, the Germanic language of its conquerors. The Franks gave their name to the land (Francia, now France) but gave up speaking Frankish and adopted the local Romance tongue, whereupon the latter took on the name "French." But the literature written in it continued to be called "romances," and they were typically filled with adventurous knights, distressed damsels, evil magicians, fiery dragons, and wild landscapes. So as the adjective "romantic" entered English it brought these associations with it. English, after all, had not been short of romances, and indeed the eighteenth century saw a revival of interest in them, notably in Spenser's *The Faerie Queene* (1596). The poets we now call Romantic used the word in extended senses to refer both to romances themselves and to the sort of thing you find in them. Wordsworth considered devoting himself to writing "some old / Romantic tale, by Milton left unsung" (1805 *Prelude* 1.179–80). In Kubla Khan's garden, as Coleridge imagined it, was "a deep romantic chasm" (12). Several poets, including Byron, called Spain "romantic," as tourism ads still do.

It was in Germany around 1800, in the circle around the Schlegel brothers in Jena, that the distinction between "romantic" and "classic" literature was established. In lectures given in 1808 and 1809, August Wilhelm Schlegel described "romantic" literature, which included Shakespeare, as modern, Christian, and filled with infinite desire, as opposed to the more contained and "perfect" literature of the Greeks and Romans and their modern imitators. Coleridge, who kept abreast of German thinking, was soon drawing a similar contrast in his own lectures, though they were not published until 1836. A greater influence in Britain and throughout Europe was Madame Germaine de Staël's book *On Germany*, translated from French into English in 1813. In 1815 Wordsworth distinguished the "classic lyre" from the "romantic harp," while in every language of the Continent the classic–romantic distinction became the hot literary topic of the day. It was nonetheless not for another generation that some of the poets we now call Romantic were so named, and not till the end of the century that all of them (except Blake) were regularly grouped together. Blake was not fully admitted into the Romantic canon until the middle of the twentieth century. Scott had been among the central members of it, but has now receded to secondary status.

Even among specialists a confusion prevails between "Romantic" as a period term, referring, say, to the time between 1789 and 1832 (dates set by political events), or to a whole century between 1750 and 1850, and "Romantic" as a set of norms, styles, and themes that characterize certain writers of the time but not all. The titles of recent anthologies reveal the confusion: *Romanticism*, *Romantic Poetry*, *English Romantic Verse*, and *Romantic Women Poets* on the one hand; *The Age of Romanticism*, *Romantic Period Verse*, and *British Women Poets of the Romantic Era* on the other. It is made worse by the famously difficult problem of defining "Romanticism" as a norm or mode. Even though a consensus has been reached, from time to time, on who the Romantics are, there has been no agreed definition of the term that defines them: an illogical state of affairs, to be sure, but one we have been muddling along with for more than half a century. The problem can be reduced if not eliminated, I think, by dispensing with the tacit assumption that definitions must be brief. If we can do so, I would propose something like this:

> Romanticism was a European cultural movement, or set of kindred
> movements, which found in a symbolic and internalized romance plot
> a vehicle for exploring one's self and its relationship to others and to
> nature, which gave privilege to the imagination as a faculty higher and
> more inclusive than reason, which sought solace in or reconciliation

with the natural world, which "detranscendentalized" religion by taking
God or the divine as inherent in nature or in the soul and replaced theological doctrine with metaphor and feeling, which honored poetry and
all the arts as the highest human creations, and which rebelled against
the established canons of neoclassical aesthetics and against both aristocratic and bourgeois social and political norms in favor of values more
individual, inward, and emotional.[2]

That is a mouthful, and not every expert will chew it happily. The clauses about
nature and the natural world leave out Blake, for whom the word "Nature" is
always negative; the clause about imagination might exclude Byron, who made
little ado about it. But it will do for a start, in order to have something in mind
as we look at individual poets and poems. Its various clauses will find many
illustrations in the chapters that follow. This book, in any case, is governed by
the idea that Romanticism was a distinct movement or trend, and that during
the period of its first flourishing (it has never disappeared) it was by no means
dominant: there were quite a few readers and writers who were impervious or
even hostile to it.

Sensibility

Some accounts of Romanticism, following the Schlegels' early definitions, contrast it with "Classicism" (or "Neoclassicism"), the literary movement of about
1660 to 1770 that took Latin poets, notably Horace and Virgil, as their models and imitated the restraint, impersonality, formal balance, wit, and grace
it found in classical culture. The two great English poets of this trend were
John Dryden and Alexander Pope. Other accounts contrast Romanticism
with "The Enlightenment" or "The Age of Reason," more or less contemporary
with Classicism and consonant with it, that saw in the achievements of Isaac
Newton in physics a model for understanding almost everything in the natural
world, and even the social world, and took the philosophy of John Locke as the
basis of understanding the human mind. Between them these two intellectual
movements encouraged reasonableness, detachment, prudence, tolerance of
religious differences, civility, formal elegance, and an aristocratic breadth of
view, though even the greatest writers of this persuasion were not always so
serenely one-sided.

If these schools of thought serve as clarifying foils for the concept
of Romanticism, another movement served as the matrix from which
Romanticism arose. Literary historians identify a distinct trend they call
"Sensibility" or "Pre-Romanticism" and date it from about 1730, though like

any other trend it has earlier precedents, and it overlapped with Romanticism well into the nineteenth century. The word "sensibility," the most frequent word for the faculty it honored, did not mean "sensibleness" but something closer to "sensitivity," a tender responsiveness to the beauty and especially the suffering of the social and natural world. The philosophers, novelists, and poets of this movement believed that our moral and social being depends on feeling much more than on reason or obedience to religious codes, and the highest kind of feeling is "sympathy" or benevolent fellow feeling. Tears ran down the cheeks of many literary characters both male and female and of many of their read-ers as well. The epistolary novel, or novel in letters, gained new prominence: Samuel Richardson's *Pamela; or, Virtue Rewarded* (1740–1) and *Clarissa; or, History of a Young Lady* (1747–8), were enormously popular; readers identified passionately with their beleaguered heroines and wallowed in their long and intimate examinations of their minds and hearts. The "Graveyard" poets, espe-cially Gray with his "Elegy Written in a Country Churchyard" (1751), the most admired English poem of the time, promoted a cult of "melancholy," where sympathy for suffering was refined by meditations among the dead. Thomas Warton, Jr., had already written "The Pleasures of Melancholy" (1747), the title of which suggests a kind of indulgence or deliberate cultivation of sad but kindly feelings. Poems of this kind are the ancestors of the meditative poems of the Romantics. The Ossian cult, too, as we shall see in Chapter 2, flourished in the fertile ground of Sensibility. A new appreciation for the imaginative and distinctive world of childhood, and a new concern for the mistreatment of children and animals, arose as natural extensions of the Sensibility domain.

As early as 1711 the Earl of Shaftesbury argued that we have an innate "moral sense" rather like taste, and that it has much more to do with our moral char-acter than with reason or obedience to a code of laws. This faculty can be cul-tivated, and as it grows we reconcile conflicting passions and harmonize them with reason. After a century of investigation in philosophy and exploration in literature the idea of the "beautiful soul" emerged, especially in Germany with the writings of Friedrich Schiller. For Schiller *die schöne Seele* is a soul that achieves a harmony between duty and inclination, or reason and sensuality, and expresses it as grace.[3]

Sometimes the poets we call Romantic can sound "sensible" or sensitive in this spirit. Wordsworth's meditations on rural tragedy and Byron's among the ruins of castles and colosseums; the poems about children by Blake and Wordsworth; and poems about suffering poets by Coleridge, Shelley, and Keats – these continue Sensibility's themes and attitudes. Wordsworth considered his mission to be the opening of the human heart or the culti-vation of human feelings, though he also stressed the importance of deep thought and the goal of philosophic calm. Many if not all of the women poets of the Romantic period seem better described as poets of Sensibility than as Romantics, though there is room for debate. Romanticism has even been defined as an episode within the larger and longer movement of Sensibility. Yet the Romantics also reacted against the cult of Sensibility. Some felt it pictured the soul as too passive and helpless before external experience, and could not serve as the basis for a moral life. Coleridge in 1796 wrote, "Sensibility is not Benevolence. Nay, by making us tremblingly alive to trifling misfortunes, it frequently prevents it and induces effeminate and cowardly selfishness." The imagination, the faculty most praised and discussed by the Romantics, is not a passive receptor of images or a trigger of emotions, but an active, creative force. All of the major British Romantics, too, were politically aware and engaged in ways untypical of Sensibility. They understood that melting with sympathy could be no more than a moment in one's path of commitment to social change. This is not to say that the Romantics were always effective agents of such change – far from it – but at least they thought and sometimes acted in a sphere larger than their own hearts, the point where the earlier movement had usually stalled. They hoped, at least between bouts of despair, that they could bring about a new social order, and that poetry and the arts could be a means to doing so. In this ambition they transcend the terms of Sensibility.

The canon

Today most anthologies and university courses dwell largely on the "Big Six" male Romantic poets – Blake, Wordsworth, Coleridge, Byron, Shelley, and Keats – and this book will do the same. It is important to remember, however, that this canon does not correspond to any list that a contemporary reader or reviewer would have come up with. It was not established until about 1950, and it has been under assault ever since. In the last forty years feminist scholars, for instance, have brought to light from nearly total neglect a number of women poets, many of whom were well known and much admired in their time, such as Felicia Hemans (who remained popular throughout the nineteenth century), Charlotte Smith, Letitia Landon, and Mary Robinson. There has been a recent effort to bring John Clare into the circle, largely because of his charming and well-observed nature poems, as well as Robert Burns, always cherished among the Scots but only loosely linked to the "major" Romantics; Walter Scott, whose poetry once seemed central and is now somewhat neglected, may be due for a revival.

It is a commonplace among literary historians today that the Romantic canon – the approved or received list of major poets – is (like every other canon) an arbitrary construction, motivated by changeable and subjective tastes, by moral, religious, and political beliefs, by conspiracies of men to exclude women, by the convenience of publishers and universities, or by sheer habit and laziness, and that it is not a set of the objectively best or most important poets. In my view this widespread opinion badly overstates the matter. While it is true that these motives can sometimes be found, and rightly assailed, and true, too, that the notion of "objective" literary value runs into great philosophical difficulties, it does not follow that the Big Six have not earned their way into the top echelon. By almost any standards that poetry lovers still invariably invoke – originality, wit, depth and complexity of thought, density of metaphor, memorability of phrasing, musicality of sound, intensity of effect, warmth of feeling – the occupants of seats in the current canon still seem preeminent. These standards may be "arbitrary" in that they cannot be grounded in some ultimate and universal set of values, but they have been widely held among many generations of readers, even among those who like to shoot down the received canon. To most readers of poetry outside the academy, as well as to most professors who teach it, these poets still seem the most rewarding, the ones most patient of frequent revisitings, the ones who "speak to our condition," as the Quakers put it, most poignantly. All six wrote some poor poems, even embarrassing ones, and many of the others jostling for attention wrote some fine ones, but all in all it is not arbitrary to dwell on the Six more than the others. Life is short, and, except for English professors, people who still love poetry do not have time to read everything. There is no avoiding a canon of some sort. This book is also short, and must exclude much more than it includes.

That said, it is better to err on the side of generosity, and some of the not quite or not yet canonical poets deserve a place in an introduction, not only because of the intrinsic interest of their poems but also because they help us see the major poets in new lights. So I will try to pay some attention to them, inadequate to be sure, but perhaps no more inadequate than my discussions of all but a few poems of the Six.

This book is titled *British Romantic Poetry* rather than *English Romantic Poetry*. Most of the poets in it were English, including five of the Six. Byron, however, had Scottish roots on his mother's side, and spent much of his childhood in Scotland. Scott and Burns, of course, were Scottish, and Burns even wrote in Scots English. Byron's friend Thomas Moore was Irish; he was much admired in England while emerging as the beloved bard of Ireland. Even among entirely English writers, moreover, there was a growing interest in the ancient Scottish, Irish, and Welsh poetic traditions. Scotland and Wales, at least, were often called "romantic" for their mountainous scenery and mysterious legends. A key instigation of early Romanticism, as will be discussed in Chapter 2, was the "discovery" by James Macpherson of the epics of the ancient Gaelic poet Ossian still sung in the Scottish Highlands; his publication in 1760 of prose translations of "fragments" of this "Northern Homer" caused a sensation across Europe. Even after they were shown to be largely the inventions of Macpherson, they continued to fascinate; Coleridge and Byron both made verse versions of Ossianic passages, and Blake not only sounds like Ossian in his diction and cadences but adapted at least one of his plots.

Reading the Romantics

The best introduction to Romantic poetry is simply to plunge in and read some Romantic poems. There is no great mystery about most of them; they yield readily to attentive reading without special preparation. William Blake's longer poems bristle with outlandish names that play parts in obscure allegories, and a few of Shelley's poems are intricate in syntax. Some of the targets of the satirical poems, though at the time they were on everyone's lips, now require footnotes. Footnotes, too, as found in most anthologies today, will give new readers the help they need with allusions to events, quotations of previous literature, and words whose meanings have changed during the last two hundred years. But, with the partial exception of Blake, virtually all the poetry of the era of Romanticism is still readily accessible. In its day, after all, it was meant to be understood by a large reading public.

And a large reading public it was, larger even in absolute terms than it is today in Britain or anywhere else, I think, in the anglophone world. More volumes of verse were published than novels, quite the opposite of today's figures. Newspapers and journals regularly carried poems, often on public themes, such as a speech by a Member of Parliament or a battle in Europe. Wordsworth, whom we think of as the timeless poet of nature and human suffering, regularly launched verse missiles to the papers on such current topics as Toussaint L'Ouverture's revolt in St. Domingo or the Tyrolese resistance to the French. Verse satires were snapped up and relished, or angrily replied to in new satires, in great numbers. Bookshop sales of poetry by the most popular poets exceeded the wildest dreams of poets now: Scott's *Marmion* (1808) sold out its first (and very expensive) edition of 2,000 copies in two months, Byron's *The Corsair* (1814) sold out its entire first printing of 10,000 copies in a single day, while the satirist "Peter Pindar" (John Wolcot), now almost forgotten, doubled even that. In any one year during the Romantic period perhaps three thousand poets were active, of whom about one-fourth were women, in a British population of about ten million.[4]

Accessible though most of it was, it was still poetry, and most poetry in English until the twentieth century was written in a poetic language that differed in many little ways from the language spoken by its readers. Even today, as the American poet Kenneth Koch has claimed, there is a special language of poetry, "a language within a language," where, for instance, the sounds of the language are very important and metaphor is routine.[5] On the other hand, the diction of poems today, the set of words found in them, usually differs little from our everyday spoken vocabulary, or what the mid-twentieth-century English poet John Wain has called "stumbling anyday speech," whereas in 1800 it often differed a great deal.[6] Wordsworth, it is true, in his "Preface" to the 1800 edition of *Lyrical Ballads*, made a case for using "the very language of men" in poetry, as against the elaborate and archaic poetic diction and abnormal phrase structures that were the peculiar inheritance of poets at that time; poetry and prose, he wrote, should have "the same human blood" circulating through them. In his own poems in this collection, especially the ballads, he by and large practiced what he preached, and he had a great influence on poetry after him. Nor was he alone, nor even the first, to move poetry toward a more current and homely diction. Yet the revolution was far from complete, and even Wordsworth relapsed at times into more ornate styles. Many readers still appreciated the traditional formalities of poetry, even as they welcomed more "prosaic" words and syntax.

Not only was there a poetic "language within a language," which the Romantics could deploy as they saw fit, but the outer language, the spoken English of the day, was not the language we speak now, though we call them both English. Nor was there a single dialect of English spoken throughout the United Kingdom. To this day there are dialects of English almost incomprehensible to my American ears; in 1800, when a Cornishman met a Yorkshireman they must each have thought the other was speaking Dutch or something. There was a standard written form, centered on London and Oxford–Cambridge, with certain conventions of spelling, punctuation, and diction, but for nearly all Britons even in London it was a second language, not a mother tongue. (Even in his ballads, Wordsworth made little effort to respell the words of the local Cumberland dialect to reveal their real pronunciation; they are assimilated into the national literary conventions.) In any case, much has changed during the last two centuries and more. To choose a word almost at random, "awful" did not mean "very bad," as it does today, but "awe-inspiring," "terrifying," "majestic," or "sublime." The modern sense, which seems to have been an Americanism, was noted in the 1830s. Indeed "awful" and "awe-some" were synonyms in 1800; now, ever since the Valley Girls' slang swept across America in the 1980s, they are antonyms. Most editions of Romantic poems will annotate "awful" and other such words, but students should get in the habit of consulting the full-sized *Oxford English Dictionary*, in paper or on line, for any word that strikes them as unusual or interesting.

These problems are not great, and it does not take long to learn the language, and the language within the language, of 1800. There are a few obstacles, however, that my students have often stumbled over. The chief of these is the use of "thou" and "thee" and "ye" and "you" as apparently random variants for the second-person pronoun. But of course that is not what they are. "Thou" and "thee" are singular, "ye" and "you" are plural; "thou" and "ye" are subjects, "thee" and "you" are objects. Dislocated word order provides other puzzles, especially when the verb is postponed to the end of a clause (and usually a line). And poetry tended to make greater use of the subjunctive mood than we do today, sometimes with ambiguous forms. Readers who want to refresh their knowledge of these matters may have a look at the Appendix in the back of this book.

Texts and contexts

The Romantic movement gave us some of the greatest poems in English (as it did in German, French, Italian, Spanish, Polish, Russian, and other European languages), but even if all its poems were mediocre the era of Romanticism would still be fascinating. The two great revolutions that define the modern world began then, and have not ended yet: the French Revolution of 1789, temporarily defeated in 1815, and the industrial revolution, which began in Britain around 1775 with the invention of the steam engine. The war that resulted from the French Revolution lasted twenty-four years, with Britain a belligerent for nearly all of it; it truly deserves the name World War I for its global scope and enormous battles. The British Empire, set back in 1781, was expanding again almost everywhere. Capitalism, now empowered by steam and a raft of new inventions, was steadily eliminating or marginalizing the remnants of feudalism. Science was on the march, especially in chemistry, electricity, and geology. The population was growing; London reached a million residents by about 1800. The two leading occupations for centuries – agriculture and domestic service – were beginning to yield to factory work. Demands for political reform rose to a near revolutionary pitch in the 1790s, and then again in the 1830s. Women still lacked most rights, but their subservience to men was under challenge by such brave writers as Mary Wollstonecraft. Slavery was abolished by the French in 1794; the slave trade was declared illegal by Parliament in 1807. Relations between England and the Celtic nations that made up the United Kingdom were complex; Ireland in particular was an unending source of conflict.

These and many other developments are inescapable contexts for the poetry of the time. Our poets were well aware of them, and weighed in on most of them. Even after they claimed to forswear politics and take refuge in rural scenery some event would draw them indignantly back into the fray. The more you know about the times the more interesting you will find the poems. With the exception of a chapter on the figures of the poet and poetess and a chapter on the French Revolution, however, this book is not organized around themes, contexts, or dates. It tries to keep the poems in the forefront, and to bring in historical contexts where they are most useful for understanding them. Many textbooks will have sections on revolution, industrialism, slavery, or colonialism; a click or two of the mouse will bring up comparable web pages; there is no need to duplicate them here.[7] As I said at the outset, many of the greatest poems do not require much in the way of background information to appreciate and understand them well.

I have organized the other chapters according to genre or kind of poetry. The poets themselves were acutely aware of the genre traditions; they experimented with them, and sometimes mocked them, but they took them seriously. Generic conventions did not seem artificial impositions but structures of feeling and thought; if they were containers of meaning, they also shaped the meaning they contained. Although some new forms, such as Coleridge's "conversation poem," may be ascribed to the Romantics, we find very little in the way of free verse, prose poems, or the like. They usually labeled their sonnets "sonnets" and their odes "odes," and sometimes organized their collected poems by their forms. I give greater weight to "lyrical" forms than narrative, since I believe that the lyric was the glory of the Romantic movement everywhere in Europe, but it is well to remember that, line for line, more narrative verse was published in this period – ballads, "poetic tales," romances, epics, "novels in verse" – than lyrical. Then again, one of the features of poetry at this time was the "lyricization" of narrative and dramatic forms, as their titles often proclaim, such as Wordsworth's and Coleridge's *Lyrical Ballads* (1798), Mary Robinson's *Lyrical Tales* (1800), and Percy Shelley's *Prometheus Unbound: A Lyrical Drama in Four Acts* (1820).

In several of the chapters I will dwell at great length on one poem and at moderate length on a few others, while trying to embrace a larger set with some generalizations and summaries. If these close readings, or slow readings, seem unduly long, I would justify them on two grounds: first, that reading serious poetry well requires a sustained attention, a focus on details as well as on the whole, free of distractions and multitasking; and secondly, that one of the hallmarks of Romanticism itself is its insistence on the unique and irreducible identity of what Blake called "Minute Particulars," both human individuals and works of art. "To Generalize is to be an Idiot," he said (*The Complete Poetry and Prose of William Blake*, Erdman edition, 641; hereafter cited as E), though I admit he was generalizing when he said that. To scan or speed-read a poem for its "ideas" or "point" is not to read it at all. I will strike a compromise between generals and particulars, and offer a few close analyses as examples of the sort of thing any reader can learn to do. I will also bring to bear a few of the approaches scholars have taken in recent years. Indeed, debates over literary theory seem to have been staged disproportionately on the terrain of Romanticism. Wordsworth's elusive eight-line poem "A slumber did my spirit seal," for example, has been the battleground of troops under various flags, such as formalism, deconstruction, Freudianism, and historicism; a whole book has been written on the debates.[8] But the poems themselves will remain in the foreground.

In this spirit I recommend reading the poems aloud. Poetry is older than writing, and the first European poems to be written down, those by Homer and Hesiod, were almost certainly composed orally, by illiterate bards, chanted to a lyre, and possibly even danced to. The link between poetry and song remained strong for millennia. Poetry right through the time of Romanticism, in fact, knows itself as song. The word "lyric" comes from "lyre"; "ode" is Greek for "song"; "sonnet" comes from the Provençal for "song," which comes from the Latin for "sound." Blake called many of his poems "songs," including a narrative of about 110 lines. Wordsworth refers several times to his as yet unnamed autobiographical poem, later known as *The Prelude*, as a song, even the song of a lark (1805 version 13.380), though it has thirteen books averaging over 650 lines each. Shelley in "Alastor," a narrative of 720 lines, asks the mother of the world to "Favour my solemn song." Examples are ubiquitous and routine. Blake seems actually to have sung his *Songs of Innocence and of Experience* to original melodies, though he wrote no musical notation. Burns tells us which traditional Scottish tunes to sing his poems to; Moore set most of his to traditional tunes but a few to tunes of his own. But the other poets, if they did not properly sing, seem to have recited poems in a way we would find artificial and almost liturgical. What evidence we have suggests they used an incantatory manner, with the meter fully expressed and with variation of pitch or tone not at all like ordinary speech.[9] Try it. Lock yourself in the bathroom, or go for a walk in the woods, and chant a few poems. However silly you feel at first, you will come closer to the experience of the poets of the time, and the poems you perform will seem more like actions than the timeless and motionless texts in your book. Though it is true that silent reading was also common at the time, and perhaps growing more so, it is important to grasp that poems are just as much like the wordless songs of nightingales as they are like the soundless legends on Grecian urns. Indeed, as I will try to show in the discussion of "Ode on a Grecian Urn" itself (in Chapter 4), the different emphases you might place on certain words or phrases, decisive for the meaning of the lines, can scarcely be appreciated without reading them aloud.

Objectivity

Except for the two that gather poems by theme (the poet and poetess, and the French Revolution), the chapters that follow offer only a modicum of historical context, however interesting it may be. That is deliberate, for I believe most of what is important about most Romantic poems is accessible to an attentive reader without esoteric knowledge or special training. My interpretations of the poems aspire to be cogent and persuasive, of course, though certainly not final. They are my "own" readings, to be sure, however much I have absorbed from predecessors, and students are invited to disagree with me, as I have sometimes disagreed with earlier interpretations, if they come up with insights that do better justice to the poems' particulars.

To say an interpretation is cogent, or does justice to the data, is to assume that there are objective standards for arriving at an interpretation or adjudicating between conflicting ones. This is not the view of many students today, I have found: they believe that all that matters is their personal response to a poem. If it arouses a feeling, or it evokes a memory of an experience, or it appeals to an idea or opinion already held, then who is to say these are irrelevant to its meaning? Anything goes, as long as the response is sincere. This personal "relativism" has been seconded by many scholars in recent years, who have earnestly warned against the belief that there is a single correct interpretation of any poem. They often accuse the now old "New Criticism," which flourished in America in the 1950s and 1960s, of assuming there could be a full, adequate, and final reading, though it might take generations of careful readers to come up with it. Such an assumption, they argue, has led to tyranny in the classroom, where most students have been intimidated into accepting the views of the manifestly better equipped professor, who would present poems as if they were intricate little bombs that only experts could disassemble without injurious embarrassment; there was only one way to do it. Whether or not this is fair to the New Critics, who in practice often made much of "ambiguities" or multiple meanings of words and lines, it now seems that most classrooms today are quite the opposite of authoritarian. Deconstruction and other poststructuralist theories have celebrated not only multiple meanings but undecidable cruxes, where a word or sentence can equally mean two contradictory things, rather like the "Copenhagen" interpretation of quantum physics, according to which light is somehow both a wave and a particle. These theories often endorse "infinite semiosis," the endless proliferation of meanings with no standard for eliminating any of them. Let a thousand flowers bloom – along with a thousand weeds, of course, for there is no inherent difference between them. The "reader-response" approach encourages the idea that each reader recreates the poem in his or her head and there is no common "objective" poem; there is no way to distinguish what a poem means from what it "means to me." Feminism, race-based approaches, postcolonial studies, and "queer theory" have promoted a group identity version of this subjectivism, arguing that there can be little commonality in the interpretations of, say, a straight white male and a black lesbian. Advocates of these theories, of course, are far less radical in their practice, whether in the classroom or in their published work, for if they allowed, for instance, that Keats's Grecian urn is really a helmet, or has nightingales depicted on it, then there really would no longer be a common text to talk about (as some theories assert) and literary studies would come to a halt, or be laughed out of the university by the other disciplines. But surely to rule out even one reading as mistaken is to invoke objective standards, however basic. There are, I believe, standards as objective as we could wish, though it behooves us to take account of what others have thought and to be open to correction. Everything I have written about poems in this book I believe is true, or at least defensible, and not just my personal "response." Having often been mistaken in the past, of course, and having learned a great deal from wiser heads, I am open to correction on anything, and I well remember that I stoutly defended some interpretations once that I have now abandoned.

Some scholars have felt that the only way to restore order or objectivity to literary criticism is to "historicize" the literary work, to place it in its original context, or set of contexts. Taking "history" in its broadest sense, the resort to history seems reasonable, indeed inevitable, if for no other reason than that we must consult the *Oxford English Dictionary* to make sure we do not attribute anachronistic meanings to words in a poem. The *OED*, however, is only the starting point. There are many contexts that might cast light, for example, on Keats's "Ode on a Grecian Urn": the tradition of the ode genre, the other odes he wrote, the journal where this ode was first published, his letters, the discussion of the Greeks and Greek art current in his day, other poems he read, the poem's reception by readers or reviewers, and so on. Under the categories of "influence," "source," "allusion," "intertextuality," or "dialogue" diligent research has turned up quite a lot of information that might bear on this poem, as it has on many other poems. We might cast the net wider to include the social structure and ideology of the times: indeed some readers have found Keats's ode an example of patriarchal morality (with its unravished brides and maidens loth). Or to include recent political events: one scholar thinks the festival depicted on the urn is haunted by the mass killings at the *Fête* of the Supreme Being in Paris twenty years earlier. On the assumption that everything is related to everything else, we could keep fishing indefinitely, but soon enough the catch will shrink to very little.

Though all literature was written (or composed orally) at a particular time and place, by a particular person (or group), in a particular language that was constantly changing, and published (or performed) for a particular audience, I do not think our grasp of a poem must remain insecure before we do a lot of research. I hope I will show that, at least for a poem written in an "English" quite similar to ours only two centuries ago, most of what matters in it will come to light when we simply read it a few times carefully and think about the interrelations of its parts. What emerges when we try to place a poem more fully in its historical setting is usually enriching rather than contradictory, though sometimes a difficult knot will come untied, or a muted nuance will speak up. We often hear that a work is "a product of its time," as if time ran a factory that bypassed real human creators. But Keats like most poets did not live in "his time" only: he was steeped in the long history of poetry and art, and thought about the future as well. His mind worked in important respects like every human mind. And like every human mind he was not always thinking, even unconsciously, about the ideologies and social problems of his day. And finally, like most poets, he wrote for "common readers," for you and for me.

Chapter 2

The poet

No feature of Romanticism is more definitive than the glory it confers on the poet. He inherits the role of prophet, preacher, and priest from the receding Christian tradition; he is seen as the creator of imaginative worlds and national myths; he becomes a hero, almost a god. In the preface to the 1802 edition of *Lyrical Ballads*, Wordsworth writes that the poet

> is the rock of defence of human nature; an upholder and preserver, carrying every where with him relationship and love. In spite of difference of soil and climate, of language and manners, of laws and customs, in spite of things silently gone out of mind and things violently destroyed, the Poet binds together by passion and knowledge the vast empire of human society, as it is spread over the whole earth, and over all time.

And that was putting it mildly. "Hear the voice of the Bard!" Blake demands, in the "Introduction" poem of the *Songs of Experience* (1794), "Who Present, Past, & Future sees / Whose ears have heard, / The Holy Word, / That walk'd among the ancient trees." Shelley concludes *A Defence of Poetry* (written in 1821, but not published until 1839) with these justly famous words expressing how poets are the vehicles of the spirit of the age, and the age to come: "Poets are the hierophants of an unapprehended inspiration; the mirrors of the gigantic shadows which futurity casts upon the present; the words which express what they understand not; the trumpets which sing to battle, and feel not what they inspire; the influence which is moved not, but moves. Poets are the unacknowledged legislators of the world."

Poets are also men. Though their images have varied through the centuries, they are almost always projected as male, and the Romantic glorification of poets did not alter the case. The female poet, or "poetess," almost always had a very different image, to which we will turn later in this chapter.

Since the beginning of recorded poetry, until quite recently, poets have exalted their role in their communities. Homer presents two bards in the *Odyssey* who are honored and well rewarded for their songs, and Odysseus himself is compared to a bard for his skill at telling his tales. Even the great warrior Achilles in the *Iliad* sings of famous deeds to a lyre. In both epics a character makes the incredible claim that the gods bring about events in order to give material to poets. Helen, for instance, the cause of all the trouble at Troy, understands that her misery was given by Zeus "that we may be a song for those to come" (*Iliad* 6.357). Pindar, whose odes were newly appreciated in the period leading up to the Romantics, hitches his wagon to the athletic stars whose victories he celebrates, and constantly harps on the power of verse and his own skill at it, as if he were a victorious athlete himself. Many later poets assumed a more becoming modesty, such as Horace, who confessed (though with tongue in cheek) that he could not soar like Pindar the swan but only flit about gathering nectar like a bee (*Odes* 4.2). But overall, if your estimate of the importance of poets over the centuries were derived only from what the poets say themselves, as the propaganda of their guild, you would be, well, a Romantic. Nonetheless, as we approach the Romantic era we see a distinct heightening of this bardic self-promotion, as well as of the corresponding despair over ridicule and neglect by an uncaring public.

The vocation of the poet

One strand in this evolution stands out: the consecration of the poet. He is more and more often described in terms that customarily belonged to pastors and priests, or to the ancient prophets: he has the highest calling, a prophetic vision, a gift of the spirit. It was easy to assimilate the classical muses to this Christian vocabulary, as John Milton had identified the muse Urania with the Holy Spirit in the invocations of *Paradise Lost* (1667). Milton indeed became the great exemplar of the sacred vocation of poet. In the eyes of many Romantics, Milton seemed to combine every poetic virtue with religious rectitude, prophetic vision, and political courage. "Milton!" Wordsworth writes in 1802, "thou shouldst be living at this hour: / England hath need of thee." Blake at about the same time engraves a sixty-plate "brief epic" called *Milton*, in which that poet returns to the earth, as Wordsworth wishes, and merges in body and spirit with Blake himself. (We will look at this astonishing poem in Chapter 9.) In the *Defence* Shelley writes, "Milton stood alone illuminating an age unworthy of him."

In Milton's wake, poets throughout the eighteenth century had been building up the image of the inspired or visionary poet. Thomas Gray's "The Progress of Poesy: A Pindaric Ode" (1757) charts the "progress" of poetry from Greece through Rome to England, where Shakespeare, "Nature's darling," was granted the vision of the unveiled face of "the mighty Mother"; where Milton "rode sublime / Upon the seraph-wings of Ecstasy, / The secrets of the abyss to spy"; and where Dryden drove his "less presumptuous" chariot "Wide o'er the fields of glory." Gray concludes by asking, "Oh! lyre divine, what daring spirit / Wakes thee now?" and hints that, though he himself, like Horace, lacks Pindar's "ample pinion," he will try his hand. William Collins asks a similar question in "Ode on the Poetical Character" (1746): "Where is the bard, whose soul can now / Its high presuming hopes avow? / Where is he who thinks, with rapture blind, / This hallowed work for him designed?" We should not underestimate the effect on the Romantic generation of these two influential poets (and they were not alone) who called out for a successor to Milton or Dryden. In an early poem, "To the Muses" (1783), Blake, who was to declare himself the vehicle or vessel of Milton twenty years later, complains that the muses have forsaken poetry: "The languid strings do scarcely move! / The sound is forc'd, the notes are few!" The lack was widely felt, and several of the Romantics besides Blake felt called upon to fill it.

Meanwhile there arose a new interest in ancient and medieval poets, not just Pindar and other Greeks but minstrels and bards, real or supposed, of Scotland, Wales, and Ireland. In medieval English "minstrel" referred to one who entertains his patrons with song, music, tales, jokes, and buffoonery, rather like the fools in Shakespeare. (The word comes from a Latin word meaning "minor official.") By the eighteenth century, however, the term had risen in dignity, shedding the clownishness. James Beattie's *The Minstrel; or, The Progress of Genius* (1771) reveals in its subtitle the assimilation of this figure into the growing cult of natural genius, as we saw in Gray's account of Shakespeare; this long poem in Spenserian stanzas tells of an honest and humble Scottish "shepherd-swain" who loved to roam in nature's wilds and play his "short pipe of rudest minstrelsy" (1.100, 139). This ennoblement of the minstrel, as well as his Scottish associations, was enhanced by Walter Scott's collection of ballads, *The Minstrelsy of the Scottish Border* (1802–3), and his own poem *The Lay of the Last Minstrel* (1805). Wordsworth called Scott himself "Great Minstrel of the Border" in "Yarrow Revisited" (1835) (1.8).

"Bard" is both Gaelic and Welsh, and was known to the Romans as a Gaulish word. The Roman epic poet Lucan (39–65 CE) wrote, "The bards (*bardi*) too – you poets who with praise send forth / Into eternity the valiant spirits cut off in war – / Then free from worry you poured out a multitude of songs" (*Pharsalia* 1.447–9).[1] Shakespeare uses the word in passing (*AC* 3.2.16); Milton calls Orpheus "the Thracian bard" (*PL* 7.34). In Lowland Scots from the sixteenth century "bard" had been in common use for a wandering minstrel, with the sense that "minstrel" also had as a minor entertainer. In Scotland and through-out Britain, however, indeed throughout Europe and North America, "bard" gained an almost mystical prestige after James Macpherson's publication in 1760 of *Fragments of Ancient Poetry, Collected in the Highlands of Scotland, and Translated from the Galic or Erse Language.* (Macpherson quotes the Lucan passage on the title page.) They purported to be the songs, still sung in the Highlands, of the third-century Gaelic bard Ossian, son of Fingal. The pub-lic response was so enthusiastic that more songs, translated into poetic prose, much longer and not very fragmentary, came out every year or two for the next decade. Soon the names Ossian, Fingal, Oscar, Selma, Cuchullin, and Oithona were as well known to readers as Achilles, Agamemnon, and Helen, and indeed Ossian was proclaimed as "the Homer of the North." The bleak Scottish landscape and even bleaker weather; the often mysterious events, sometimes only implied as backgrounds to the tragic love affairs and murders of the foreground; the elegiac mood, as Ossian and the other bards sing of the great warriors and bards of days gone by; the supernatural visitations of these past heroes; and the utter absence of gods (in this respect very unlike Homer) or any sort of consolation for the tragedies of this world – these sent readers into raptures across Europe.

There were doubters from the first, and Macpherson was unable to produce most of the original Gaelic texts from his notes. The best-known early skep-tic was Samuel Johnson, who declared the poems "as gross an imposition as ever the world was troubled with." A generation later, in 1815, Wordsworth mocked Macpherson as "Sire of Ossian" and wrote, with echoes of Johnson's phrase, "Having had the good fortune to be born and reared in a mountainous country, from my very childhood I have felt the falsehood that pervades the volume imposed upon the world under the name of Ossian. From what I saw with my own eyes, I knew that the imagery was spurious." The consensus today is that Macpherson did indeed hear some Gaelic songs with some of the char-acters and events he presents in his "translations," but most of it, guided by his theory that the songs were fragments of an ancient epic cycle, was his inven-tion. Despite the widespread doubt, many readers, including many Romantic poets, believed in Ossian's authenticity, and even when they were disabused they continued to admire Macpherson's work. Blake proclaimed his faith in Ossian despite Wordsworth's dismissal, having already written a poem, *Visions of the Daughters of Albion*, based on the plot situation of one of the "songs." Coleridge and Byron each versified a couple of passages. Goethe did the same in Germany, as did almost every poet of note throughout the Continent, and some of them formed clubs and named themselves "bards."

It takes a leap of sympathetic imagination (though that is a Romantic virtue, surely) for a reader today to overcome his or her tastes and enter into the world of Ossian. Here is the opening and closing of fragment VIII from the first collection, just a page in length:

> By the side of a rock on the hill, beneath the aged trees, old Oscian sat on the moss; the last of the race of Fingal. Sightless are his aged eyes, his beard is waving in the wind. Dull through the leafless trees he heard the voice of the north. Sorrow revived in his soul: he began and lamented the dead.
>
> How hast thou fallen like an oak, with all thy branches round thee! Where is Fingal the King? where is Oscur my son? where are all my race? Alas! in the earth they lie. I feel their tombs with my hands. I hear the river below murmuring hoarsely over the stones. What dost thou, O river, to me? Thou bringest back the memory of the past.
>
> The race of Fingal stood on thy banks, like a wood in a fertile soil. Keen were their spears of steel. Hardy was he who dared to encounter their rage. Fillan the great was there. Thou Oscur wast there, my son! Fingal himself was there, strong in the grey locks of years. Full rose his sinewy limbs; and wide his shoulders spread. The unhappy met with his arm, when the pride of his wrath arose.
>
> [Fingal fights and captures a challenger, then releases him to his pleading sister.]
>
> Such, Fingal! were thy words; but thy words I hear no more. Sightless I sit by thy tomb. I hear the wind in the wood; but no more I hear my friends. The cry of the hunter is over. The voice of war is ceased.

In small sections this sort of obsessive, gloomy, nostalgic lamentation is evocative enough, even moving, but Macpherson "discovered" a great deal of it, and though the stories grow longer this scene is typical of their tone, style, and framework: old blind Oscian (Macpherson changed its spelling in later editions, along with Oscur) sits outside on a wind-beaten hill, haunted by the dead. Questions to himself, usually on the *ubi sunt* theme ("Where are they?"), and apostrophes to rivers and winds; short sentences, with little subordination of clauses; adjectives and adverbs early in the sentences ("Sightless are his aged eyes"; "Hardy was he"; "Full rose his sinewy limbs"); and conventional similes from nature ("fallen like an oak") permeate the poetic prose. Many were the readers who thrilled to these songs. Like gentle streams tears flowed down their cheeks. Soundless now are their sad sighs; gone are the readers of Ossian.[2]

But the idea of the "bard" had arrived. Its reception was seconded by a revival of interest in Welsh bards due in part to Gray's "The Bard: A Pindaric Ode" (1757), which Macpherson doubtless knew. It tells of an aged poet ("Loose his beard and hoary hair"), the last of his line, standing on a rock overlooking the River Conway and laying a mighty curse on the invading army of England's King Edward I before leaping to his death. Bards, then, acquired something of a political edge, or at least the aura of a natural untutored rural visionary free of the taint of court flattery or London sophistication. Robert Burns, the poet of Ayrshire, Scotland, who really did work a farm, made the most of the label, though he often preferred the more cheeky "bardy," a "wee bard," with a pun on the Scots dialect word "bardy," which means "bold" or "impudent." Though he had to be cautious, his contempt for the Hanoverian dynasty was well known, along with his nostalgia for the Scottish Stuart line, whose last attempt to revive its fortunes was defeated by the English in 1745, and his sympathy for the French revolutionaries after 1789.

Meanwhile a fresh look at the literary qualities of the Old Testament, ignited by Robert Lowth's *Lectures on the Sacred Poetry of the Hebrews* (1753), led to a new estimation of David, the purported author of the Psalms, as an inspired poet. His example conferred the highest religious authority on the bard type, and the Psalms were taken increasingly often as models for the hymn and ode. This convergence of traditions – Pindaric flights, Old Testament prophecy and hymn, Miltonic sublimity, and primitive bardic genius – with the feeling that a new great poet is overdue, raised expectations, and self-expectations, on the part of the Romantics, inciting them to ambitious efforts while burdening them with an unmatchable past.

If a single poet stands as the central figure of Romanticism it is William Wordsworth, and his sense of vocation, his summons to be a poet, is central to his work, especially to the "poem to Coleridge," the quasi-epic autobiography in blank verse that reached its full length of 8,500 lines in 1805 but remained untitled and unpublished until his death in 1850, when it appeared as *The Prelude*. Late in the poem, which we will discuss more fully in Chapter 9, he summarizes its theme: "the discipline / And consummation of the poet's mind" (1805 version 13.270–1). It is both a test of his powers, anxiously undertaken, and a proof or credential, triumphantly submitted at the end, that he has acquired them. Even in the opening he has a moment when "poetic numbers came / Spontaneously, and clothed in priestly robe / My spirit, thus singled out, as it might seem, / For holy services" (1.61–4). "I was a chosen son" (3.82), with "holy powers" (83) and "god-like hours" (192). Authentic poets' minds, he says later, endowed with imagination and tutored by Nature, "are truly from the Deity, / For they are powers" (13.106–7). This religious language reaches its own consummation at the end. Turning explicitly to Coleridge, the addressee throughout, Wordsworth promises that the two of them, faced with the backsliding of men to idolatry and servitude, will be "joint labourers in the work— / Should Providence such grace to us vouchsafe— / Of their redemption, surely yet to come" (13.439–41). Redemption by philosophic poetry! It is a startling claim, no doubt blasphemous to many Christians, but a frequent feature of the Romantic worldview.

For his part, Coleridge was never as confident of his own calling or gifts, and in despair over his waning powers he passed the torch to Wordsworth and coached him, perhaps unwisely, to attempt the great philosophic poem that *The Prelude* was a prelude to. Nonetheless, at the conclusion of "Kubla Khan" (published in 1816) Coleridge left us the period's most famous description of the divinely inspired poet. If he could revive the vision he once had of a muse-like "damsel with a dulcimer," he says, he would rebuild Kubla Khan's dome in music,

> And all should cry, Beware! Beware!
> His flashing eyes, his floating hair!
> Weave a circle round him thrice,
> And close your eyes with holy dread,
> For he on honey-dew hath fed,
> And drunk the milk of Paradise.

Blake sometimes felt doubts, but he had fewer inhibitions over making grandiose claims than either Wordsworth or Coleridge. At the climax of his two-book "brief epic" *Milton* the hero descends to this world "in Self-annihilation & the grandeur of Inspiration" (41.2) in order to transform himself into the poet he had not quite been during his former life. In his new form, united with Blake himself, he will transform "Albion" as well, the personification of Britain, by means of imagination and inspiration, that is, poetry:

> To take off his filthy garments, & clothe him with Imagination
> To cast aside from Poetry, all that is not Inspiration
> That it no longer shall dare to mock with the aspersion of Madness
> Cast on the Inspired, by the tame high finisher of paltry Blots,
> Indefinite, or paltry Rhymes; or paltry Harmonies.

(41.6–10)

There is more to it than this, but in Blake's view the redemption of Britain depends on purging poetry of rhyme, painting of "Blots," and music of harmony. The savior of humanity incarnates as a certain kind of poet, painter, or musician.

The young Percy Shelley, too, envisaged the redemption of the world in an epic of 4,800 lines of Spenserian stanzas called *Laon and Cythna* (later *The Revolt of Islam*) (1818). The hero and heroine are both singers and orators. Having learned the "holy and heroic verse" Laon composes (934), Cythna stirs the longings and resolve of people everywhere to throw off their chains. In "Ode to the West Wind" (1820) Shelley pleads with the wind to "Drive my dead thoughts over the universe / Like withered leaves to quicken a new birth!" and "Be through my lips to unawakened Earth / The trumpet of a prophecy!"

Not all the poets in the usual Romantic canon made such sweeping claims or expressed such anguished hopes for poetry's power of salvation. Byron, notably, did not, but even this most worldly and ironic of the Romantics created "Byronic heroes," such as Childe Harold, whose feelings for the natural world and alienation from most of the human race make them kin to the inspired but outcast poet. Keats usually thought poetry "should be a friend / To sooth the cares, and lift the thoughts of man" ("Sleep and Poetry" [1817], 246–7), more at home in quiet bowers than on windy mountaintops, but this modest purpose did not call into question poetry's luminous force: "A drainless shower / Of light is poesy; 'tis the supreme of power" (235–6).

Rapture

One of the feelings characteristic of Sensibility, and no less of Romanticism, is rapture, especially as it describes the state of mind of a poet or his audience. In poem after poem from the early eighteenth century well into the nineteenth we hear of a poet or his readers rapt, ravished, transported, charmed, entranced, ecstatic, enthusiastic, or spellbound; it becomes a predictable cliché. The idea of an entranced audience, it is true, is as old as Homer, who twice describes the spell Odysseus casts as he tells his tales: "So he spoke, and all of them stayed stricken to silence, / held in thrall [*kelethmō*] by the story all through the shadowy chambers" (*Odyssey* 11.333–4, 13.1–2).[3] The word *kelethmos* means "enchantment" or "fascination," with a suggestion of magic. And the notion of the enraptured poet goes back to Plato, who describes the possession and madness (*mania*) that come from the Muses (*Phaedrus* 245A). But the idea of poetic rapture reemerges with great force in the early eighteenth century.

Its immediate sources are not only these classical passages but mystical ecstasy within Christianity as well, and particularly the experience of religious music and song. In "On the Morning of Christ's Nativity" (1629) Milton recounts how the shepherds heard such sweet music "As all their souls in bliss-ful rapture took" (98), while in *Paradise Lost* he tells of a song sung by the fallen angels that "took with ravishment / The thronging audience" (2.554–5). Thomas Warton, Jr., likes to attend vespers sung by a choir "Till all my soul is bath'd in ecstasies" as the sounds "reach my ravish'd ear" ("Pleasures of Melancholy" 200, 205); he is echoing Milton's "Il Penseroso" (1631), the proto-type of the poem of philosophical melancholy, where the speaker asks the organ and choir "through mine ear" to "Dissolve me into ecstasies" (164–5).

To take the inevitable step from religious music to secular song or verse as cause or product of rapture is to confer a religious aura on the latter and to promote the emergence of the poet as the modern priest, prophet, or psalmist. In his invocation to "Inspiration" at the opening of "Summer" (1727), James Thomson rings the changes that soon became (and perhaps already were) commonplace, while connecting poetic power with the religious origins of rapture:

> Come, Inspiration! from thy hermit-seat,
> By mortal seldom found: may fancy dare,
> From the fixed serious eye and raptured glance
> Shot on surrounding Heaven, to steal one look
> Creative of the poet, every power
> Exalting to an ecstasy of soul.
>
> (15–20)

Many of the Sensibility poets use similar terms. Edward Young, reading Homer and Milton at night, laments, "How often I repeat their Rage divine, / To lull my Griefs, and steal my Heart from Woe! / I roll their Raptures, but not catch their flames" (*Night-Thoughts* [1742] 1.446–8). In his "Elegy" Gray imagines a neglected poet who might have "waked to ecstasy the living lyre" (48). At the opening of "The Progress of Poesy" (1757) he calls on his own lyre to awake and "give to rapture all thy trembling strings" (2); later he describes Milton as riding "Upon the seraph-wings of Ecstasy" (96). The "sainted sage" and "bard divine," he tells us in "Ode for Music" (written 1769), are "Rapt in celestial transport" (15, 18). When Collins, as we saw, asks where the next great poet will come from, he does not fail to assume that the poet will be gripped by this same state of mind: "Where is he who thinks, with rapture blind, / This hallowed work for him designed?" ("Poetical Character" 53–4). Already by 1737 Mark Akenside is satirizing this poetic ecstasy in "The Poet: A Rhapsody": "Rapt in thought, / Fancy presents before his ravished eyes / Distant posterity, upon his page / With transport dwelling" (99–102). The poet is rapt at the thought that others will be rapt reading his poems! But for most poets, of course, the claim to feel rapture, and the hope of arousing it, are avowed in earnest.

It remains so among the Romantic poets. Wordsworth, for example, remembers the "raptures" and "ecstasy" he felt, "Even unto tears," when reading poems as a young man, and hopes that he himself as a poet will "teach, / Inspire, through unadulterated ears / Pour rapture, tenderness, and hope, my theme / No other than the very heart of man" (1805 *Prelude* 5.569–70, 614; 12.237–40). The word "rapt" is not only assigned to the poet and his audience but sometimes projected on to the mental faculty or musical instrument that causes rapture. So in Wordsworth we find "rapt imagination" and "rapt Fancy"; in Mary Robinson not only "rapt minstrel" but also "rapt fancy" and "rapt lyre"; and in Shelley not only "rapt poet" but also "rapt poesy."

It is difficult to decide how far this poetic rapture is conventional, outliving its social origin as almost formulaic epithets and conceits, and how far it registers genuine experiences at the time. I believe it is real enough, though doubtless exaggerated and at times merely routine. We should not underestimate how important poetry was to many people then, in an age with far fewer media than we take for granted today, and we should remember that it was commonly read aloud in dramatic and incantatory fashion. In public readings today, in my view, poets often understate their poems, reducing their rhetorical charge, as if they are faintly embarrassed by them or just uncomfortable before an audience. (Recently, however, we have seen the rise of "performance poetry" and rap music which, whatever their merits as poetry as it stands on the page, at least recapture something of the older mode of recital.) In the Romantic era, as in all eras before it, poets were usually performers, chanters of their verse and enchanters of their audiences, who in turn were ready to be gripped. Even when reading silently in solitude, readers could summon in their inward ear the sounds and drama of a performance. And thus poetry, so realized, seemed to have the high seriousness, moral force, and emotional penetration of a religious service among believers.

Eagles

Since the time of the Greeks poets have likened themselves to nightingales. Hesiod called himself a nightingale, and Theocritus called Homer a nightingale. The bird sang through the lovelorn songs of the Provençal troubadours and German Minnesängers. Milton compared himself to one, for he sang in the dark. Keats's bird, the most famous in English, sings in full-throated ease while Keats listens ("Ode to a Nightingale," 1819). Since the time of the

Romans poets have also been swans. Horace called Pindar the "swan of Dirce," and thereby launched two millennia of clichés whereby Shakespeare is the Swan of Avon and every other poet is the swan of some river or other. Swans supposedly sing at their death, so the "swan song" became another cliché after Ovid declared the final book of his *Tristia*, written in his lonely exile by the Black Sea, to be the sad song of a swan. Shelley was particularly given to swan imagery. Since the Middle Ages, finally, poets have sung like larks. Wordsworth wrote two skylark poems, while Shelley's "To a Sky-Lark" (1820), in which he compares the little bird to a "Poet hidden / In the light of thought," is as nearly well known as Keats's "Ode to a Nightingale."

All these birds chirp and chant through Romantic poetry, just as we would expect, but they are almost overshadowed by the arrival of the eagle. Nothing much had been heard from eagles as poets since Pindar compared himself to one (twice), and then Dante called Homer an eagle in the *Inferno*. It may show up here and there – Elizabeth Thomas likens Virgil to an eagle in "The Dream" (1722) – but it is rare until Gray in his "Progress of Poetry" (1754) names Pindar "the Theban eagle," "sailing with supreme dominion / Through the azure deep of air"; after that it grows more and more frequent. Beattie calls Gray himself an eagle, soaring "Pindaric heights" ("On the Report of a Monument" [1766], 33–4). If Dante called Homer an eagle, Byron calls Dante an eagle in "The Prophecy of Dante" (1819) (3.70–1). Byron is described as an eagle by Shelley if we take the character Maddalo as Byron: "The sense that he was greater than his kind / Had struck, methinks, his eagle spirit blind / By gazing on its own exceeding light" (*Julian and Maddalo* [1819] 50–2). Shelley neatly turns the ancient myth that the eagle renews its sight by staring at the sun into an image of narcissism and pride. In his poem "Genius" (1835), John Clare writes: "Byron, like an eagle, flew / His daring flight, and won" (21–2). Several French poets, such as Lamartine and Delavigne, also see Byron as an eagle; Lamartine dwells on the brutal side of the eagle, as it takes pleasure in the cries of its prey ("L'Homme" 19). English poets, too, spoke of the prey of the poet-eagle. "But the muse, eagle-pinion'd," Cowper writes in 1782, "has in view / A quarry more important still than you; / Down, down the wind she swims, and sails away; / Now stoops upon it, and now grasps the prey" (*The Progress of Error* 331–4). The muse's prey must be her subject matter! Shelley makes a similar flight: "My soul spurned the chains of its dismay, / And in the rapid plumes of song / Clothed itself, sublime and strong; / As a young eagle soars the morning clouds among, / Hovering in verse o'er its accustomed prey" ("Ode to Liberty" 5–9) (1820).

The presence of all these eagles, and there are many more, raises interesting questions. Eagles are not songbirds, whereas surely the chief characteristic of poets is that they sing. Eagles are predators that might well kill a songbird. In Greek and Latin literature the eagle is the king of birds and the bird of the king of the gods, Zeus or Jupiter. It is the lord of the sky. For a mere poet, whose traditional role was to sing for his supper at the courts of the real lords, to proclaim himself or another poet an eagle might seem ridiculous if not dangerously presumptuous. But by the mid eighteenth century the status of poets was changing as they relied less on aristocratic patronage and more on the growing middle-class reading public for their livelihood and saw themselves, as we have noted, as having a consecrated mission that far transcended that of entertainer or chronicler. As they expressed that mission, the eagle appealed to poets as a symbol more suitable to the role of prophet and visionary than a nightingale or lark. The eagle soars high in the sky and has excellent vision. It has long been the emblem of St. John the Evangelist, whose Gospel is the most "visionary" and whose dominant image, at least in the opening, is light.

The French Romantic poets make even more frequent use of eagles than the British (it is also common among German and Russian Romantics), and one eagle story they remembered was that of Ganymede, the beautiful Trojan youth carried off by Zeus's eagle, or by Zeus in the guise of an eagle, to Olympus and kept there to be Zeus's cupbearer. This brings us back to "rapture," for the abduction of Ganymede was a rapture in the literal sense, carried out by the great raptor of the heavens. Lamartine and others describe their poetic enthusiasm as a kind of helpless passivity in the grip of an outside force. In British poetry we occasionally find "rapture" as flight, as in Susan Evance's sonnet "To Melancholy" (1808) where "My raptured spirit soars on wing sublime," or in Wordsworth's sonnet "The Source of the Danube" (1820) where "Fancy … mounts on rapt wing," but these are not like Ganymede, who did not fly with his own wings. Ganymede, unless I have missed something, was not invoked for this purpose by British poets until well after the peak of Romanticism, when Martin Farquhar Tupper, in "Imagination" (1851), writes, "Wing'd with ecstatic mind, and carried away / Like Ganymede of old" (145–6), or, with greater flair and wit, Elizabeth Barrett Browning in *Aurora Leigh* (1856):

> poetry, my life,
> My eagle, with both grappling feet still hot
> From Zeus's thunder, who hast ravished me
> Away from all the shepherds, sheep, and dogs,
> And set me in the Olympian roar and round
> Of luminous faces for a cup-bearer,
> …
> We drop the golden cup at Here's foot
> And swoon back to the earth—and find ourselves

> Face-down among the pine-cones, cold with dew,
> While the dogs bark, and many a shepherd scoffs,
> "What's come now to the youth?" Such ups and downs
> Have poets.

(1.918–34)

In British poetry the poet is usually the eagle, not its prey, but sometimes the poets recognize their weaknesses or failures in aquiline terms, as an eagle wounded, sick, or caged. Keats, who called Wordsworth an eagle in a letter to Reynolds in May 1818, saw himself as "a sick eagle looking at the sky" in his sonnet "On Seeing the Elgin Marbles" (1817). Felicia Hemans' "The Wounded Eagle" (1830) is one long simile for the destiny of "gifted souls and high," while in "The Storm-Painter in his Dungeon" (also 1830) Hemans describes an artist (Pietro Mulier) in prison as an eagle caged. Sometimes as a simple gesture of modesty a poet might say, with Keats, "I have not eagle's wings" ("To Haydon, with a Sonnet / Written on Seeing the Elgin Marbles") (1817). A more elaborate gesture of humility is found in a poem Caroline Bowles included in her novel *Ellen Fitzarthur* (1820), which begins:

> Parnassus! to thy heights sublime,
> Thy awful steep, I may not climb
> Where rays of living light surround
> Thy sacred fane, with laurels crowned,
> And gushes with melodious flow
> Thy fountain, from its source below.
>
> I may not look with eagle gaze
> Unshrinking, on those living rays;
> I may not soar on eagle's wing,
> To drink of that celestial spring[.]

Instead she is content to haunt the vale below, catch a distant glimpse of the mount, and weave a chaplet of wildflowers.[4]

Aeolian harps

In 1650 the German Jesuit Athanasius Kircher described an invention of his called the "aeolian harp" or wind harp (or lyre). It was a long, narrow wooden box with eight to ten strings stretched over two bridges and tuned in unison; it was meant to be placed in a window where the wind would draw out harmonious sounds – not always the same note but overtones in octaves, fifths, and thirds. In the next century a Scottish cellist and composer named James Oswald made a wind harp, and it soon became popular among those who could afford one; by mid century it appears in poetry across Europe. It was an irresistible symbol of the "sensible" or sensitive soul, responsive to every passing breeze, but especially the soul so cultivated or "attuned" as to react with beauty or grace to its experiences. It seemed more than a metaphor, in fact; it was a model of the human brain and spinal column, and perhaps the heart, which philosophers and physicians commonly described as sets of nerves that vibrated when stimulated and that communicated their vibrations to one another, thereby generating the "association of ideas" that John Locke and others investigated. We still resort to this model today, as when we speak of good or bad "vibes," of something "striking a chord," or of someone "too high-strung" or "uptight." A letter from Robert Burns to a friend in 1787 uses another term still common now: of the first girl he loved he writes, "Indeed I did not well know myself … why the tones of her voice made my heartstrings thrill like an Eolian harp."[5]

Because the sounds produced by the harp were invariably soft and usually brief, and perhaps because they did not have much structure, they sounded plangent and "melancholy" to most ears. Here is James Thomson's description of them in *Castle of Indolence* (1748), probably the first in English poetry:

> A certain music, never known before,
> Here lull'd the pensive, melancholy mind;
> Full easily obtain'd. Behoves no more,
> But sidelong, to the gently waving wind,
> To lay the well tuned instrument reclined;
> From which, with airy flying fingers light,
> Beyond each mortal touch the most refined,
> The god of winds drew sounds of deep delight:
> Whence, with just cause, the harp of Æolus it hight.

> (1.352–60)

(The phrase "it hight" is archaic English for "it was called.") So the wind harp chimed nicely with the mid-eighteenth-century cult of melancholic meditation, which lasted well into the nineteenth. The harp still sounded sad, for instance, to Letitia Landon in 1824:

> A dying tone, a plaining fall,
> So sad, so wild, so musical—
> As the wind swept across the wire,
> And waked my lone Æolian lyre,
> Which lay upon the casement …

> (The Improvisatrice, 494–8)

Nearly every poet of Sensibility and Romanticism, it seems, had a go at it. "Come soft Aeolian harp," a sonnet of Mary Robinson's begins, "while zephyr plays / Along the meek vibration of thy strings, / As twilight's hand her modest mantle brings, / Blending with sober grey the western blaze!" ("To the Aeolian Harp," from *Sappho and Phaon* [1796]). Coleridge was much taken with it. He devoted one of his "conversation" poems to it ("The Eolian Harp," 1795), in which he tentatively offers an extraordinary metaphysical speculation inspired by it:

> And what if all of animated nature
> Be but organic harps diversely framed,
> That tremble into thought, as o'er them sweeps,
> Plastic and vast, one intellectual breeze,
> At once the Soul of each, and God of All?

(44–8)

In "Dejection: An Ode" (1802; there were several later versions) Coleridge likens himself to the harp: he describes a light wind, "the dull sobbing draft, that moans and rakes, / Upon the strings of this Eolian lute, / Which better far were mute" (6–8).

The trouble with the symbol is that it makes the soul passive, a plaything of the gusts of life. Near the end of the century Oscar Wilde was to invoke it as a metaphor for just such passivity in his sonnet "Hélas!" (1881), where he feared his fate was "To drift with every passion till my soul / Is a stringed lute on which all winds can play." The metaphor well suits the outlook of Sensibility, and goes well with the primary notion of "rapture" as something that comes over the soul or seizes it, but it sits uncomfortably with the characteristically Romantic idea of the creative imagination as a sovereign power that makes worlds from its own inner fire or fountain. Shelley states the problem neatly in his *Defence of Poetry* (1821):

> Poetry, in a general sense, may be defined to be "the expression of the imagination": and poetry is connate with the origin of man. Man is an instrument over which a series of external and internal impressions are driven, like the alternations of an ever-changing wind over an Æolian lyre, which move it by their motion to ever-changing melody. But there is a principle within the human being, and perhaps within all sentient beings, which acts otherwise than in a lyre, and produces not melody alone, but harmony, by an internal adjustment of the sounds and motions thus excited to the impressions which excite them. It is as if the lyre could accommodate its chords to the motions of that which strikes them, in a determined proportion of sound; even as the musician can accommodate his voice to the sound of the lyre.

One might think even this correction is not enough for a Romantic. Wordsworth went further, positing not an internal adjustment of the chords but an internal wind, inspired, it is true, by an external wind but capable of independent motion. So *The Prelude* (1805) begins with a breeze, like a muse:

> Oh there is blessing in this gentle breeze,
> That blows from the green fields and from the clouds
> And from the sky; ...
> ...
>
>   ... I breathe again—
> Trances of thought and mountings of the mind
> Come fast upon me ...

The poet thinks about where he might go, and to the tasks he has chosen, and feels this hour has brought a gift:

> For I, methought, while the sweet breath of heaven
> Was blowing on my body, felt within
> A corresponding mild creative breeze,
> A vital breeze which travelled gently on
> O'er things which it had made,

and bringing with it "vernal promise" of accomplishment in "The holy life of music and of verse" (1.1–54). The inspiration does not last; his soul tries her new strength, "nor did she want / Eolian visitations—but the harp / Was soon defrauded" and falls silent (1.103–5). It is telling that Wordsworth resorts to the commonplace image of the aeolian harp only when his creative powers are waning; when it is in full career he uses the original and more interesting metaphor of the corresponding breeze. As we will see in "Tintern Abbey" (Chapter 3 below), Wordsworth believed that nature and our minds are joint creators of our world; here we see they are also joint creators of our poetry. Nature may take the initiative, but our response is not just an echo of it, a sigh of sympathy with it, or a harmonizing of its melody. It is an inner version of nature herself. It was Wordsworth, then, even more than Shelley, who transcended the aeolian harp metaphor from within, showing that its implications are largely confined to Sensibility.[6]

Dying poets

It is still a common image of the Romantic poet or artist that he dies young, preferably of tuberculosis, of suicide, of a duel, of starvation in a garret, or in exile. The "second generation" of poets, Keats, Shelley, and Byron, has engraved that pattern deeply in our minds, even though the first generation, Blake, Wordsworth, and Coleridge, lived long lives. Keats died of tuberculosis in Rome at age 25, Shelley drowned in the Bay of Lerici at 29, and Byron died of fever in Greece at 36. Burns also died young, at 37. But the Romantics themselves had already worshipped at the shrines of poets prematurely cut off from their promise, and of these the prototype, or at least the most celebrated, was Thomas Chatterton. He certainly died the youngest.

Born in 1752 in Bristol, as a boy he haunted the church of St. Mary Redcliffe and read Chaucer, Spenser, and other old authors. By the time he was 12 he was forging poems in archaic English and passing them off as medieval. Moving to London in 1770, his "Rowley" poems, which he attributed to a fifteenth-century monk named Thomas Rowley, were noticed and admired. His finances were precarious, and he might soon have been exposed as a forger – for these or perhaps other reasons he seems to have committed suicide by poison. He was 17.

When he was barely a year older than Chatterton at his death, Coleridge wrote a "Monody on the Death of Chatterton" (*c.* 1790),[7] in which he blames "Want and cold Neglect" for the boy's tragic fate, as well as "the keen insult of th'unfeeling Heart, / The dread dependence on the low-born mind," the mind of the public and publishers, it would seem, too dull to recognize his genius. But he is now a "Spirit blest," pouring forth his hymn among the Cherubim, "Or, soaring through the blest Domain, / Enraptur'st Angels with thy strain." When Coleridge and his friend Southey married the two Fricker sisters, the wedding ceremony took place in St. Mary Redcliffe Church.

In "Resolution and Independence," written in 1802, Wordsworth reports his bleak thoughts while walking on a moor:

> I thought of Chatterton, the marvellous Boy,
> The sleepless Soul that perished in its pride;
> Of Him who walked in glory and in joy
> Behind his plough, upon the mountain-side [Robert Burns]:
> By our own spirits are we deified;
> We Poets in our youth begin in gladness,
> But thereof comes in the end despondency and madness.

Mary Robinson, like Coleridge, wrote a "Monody to the Memory of Chatterton" (1806) that wrings as much pathos as possible from his poverty and neglect. She makes him a flower, blighted in the bud: "So the pale primrose, sweetest bud of May, / Scarce wakes to beauty ere it feels decay." Keats delighted in reading Chatterton's verse aloud, and felt, as well he might, a kinship with his story of budding promise blasted. "Thou didst die / A half-blown flower," Keats writes in one of his first sonnets, "Oh Chatterton!" (1815), but, like Coleridge and Robinson, Keats places him in heaven, where "to the rolling spheres / Thou sweetly singest." Three years later Keats dedicated to Chatterton his first effort at an epic poem, *Endymion*. William Henry Ireland produced a set of poems called *Neglected Genius* (1812), one poem each on the greatness and suffering of Spenser, Milton, Dryden, Thomson, Goldsmith, and several others, concluding with Chatterton:

> Great *Chatterton* awakes my pensive song,
> Sublimest stripling of the muse's throng;
> Prolific prodigy of fancy's womb,
> Born but to blaze, then moulder in the tomb.

These lines may reveal why their author's own genius has been neglected, but they deserve notice for their digesting and disgorging of poor Tom Chatterton as an icon, performed with less talent than Coleridge's or Keats's, perhaps, but no more caught up in the Chatterton cult than they. It is as if all these poems (and there were many more) were votive candles lit at a shrine to ward off despondency and madness, or perhaps warning shots fired across the bows of hard-hearted critics.

Keats died in 1821 in Rome, where he had gone in the hope that the climate would benefit his "consumption" (tuberculosis), but it was believed that a hostile review of *Endymion* had brought on his first symptoms. Shelley took this idea as a given in his elegy for Keats, *Adonais* (1822), in the preface to which he denounces the anonymous reviewer as a miserable murderer. In the poem itself he laments that Adonais was "pierced by the shaft which flies / In darkness" (11–12), in an act not only murderous but cowardly. He elaborates the predictable flower metaphor: "The bloom, whose petals nipt before they blew [bloomed] / Died on the promise of the fruit, is waste" (52–3). And he places Adonais–Keats among others of "unfulfilled renown": the Roman poet Lucan (39–65), Sir Philip Sidney (1554–86), and Chatterton.

Fame

Dying young is not the only unhappy fate that might befall a poet. Milton's blindness and his ostracism (and threat of execution) after the Resoration of the monarchy in 1660 were often in the minds of the Romantics. So was the madness of Tasso.

Legend tells that Torquato Tasso (1544–95), the great Italian poet, author of the epic *Jerusalem Liberated* and many sonnets, fell in love with Leonora, the sister of the Duke of Ferrara, and was confined as a madman for seven years. After Tasso's release, Pope Clement VIII planned to crown him Poet Laureate at the Capitol, but the poet died before the ceremony. Illicit love, madness, the cruelty of a tyrant, genius recognized too late – this was irresistible Romantic material. Byron wrote about Tasso both in *Childe Harold* canto four and in "The Lament of Tasso" (both 1817), the latter a long epistle to Leonora where the poet, the "eagle-spirit of a Child of Song," bemoans his long captivity but takes some consolation in knowing that, when the castle of Ferrara has crumbled, "A poet's wreath shall be thine only crown, / A poet's dungeon thy most far renown." Shelley planned a play on Tasso and wrote a scene and song for it (1818), while Felicia Hemans wrote "The Release of Tasso" (1823) and "Tasso and his Sister" (1826).

Yet it sometimes seems that the worst fate that could befall a poet, in the Romantic scheme of things, is to fail to gain the recognition he deserves, to miss his rightful place as a star in what Shelley called "the heaven of fame" ("Ode to Liberty" 10). Tasso and Milton, whatever their sufferings, were famous by the time of the Romantics, who in turn were doing their best to promote Chatterton and Burns. Byron rightly asserts that the castle of Ferrara was remembered only for having the dungeon where Tasso was kept (Percy and Mary Shelley visited it in 1818). "To be remembered after we are dead," however, as the essayist Hazlitt writes, "is but poor recompense for being treated with contempt while we are living" (*Characteristics*), a remark which echoes the Roman poet Martial's epigram "To the dead fame comes too late" (1.25.8). The main Romantic poets wanted to be famous in their own day, though as they faced public indifference or hostility they appealed to the esteem of posterity as the better sort of renown.

This, too, has an ancient pedigree, as Martial's saying reminds us. Homer made no claims for himself, though he had much to say about fame and the bards' power to confer it, but Pindar could scarcely write an ode without a little self-puffing, not only claiming to be an eagle but trusting that he would be "foremost in wisdom among Hellenes everywhere" (*Olympian* 1.115–17). Ovid made clear "My quest is for everlasting fame" (*Amores* 1.15.7). So did Horace, who ends his first ode with the wish that his patron Maecenas would make him the equal of Pindar and the other Greek lyrists, and who in the final ode of the third book (3.30 *Exegi monumentum*) announces he has made a monument more lasting than bronze and his fame will grow as long as Rome lasts. (The great Russian Romantic poet Alexander Pushkin wrote a version of this poem about his own fame.) With the establishment of Christianity, however, the desire for worldly fame was officially frowned on: such vainglory idolized what Dante called "a breath of wind that blows now here, now there"

(*Purgatorio* 11.100–1), of no weight beside the heavenly glory that the righteous earn. After the Renaissance and its recovery of classical "humanist" texts the fame of poets grew more respectable as a theme, but an ambivalence remained in most writers. Milton echoes Horace's *Exegi monumentum* in his poem "On Shakespeare" (1630): Shakespeare, whom he calls "great heir of Fame," needs no pyramid or other monument other than his book, which is so great "That Kings for such a Tomb would wish to die." In his early writings Milton reveals his own hopes for fame, but they were usually counteracted or transcended by his Christian belief that, as he states in "Lycidas" (1637), "Fame is no plant that grows on mortal soil" (78); worldly fame may be "That last infirmity of Noble mind" (71) but only God will decide our glory in heaven. Those who still felt infirm, or whose Christian faith was shallow or lost, usually made a parallel distinction between immortal fame, which is the slowly growing judgment of posterity, and "popularity" or "reputation," which is evanescent, delusory, and worse for the creative soul than outright neglect.

Keats, though he died before he attained much of it, is the Romantic now most notorious for his explicit ambition to gain poetic fame. He would often dwell on the glory of being a poet: "what a thing to be in the Mouth of Fame" (letter to Leigh Hunt, May 10, 1817). His early wide-eyed hopes were chastened by bad reviews, especially of his first long poem, *Endymion* (1818), but even in the wake of such reviews he could write, "I think I shall be among the English Poets after my death" (letter to George and Georgiana Keats, October 1818). He wrote two sonnets on fame (1819) in which he wrestles with himself over this fickle and unworthy temptation, but even in his most self-effacing moods he cherished the hope of poetic immortality. In one of his last letters to Fanny Brawne, written while in his final illness, he quotes Milton as he acknowledges that he divides his thoughts between her and his waning hope for fame, the "last infirmity of noble minds" (February 1820).[8]

In a verse "Letter to Maria Gisborne" (1820) Shelley likens himself to a silk-worm spinning a cocoon out of "fine threads of rare and subtle thought" so that, when he dies, "Memory may clothe in wings my living name / And feed it with the asphodels of fame" (7–12). A generation earlier, Burns wrote in his commonplace book, "Obscure I am, & obscure I must be, though no young Poet, nor young Soldier's heart ever beat more fondly for fame than mine."[9] A few years after Shelley's poem, the young Tennyson told his brother, "Well, Arthur, I mean to be famous."[10]

These examples are enough to show the extent of personal ambitions, but we must also remember that the ambitions were much more often channeled more decorously into poems of praise for other poets, such as those about Chatterton or Tasso. Coleridge, for example, imagines Wordsworth even now

(1807) "in the choir / Of ever-enduring men" ("To William Wordsworth" 49–50). Keats also puts Wordsworth first among the spirits in his sonnet beginning "Great spirits now on earth are sojourning" (1817), and adds the poet Leigh Hunt and the painter Benjamin Robert Haydon. Keats himself is the subject of Shelley's elegy "Adonais." They made other poets into stars in the skies where they hoped to shine themselves.[11]

"The poetess"

Though we have quoted a few women poets in this chapter, the tacit assumption about poets at the time, even in poems by these same women poets, is that they are men. But of course they were not all men: about a quarter of those who published were women, and many of them projected an image of the female poet, often called "the poetess," that differed in several ways from the male. We would not use the term "poetess" today, of course – it dropped out of common usage before many of the other "-ess" words – but we will retain it here to refer to the image, not the reality. They were sometimes called Muses, as when Susanna Blamire was known as "the Muse of Cumberland," surely a less justifiable term, since the ancient Muses were mainly the inspirers or teachers of poetry and the other arts to men, though an epigram ascribed to Plato calls Sappho the tenth Muse. Even more condescending terms were sometimes deployed, such as Samuel Johnson's word for Hannah More, "versificatrix," about which the less said the better.

That these terms were in the air suggests the difficulty faced by women poets who wished to be taken seriously. It is not surprising, then, that when they dealt with their own calling or that of other women, they usually made modest and deferential claims, as Mary Tighe does in the "Proem" to her Spenserian epic-romance *Psyche* (1805), where she "for cruel battles would not dare / The low-strung chords of her weak lyre prepare" (4–5), or as Caroline Bowles does in the poem we quoted earlier, where she protests she cannot soar like an eagle. More prominent is their disavowal of fame: not only are they not seeking it, but they see it as a positive evil, a snare and a delusion, distracting them from their true heart's home, the home. Mary Robinson concludes her lightly ironic poem "The Poet's Garrett" (1809) by imagining him (it is a male poet, of course) far above the cares of the world and endowed with the power to "fill thy lines / With the all-conqu'ring weapon Heav'n bestows / In the grey goose's wing which, tow'ring high, / Bears thy rich fancy to immortal fame!" The divine pen is mightier than the worldly sword. But many of her fellow poetesses agreed, or pretended to agree, with Mary Browne, whose poem "The Poetess"

(1828) tells of a woman crowned and praised and flattered for her poetry, but her heart is still a woman's and she turns from "Glory's false star" that men seek to the warmth of home and the private happiness of the "silent ocean cave" of her heart. Maria Smith Abdy tells a similar story in "The Dream of the Poetess" (1836):

> 'Tis true, when the banner of Fame is unfurled,
> Man finds his reward in the smiles of the world;
> But Woman, though raised by that world to a throne,
> Will languish, if destined to fill it alone.

In her elegy "Felicia Hemans" (1838) Letitia Landon praises the poetic gifts Hemans brought us, but then asks, "Was not this purchased all too dearly?— never / Can fame atone for all that fame hath cost." Now in her grave, Hemans is free of "Fame's troubled hour," but she has a kind of fame after all, her "gentle sway" extending even to America and her grave now "a shrine."

The thought of home with its duties and blessings, the wish to shun the glare of public renown and flourish in the light only of husband or family – these usually win out over the desire to join the ranks of the poets shining in the heaven of fame. The very fact that so many poems proclaiming the joys of domestic retirement were *published* would be enough to imply the conflicting feelings of their authors, but these feelings are evident in the poems themselves, as the passages we have quoted suggest. The figure on whom many women poets (and even some men poets) projected these conflicts was the early sixth-century Greek poet Sappho of Lesbos, whom we have mentioned already. She played a role for female poets comparable to that played by Milton or Tasso for male poets: she was a great lyric poet, honored by the ancients as one of their best, even a "Muse," but she suffered greatly. She was not seen, for the most part, as a "lesbian" as we use the word today; what she was known for, besides a few surviving scraps of brilliant verse, such as her "Ode to Aphrodite," was her suicide by leaping off the Leucadian cliff after she was abandoned by her lover Phaon, a man. Ovid had told the story in his *Heroides* 15, a letter from Sappho to Phaon. She is alone, her father dead, her brother gone, and Phaon far away in Sicily; she takes no pleasure in the fact that her fame as a poet is known in every land. She has rent her clothes, wept in grief, and wandered frenzied through the caves and woods where they once made love. She pleads with Phaon to return. If he does not, she vows to leap from the high cliff of Leucas, in the Ionian Sea. In part mediated by Alexander Pope's version (1712), this heart-rending letter fired the imagination of numerous women poets.

Mary Robinson in 1796 wrote a sequence of forty-four sonnets entitled *Sappho and Phaon* that meticulously charts her life, her passion for Phaon, his departure, her voyage to Sicily, her confrontation with the false Phaon, her resolution to die, and her final thoughts as she stands on the Leucadian cliff. (We shall look at one of these sonnets in Chapter 6.) In 1824 Letitia Elizabeth Landon wrote "Sappho's Song" and Catherine Grace Godwin wrote *Sappho: A Dramatic Sketch*, not to mention works by French and Russian women. In 1831 Felicia Hemans produced "The Last Song of Sappho." Men throughout Europe were taken with the theme almost as often as women, and it would be interesting to know why this was so. In 1793, for example, Southey in England and Kleist in Germany wrote dramatic poems about Sappho, Byron treated her in *Childe Harold*, canto two (1812), and Giacomo Leopardi poured his despair into "Ultimo canto di Saffo" in 1822.

The purport of these works varies, but again and again they dwell on the hollowness of poetic fame in comparison with love. Yet passionate and erotic love, like Sappho's, is also shown to be dangerous and irresponsible in comparison with tender domestic devotion. Admirable though she is, Sappho's case is a warning, and a warning more to female poets, of course, than to male. It is true that Byron once claimed that he would give up all his laurels if he could win the love of a beautiful young woman ("Stanzas Written on the Road between Florence and Pisa"), and he frequently gestured at the meaninglessness of fame when he had a lot of it, but the moral of Sappho's sacrifice was mainly directed at women, for whom love and duty to a man were expected to be the center of their existence.

The Sappho theme received a powerful but complicated impetus in Madame de Staël's novel *Corinne, or Italy* (1807, with two English translations the same year). Its title character is an astonishing young woman, beautiful, brilliant, independent, cosmopolitan, an accomplished actress, poetess, and *improvisatrice* (one who improvises verse before audiences who propose subjects), whom we meet in the opening chapter as she is being crowned with laurel in Rome before an admiring crowd. She is a new Sappho: indeed her name evokes the ancient poet Corinna of Tanagra, said to have been the teacher and rival of Pindar; she is a new sibyl, a prophetess of a restored Italy (then under domination by Napoleon); and, as the subtitle suggests, she is an embodiment of Italy herself, glorious but powerless. She meets Lord Oswald Nelvil, a brave and intelligent Englishman harboring an obscure guilt and a commitment to a woman at home, and they fall in love. They do a great deal of sightseeing and have many discussions of Italian, French, and British literature and culture; they spend some hours on the rim of smoldering Vesuvius, where Oswald reveals his troubled history; there are revelations on her part a week later (she turns out to be the half-sister of Oswald's intended!); they both struggle with the question of whether she could still perform as a poetess if she were a wife

and a mother. Then the inevitable happens: he must return to England. She follows in secret, there are misunderstandings, and a long train of suffering and
renunciation lumbers to its tragic end. The plot is absurdly unlikely and melo-
dramatic, and it carries too much allegorical freight; the moral, to the extent
that it can be extracted, would be depressingly familiar to women of that time
who sought independence and a chance to express their genius; but Corinne
is irresistibly interesting and attractive. She seems to transcend the plot that
humbles her and to retain her power over the reader long afterward, or so she
evidently did to many women throughout Europe and America. They must
have rewritten the story in their heads to make it possible for love and literary fame to cohabit, as it seems to have, fitfully, in the life of Madame de Staël
herself, but in their poems they seem to scold Corinne for even imagining she
might find happiness as a poetess.

Letitia Landon turns to the subject several times, in "Corinna" (1821), "The
Improvisatrice" (1824), and "Corinne at the Cape of Misena" (1832). The last
of these, based on an engraving of François Gérard's painting with that title,
holds that Corinne's many afflictions include the disappointments of poetic
ambition:

> The thirst of praise that ends in bitterness;
> Those high aspirings which but rise to find
> What weight is on their wings

(50–2)

A decade earlier Jane Taylor, in "To Mad. De Staël" (1822), admits her kinship with Corinne but then urges "meek submission" to the Christian call to
domestic duty:

> Yes, too much
> I've felt her talent's magic touch.
> Return, my soul to that retreat
> From sin and woe—Thy savior's feet!

Felicia Hemans joins in with "Corinne at the Capitol" (1830), which ends in a
typical way:

> Radiant daughter of the sun!
> Now thy living wreath is won.
> Crowned of Rome! Oh! art thou not
> Happy in that glorious lot?
> Happier, happier far than thou,
> With the laurel on thy brow,
> She that makes the humblest hearth
> Lovely but to one on earth![12]

Responses like these to the more divided impact of the original character seem like attempts to stifle the free and creative spirit of women. With the often terrible fates of the male poets in mind, not to mention their often scandalous conduct, one can almost sympathize with this retreat into piety and propriety. But to repress the poetic genius is to repress Romanticism, and it is fair to ask whether the "poetesses" who felt they should do so belong in a book about Romantic poets. There are other features of their work that overlap with those of the Romantics, and they may serve as an instructive contrast to Romanticism, perhaps even a salutary rebuke to it, but they seem to have placed themselves, no doubt under great pressure from a society still only slightly softened from its harsh and ancient patriarchal laws and customs, in a different world.

Chapter 3

"Tintern Abbey"

In 1798 a book of poems appeared that, more than any other, marks the beginning of the Romantic movement in Britain: *Lyrical Ballads, with A Few Other Poems*. The author is unnamed; in the second edition (1800), which has many more poems, and in the two later editions (1802 and 1805), the author is given as "W. Wordsworth," but it is explained in the preface that some of the poems were written by a "friend," who was soon known to be S. T. Coleridge. The first poem in it, soon the most famous of the lot, is Coleridge's "The Rime of the Ancyent Marinere." The great length of that poem (658 lines) is probably what justified the otherwise misleading title of the volume, for by one count there are twelve ballads and eleven "other poems," though it is difficult to sort them out since some poems are in ballad form but with most unballad-like subjects and some are just the opposite. Five of the "other poems" are called "Lines" with various subtitles, and the last of these, the last poem in the book, is arguably the most important single poem of British Romanticism, both for its intrinsic greatness and for its impact on later poets: "Lines Written a Few Miles above Tintern Abbey, on Revisiting the Banks of the Wye During a Tour, July 13, 1798." It is by William Wordsworth.[1]

The long and awkward title (though it is no longer than one of the other "Lines" titles) begged for a shorter version, and of course it has been known ever since simply as "Tintern Abbey." That is unfortunate, for many casual readers of the poem are under the impression that the poem was written beside the great and beautiful ruin of the Cistercian abbey near Tintern, Wales, closed down by Henry VIII, or that the poem deals with it in some way. When I last visited the abbey, in the 1980s, Wordsworth's poem was hanging in the museum, and when I asked the custodian where he thought Wordsworth composed his poem he pointed to a spot a hundred yards away on the banks of the Wye. From a few miles "above" (upstream), however, the ruin is not visible, and nothing is said about it in the poem. Whether or not Tintern Abbey is nonetheless somehow "in the poem" remains an interesting question, to which we shall return.

Wordsworth – we shall call him "Wordsworth" though to be strict we should call him the speaker or *persona* of the poem – returns to a spot he last visited five years earlier, and describes it in some detail. He remembers how his earlier experience here had refreshed or restored him when he was wearied by his life in the city; it gave him feelings both of pleasure and of something more sublime, and both feelings had moral or spiritual effects on him. He then thinks that his present visit will give the same benefits in the future, even though he has changed from what he was five years ago. Then he was more spontaneously or instinctively responsive to nature than he is now, but though he has lost that state of being he believes he has gained something as well, a more philosophical and subdued understanding of the human and natural worlds. Wordsworth then turns to his sister, who has been at his side, unbeknownst to us, all the while. In her he sees and hears "what I was once," and then prays that nature will nourish her as it did him so that she too will be protected against the dreariness of social life. He concludes by imagining that, if they are parted in the future, she will remember this place and what he has said to her about it.

That is more or less the "plot" of the poem, and it will be useful to keep its outline in mind as we look at some of the rich details. The poem is both an exercise of memory and a meditation on memory's healing power. It courses back and forth between memory and anticipation, but the anticipation is about memory, too: just as Wordsworth remembers remembering his earlier visit, when he sat in lonely rooms, he also anticipates his sister's remembering the present moment one day when she too is alone. Some readers have thought that Wordsworth could have drawn the same lessons and the same nourishment from almost any natural spot, for what it provides is general, but Wordsworth insists strenuously that it is a particular spot that has meant so much to him, and will mean so much to his sister, while the two gifts it has given him correspond to two physical features of the scene.

> Five years have past; five summers, with the length
> Of five long winters! and again I hear
> These waters, rolling from their mountain-springs
> With a sweet inland murmur—Once again
> Do I behold these steep and lofty cliffs,
> Which on a wild secluded scene impress
> Thoughts of more deep seclusion; and connect
> The landscape with the quiet of the sky.
> The day is come when I again repose
> Here, under this dark sycamore, and view
> These plots of cottage-ground, these orchard-tufts,

Which, at this season, with their unripe fruits,
Among the woods and copses lose themselves,
Nor, with their green and simple hue, disturb
The wild green landscape. Once again I see
These hedge-rows, hardly hedge-rows, little lines
Of sportive wood run wild: these pastoral farms,
Green to the very door; and wreathes of smoke
Sent up, in silence, from among the trees,
With some uncertain notice, as might seem,
Of vagrant dwellers in the houseless woods,
Or of some hermit's cave, where by his fire
The hermit sits alone.

(1–23)

That it must be this place, and this time, Wordsworth could hardly be more emphatic. The poem begins in an explosion of what linguists call "deictic" words, pointing words, words whose referents depend on the situation of the speaker: *these* waters, *these* cliffs, *here*, *this* sycamore, *these* plots, *these* orchard-tufts, *this* season, *these* hedge-rows, *these* farms. He specifies the length of time he has been away, five years, and then repeats it by season, five summers and five winters, to make it seem more exact as well as longer. He says "again" four times, a repetition the poet Tennyson deplored in a poem he otherwise admired. Wordsworth seems to want to convey, in almost helpless gestures of pointing to things, the magical power of this place as he hears and sees it at this time, and his feeling as he notes how exactly it corresponds to his memory of it. He might have tried to name his emotion, but even though he is self-conscious enough ("I hear," "I behold"), he is also closely attending with ear and eye almost exclusively to what is before him.

What he hears and sees seems to have two aspects, wild and cultivated (he uses "wild" three times), the "steep and lofty cliffs" and the "plots of cottage-ground" or "pastoral farms," and they in turn correspond to the two kinds of feelings he will say he owes to his previous visit, the "sensations sweet" (28), which echoes the "sweet inland murmur" of the waters, and a more "sublime" and "blessed" mood (38) which leads to a visionary trance.[2] Twice he notes how his perceptions rouse his thoughts. First he beholds "these steep and lofty cliffs, / Which on a wild secluded scene impress / Thoughts of more deep seclusion," an interesting tangle of theories of perception, suggesting a struggle to understand the mind's relationship to nature or the external world. According to John Locke, whose theory of how we come to know things dominated British thinking, the cliffs would "impress" the beholding mind, which would associate these sense impressions with ideas in its memory and generate appropriate thoughts. But here it is the thoughts that are impressed on the secluded scene, making it seem more secluded; the mind does the impressing, not the cliffs. And yet it is the cliffs after all that enlist the thoughts and impress them on the scene, as if Wordsworth's mind is a mere vehicle of the cliffs' activity, or as if the cliffs themselves think these thoughts. This short-circuiting of the prevalent theory, if I have read it right, anticipates the passage later in the poem where Wordsworth writes that he loves "all the mighty world / Of eye, and ear, both what they half create, / And what perceive" (106–8), and thereby suggests that the cliffs and his mind work together, as joint creators of what he beholds.[3] Second, he lets his imagination people the woods with "vagrant dwellers," plausibly enough, and then, less credibly, with a hermit sitting in his cave alone, as if Wordsworth is revisiting Arcadia, the idealized classical realm of poetic shepherds where one might also meet a hermit. It is the solitary hermit that seems to trigger his memory of living unhappily in "lonely rooms" (26) in the next section of the poem. The poem is not only about *what* a natural spot can teach us but *how*.

This particular scene, then, at this particular season and even this particular day, is all-important to Wordsworth; much of the remainder of his poem grows out of this seedbed, and out of his memories of places that were the opposite of this one and for which this one acted as antidote and cure. Let us return to the title, which names the spot, somewhat vaguely, and the day, very precisely, when he wrote the poem. (In fact, as Wordsworth told a friend many years later, in 1842–3, he spent several days composing his poem as he walked and boated back to Bristol with his sister, putting nothing down on paper until he arrived, but the poem represents or enacts a single speech-act of a few minutes' length. When it appeared in editions of his collected poems, Wordsworth substituted "composed" for "written" in the title.)[4] It is as if we have a diary entry, or perhaps a (rather long) tablet to be erected on the spot to commemorate a remarkable event. Is it presumptuous of Wordsworth to think we care at all about his actual experiences and thoughts on that day? Today, of course, a legion of scholars cares very much about these things, and some scholars have read into the poem their ideas about them, as we shall see later, but I think, as he was hardly known at the time and the poem was anonymous in its first printing, his title is meant simply to underscore the unique "this-ness" of the place and time. It does not imply that this place among all places will bring revelations to every tourist who happens along, but it suggests that we might all have such a place in our lives. The particularity of this place is generalizable in that way, for we have all of us, as he said elsewhere, one human heart.

And the abbey? In view of the to-do Wordsworth himself makes of the spot on the Wye it is fair to ask if the abbey is anything more than the nearest

prominent landmark, part of the generalizable particularity I have been trying to bring out. Wordsworth himself, apparently, did not think of the poem
as connected with the abbey, for a note in the 1800 edition of *Lyrical Ballads*
is headed "NOTE to the Poem ON REVISITING THE WYE," and in 1815
he referred to it as "the poem upon the Wye." Coleridge, in his *Biographia
Literaria* (1817) names it "the lines written near Tintern Abbey" (in quotation
marks) and then in the same paragraph just "Tintern Abbey" (70), but then a
few pages later in the same chapter (79) he calls it "his lines 'on re-visiting the
Wye." It would seem, then, that its author and his closest collaborator thought
of it as the poem about the Wye, but the presence of "Tintern Abbey" in the
title provided an irresistibly handy label for it.[5] Some scholars think the abbey
is present and active in the poem at a deep and "suppressed" level. The date,
too, which seems to allude to the anniversary of the beginning of the French
Revolution, though, oddly, one day before *le quatorze juillet*, seems to these
scholars another clue to subterranean thoughts and fears at work in the poem.
To these suspicions we shall return.

>   Though absent long,
> These forms of beauty have not been to me,
> As is a landscape to a blind man's eye:
> But oft, in lonely rooms, and mid the din
> Of towns and cities, I have owed to them,
> In hours of weariness, sensations sweet,
> Felt in the blood, and felt along the heart,
> And passing even into my purer mind,
> With tranquil restoration:—feelings too
> Of unremembered pleasure; such, perhaps,
> As may have had no trivial influence
> On that best portion of a good man's life;
> His little, nameless, unremembered, acts
> Of kindness and of love. Nor less, I trust,
> To them I may have owed another gift,
> Of aspect more sublime; that blessed mood,
> In which the burthen of the mystery,
> In which the heavy and the weary weight
> Of all this unintelligible world,
> Is lightened:—that serene and blessed mood,
> In which the affections gently lead us on,
> Until, the breath of this corporeal frame,
> And even the motion of our human blood
> Almost suspended, we are laid asleep
> In body, and become a living soul:

> While with an eye made quiet by the power
> Of harmony, and the deep power of joy,
> We see into the life of things.
>
> (23–50)

The poem's second section begins in mid-line, as all but one of the four sections (not counting the first) begin. These are not stanzas. They vary in length from eight lines and a fraction to fifty-two and a fraction. As printed they are separated by a space, but the ending fraction of one section and the beginning fraction of the next make a full line of iambic pentameter. There are no rhymes: this is blank verse, the medium Shakespeare used in most of his plays and Milton used in *Paradise Lost*. By the eighteenth century both drama and epic had largely abandoned blank verse, but it had been adopted in such long meditative or philosophical poems as James Thomson's *The Seasons* (1726–46), Thomas Warton, Jr's *The Pleasures of Melancholy* (1747), and William Cowper's *The Task* (1785), all of which Wordsworth knew well. In the 1798 *Lyrical Ballads* there are six blank-verse poems, three each by Coleridge and Wordsworth; one of Coleridge's, called "The Nightingale," has the subtitle "A Conversation Poem," and it is addressed to "My Friend, and my Friend's Sister" (40). "A Conversation Poem" would be an apt subtitle for "Tintern Abbey," which is addressed, at least at the end, to the same sister, though it is certainly a one-sided conversation. Blank verse seemed to lend itself better than all other verse forms to conversational speech, to "real" speech, and could register the shifts of subject and tone appropriate to a meditative discussion better than verse with shorter, irregular, or rhymed lines. Wordsworth made it his own, not only here but in his tragic story "Michael" and his epic-length autobiography *The Prelude*, but it is not as easy as it looks: he was to say many years later that it is "infinitely the most difficult metre to manage."[6]

This section of slightly over twenty-seven lines Wordsworth fills with just two sentences of roughly equal length, which thus give equal time to the two gifts he has "owed" to the "forms of beauty" he is now beholding again: the sweet sensations and pleasure, on the one hand, which not only restored him to tranquillity but made him a better man with his little acts of kindness and of love; and on the other hand a deeper, "blessed" mood, which has given him the powers of harmony and joy through a sort of visionary trance during which he could see into "the life of things." Both sentences seem to come to an end or "period" syntactically, but both, after a colon and a dash, start again with a noun phrase that either adds a parallel to the preceding one ("feelings" supplementing "sensations") or restates it ("that serene and blessed mood"). It is worth noting the dashes, colons, and semicolons with which Wordsworth tries throughout his poem to keep his long sentences aloft. They help him in his skillful management of the rhetorical arc of his sections, the pacing, tone, and what we might call the music of his syntax. Both sentences come to a climax with moving and memorable phrases or clauses. The first is "that best portion of a good man's life; / His little, nameless, unremembered, acts / Of kindness and of love." These nameless acts are named generically, and it may be precisely their grouping under one general category that gives them their weight and dignity as moral acts. In "The Old Cumberland Beggar," which was added to the 1800 *Lyrical Ballads*, Wordsworth fleshes out what these acts might be as he tells of a woman, though pressed by wants herself, who nonetheless every week gives an "unsparing handful" of meal to the wandering beggar (147–54), while the beggar serves as "a record which together binds / Past deeds and offices of charity / Else unremember'd" (81–3). In "Simon Lee" (in the 1798 edition) Wordsworth reports how he helped an old man struggling with a mattock to cut a tangled root. But the decorum he establishes in "Tintern Abbey" requires generals rather than particulars. It is striking that the only particular in the poem is the scene where it is spoken (as well as the date and place in the title); it is the particular virtue of *this* spot at *this* moment that it gives the poet the distance from which to summarize his moral life in general terms.

The second climax is grander, as befits a gift of "aspect more sublime," a "blessed mood" that draws him into a state where our body seems to sleep and we become a "living soul" with a "quiet" eye endowed with unusual vision. When he returns to these two states of mind he again uses the word "sublime" of the second one (96), so we shall pause here to consider what the sublime was. It was of the greatest importance to the Romantics.

In the sixteenth century an ancient Greek treatise attributed to Longinus was rediscovered and published; it was called *Peri Hypsous*, that is, *On Loftiness* or *On the Sublime*. It was about grandeur in style, or how to achieve deeply moving effects in oratory. Longinus said the soul was raised by hearing a sublime passage, elevated even to ecstasy. As European writers discussed the idea, it got attached to natural scenery as well as to verbal descriptions of it, and especially to mountains, great vistas, and stormy seas and skies. Joseph Addison, writing in 1712, claimed "Our Imagination loves to be filled with an Object, or to grasp at any thing that is too big for its Capacity. We are flung into a pleasing Astonishment at such unbounded Views, and feel a delightful Stillness and Amazement in the Soul at the Apprehension of them." This "stillness" seems quite like the serenity and quietness Wordsworth describes, but a common view of the sublime after Addison put greater weight on the terror of it. "Whatever is fitted in any sort to excite the ideas of pain, and danger," In 1757 Edmund Burke wrote in *Enquiry into the Sublime and the Beautiful*:

that is to say, whatever is in any sort terrible, … or operates in a manner analogous to terror, is a source of the *sublime*; that is, it is productive of the strongest emotion which the mind is capable of feeling … When danger or pain press too nearly, they are incapable of giving any delight, and are simply terrible; but at certain distances, and with certain modifications, they may be, and they are delightful, as we every day experience.

Burke goes on to say, using a phrase Wordsworth seems to echo:

The passion caused by the great and sublime in *nature*, when those causes operate most powerfully, is Astonishment; and astonishment is that state of the soul, in which all its motions are suspended, with some degree of horror. In this case the mind is so entirely filled with its object, that it cannot entertain any other, nor by consequence reason on that object which employs it.

In Wordsworth's account it is the motion of the body, even its pulse, that is "suspended," not that of the soul, which is not astonished but serene, joyful, and "living" as it penetrates into "the life of things."

The sublime was commonly contrasted with the beautiful, which categorized pleasing, gentle, inviting scenery, cultivated as opposed to wild, and feminine as opposed to the masculine sublime. These two aesthetic categories seem to govern the distinction between the "gifts" Wordsworth has received from this place.

Many writers considered the sublime to belong to God and his works, to the language of parts of the Bible, and to the emotion of religious awe. Wordsworth's language will take a religious turn later in his poem, but here it is only lightly evoked in the word "blessed" (twice). Nonetheless the trancelike state he describes is akin to the transport or ecstasy of a Christian mystic, who strives through meditation or prayer or fasting to unite with God. There is no God in this poem. The "harmony" that descends on him is not explicitly *with* anything, God or otherwise; it is just harmony itself, seemingly an inner state. And what he sees is not God or a type or symbol of God but "the life of things." His "living" soul is in harmony, we might say, with this "life," and nature or natural things share something living with him. Beyond that it is difficult to say just what he experiences.

We shall return to this question when the poem does, but it is important to notice, in the third and shortest section, that Wordsworth seems to lose his nerve for a moment, to shrink back from his surge of sublime rhetoric and to doubt his own powers.

                    If this
Be but a vain belief, yet, oh! how oft,

In darkness, and amid the many shapes
Of joyless day-light; when the fretful stir
Unprofitable, and the fever of the world,
Have hung upon the beatings of my heart,
How oft, in spirit, have I turned to thee
O sylvan Wye! thou wanderer thro' the woods,
How often has my spirit turned to thee!

(50–8)

It does not seem possible that he would concede that his intense insight into "the life of things" might be a vain belief unless he were admonished by someone that his belief is not entirely orthodox (here is a hint that this is indeed a "conversation" with his sister), but I think we must attribute this concession to a tendency toward doubting in his own mind, signs of which we have already heard, such as "perhaps" (32) and "I trust" (36), and will hear again, with "I dare to hope" (66), "no doubt" (67), "I would believe" (88), and "perchance" (147). They might be mere filler, for he is composing verse, after all, and needs five feet in each line, but his cautious, almost pedantic, qualifications of otherwise bold assertions lend an air of reasonableness to the whole poem. Perhaps too much reasonableness, we might feel, yet when he returns in the next section to just what happens in his "sublime" state of mind he does not hesitate to press a belief quite far from orthodox Christian teaching. This reasonableness, then, might be calculated to disarm in advance those who might object to his "vain belief." A similar effect can be attributed to the many negative phrases, such as "have not been to me" (23), "no slight or trivial influence" (32), and "nor less" (35), and to the many negative words, such as "unripe," "uncertain," "unremembered" (twice), "unintelligible," "joyless," "unprofitable," and the like, over thirty such constructions in all. The tone that results suggests a man sobered by the passage of time and the wearying experiences he describes, "the fretful stir / Unprofitable, and the fever of the world," and tentative about what they all mean as he marks an anniversary on this day, but a man still given to surges of rapturous feeling and hopeful belief. The uneasy balance between these two moods is characteristic of Wordsworth at his best; a few years later, many readers have felt, the balance tips toward caution and restraint, and he loses much of his poetic power.

In the most puzzling clause of this little section, Wordsworth says the stir and fever "Have hung upon the beatings of my heart." I don't know how to paraphrase this so that it makes sense, but it seems tied to the two gifts he owes to the place: the "sensations sweet, / Felt in the blood" (28–9) and the "blessed mood" where "the motion of our human blood" is "almost suspended" (45–6). His three contrasting states of mind correspond, metaphorically if not medically, to three levels of blood pressure. This section, too, has the only apostrophe in the poem, a direct address to a nonhuman entity, the "sylvan Wye," who like Wordsworth himself five years ago, as we will see, is a "wanderer thro' the woods." It is perhaps a "literary" touch, the sort of thing conventional in odes, but it seems heartfelt. Wordsworth allows that his notion of seeing into the life of things may be mistaken, but he insists he gained something from his earlier visit to this spot overlooking this river.

In the next section he returns to his "deictics" (*now, here, this moment, these hills*) as if to reorient himself before resuming his wandering meditation.

> And now, with gleams of half-extinguished thought,
> With many recognitions dim and faint,
> And somewhat of a sad perplexity,
> The picture of the mind revives again:
> While here I stand, not only with the sense
> Of present pleasure, but with pleasing thoughts
> That in this moment there is life and food
> For future years. And so I dare to hope,
> Though changed, no doubt, from what I was, when first
> I came among these hills; when like a roe
> I bounded o'er the mountains, by the sides
> Of the deep rivers, and the lonely streams,
> Wherever nature led; more like a man
> Flying from something that he dreads, than one
> Who sought the thing he loved. For nature then
> (The coarser pleasures of my boyish days,
> And their glad animal movements all gone by)
> To me was all in all.—I cannot paint
> What then I was. The sounding cataract
> Haunted me like a passion: the tall rock,
> The mountain, and the deep and gloomy wood,
> Their colours and their forms, were then to me
> An appetite: a feeling and a love,
> That had no need of a remoter charm,
> By thought supplied, or any interest
> Unborrowed from the eye.

(59–84)

Wordsworth now looks forward briefly, hoping to repeat in the future the enjoyment of the same "life and food" from this place that he garnered five years ago and has drawn on ever since, but in the remainder of this section he looks back, and this time he attempts to say something about what he was like then. When he came here five years ago he was no longer a boy with "glad animal movements," he tells us, but he must not have outgrown his boyish days by much for he nonetheless bounded like a roe in pursuit of nature. Nature then was all in all, sufficient unto itself, with no need of "thought" or reflection to supply charm or interest. Now he has "thoughts" as he looks upon the scene, both pleasing, as he thinks about future benefits, and sad, as he feels perplexed, for unstated reasons. We might be perplexed ourselves at his comparison of his former self as "more like a man / Flying from something that he dreads, than one / Who sought the thing he loved." Some readers, as we shall see, have taken this simile as a clue to something lurking behind or beneath the poem that Wordsworth wanted to suppress. Here it is enough to take in the unexplained hint of something unhappy in his previous visit, as if that bounding roe were fleeing a wolf or hunter. On the basis of what the poem itself gives us, we can easily imagine Wordsworth fleeing the city, with its joylessness and fever, its loneliness and din, but "dread" strikes us as a little too strong a word for his feeling about it.

This section continues, relaunched by a dash.

> —That time is past,
> And all its aching joys are now no more,
> And all its dizzy raptures. Not for this
> Faint I, nor mourn nor murmur: other gifts
> Have followed; for such loss, I would believe,
> Abundant recompence. For I have learned
> To look on nature, not as in the hour
> Of thoughtless youth; but hearing oftentimes
> The still, sad music of humanity,
> Nor harsh nor grating, though of ample power
> To chasten and subdue.

(84–94)

Whatever dread was suggested in his simile, the "time" five years ago, full of joys and raptures, is irrevocably past. The poem grows sadder, more chastened, and subdued. Wordsworth claims he does not mourn or murmur, but he sounds mournful here over his "loss," and even when he claims to have found "abundant recompence" for it he murmurs another qualifying clause, "I would believe," which undermines his claim. What has he gained in recompence? Thought, to be sure, for he is no longer "thoughtless," but also a more acute power of hearing, he says, for he can hear "the still, sad music of humanity." It is still, or inaudible, presumably, to thoughtless ones, like his former self, but he can hear it now that thought has amplified its music. It is a memorable line, but like the memorable "little, nameless, unremembered, acts / Of kindness and of love" it is very general, and invites us fill it with our own associations.

Its abstractness lends it distance, and indeed Wordsworth has withdrawn into his mind so far that human sadness, which heard close up might sound harsh and grating, now sounds like music, a dirge, to his tutored ears. We recall the "eye made quiet by the power / Of harmony" that lets him "see into the life of things" (48–50); when he *hears* into the life of things he finds the music of humanity.

But just as the "sensations sweet" recalled in his lonely rooms (28) yielded to a deeper and "more sublime" feeling (38), so this sad music gives way to something sublime and elevated:

> And I have felt
> A presence that disturbs me with the joy
> Of elevated thoughts; a sense sublime
> Of something far more deeply interfused,
> Whose dwelling is the light of setting suns,
> And the round ocean, and the living air,
> And the blue sky, and in the mind of man,
> A motion and a spirit, that impels
> All thinking things, all objects of all thought,
> And rolls through all things.

(94–103)

This "something" is even vaguer than "the life of things" and, we may ask, "far more deeply interfused" than what? But there it is, and it is not a passing phrase, for Wordsworth rises to his most sublime rhetorical pitch in describing it, with the chain of appositions connected by "and" and the climax with "all" four times in the final two lines. It ends, like the comparable passage earlier, with the word "things." One line of this passage, "Whose dwelling is the light of setting suns," struck Tennyson as "almost the grandest in the English language, giving the sense of the abiding in the transient";[7] its grandeur is not diminished if we also catch in it a suggestion that Wordsworth feels he has entered the evening of his life.

So what is this "something," this motion or spirit? It "impels" all things thinking and all things thought, human things and inanimate, subject and object, and it "rolls" through them all. This is not God, certainly not the transcendent God of most versions of Christian belief. It seems most like the "God" of pantheism, the doctrine traceable to Benedict Spinoza (1632–77), who argued the identity of God and Nature as two aspects of one universal substance. We know Coleridge had been talking about Spinoza with Wordsworth as they ambled about the English countryside during the incubation of the *Lyrical Ballads*, but he would have talked about a hundred other philosophers as well, and in fact several French materialists and British empiricists had described nature, and the spirit of nature, and even God, in terms similar to Wordsworth's. Later readers of the poem found pantheism in the poem and complained about it. But just what philosophical doctrine Wordsworth invokes here, if any, is less important than the experience he is laboring to convey. It is disturbing and stirring, and a source of joy, as well as a gift of seeing more deeply into the universe. And surely it is important that he refuses to use the word "God" in both passages that describe this elevated state of mind; nor does he use it late in the poem when his language otherwise grows religious.

The anti-romantic critic T. E. Hulme (1883–1917) called Romanticism "spilt religion,"[8] and more recent scholars more sympathetic to it, such as Northrop Frye and M. H. Abrams, have stressed the characteristic way Romanticism redefined or reshaped traditional Christian doctrine. One may figure the traditional view as a triangle, with God at the apex and the soul (or self) as one lower corner and nature (or matter or "flesh") as the other. God is the transcendent creator of both soul and nature, and the chief business of the Christian soul is to have as little to do with nature as she can during her perilous walk through this life. At best, nature, as God's handiwork, can teach us something about him, but it is also the source of distraction and sin. The goal is to reunite with God, certainly in heaven after death, and possibly also through mystical contemplation in this fallen world. The philosophers of the Enlightenment dethroned God, making him at best the creator of the universe and its laws but not an intervener with "miracles" or a responder to prayers; he is an abstract prime mover, not a personal being, and is not concerned with us. This "Deism" or "natural religion" had no room for heaven and hell, Christ as incarnation of God, the Trinity, the miracles of the Bible, and all the rest of Christian theology.

Romanticism by and large accepted this critique of traditional belief but not its cool rationality; it saw God as dead but his "divinity" as bequeathed to the soul and nature. The soul had something divine or holy in it, and so did nature. "God becomes as we are," Blake wrote in 1788, "that we may be as he is." Wordsworth wrote, "By our own spirits are we deified" (1802). In Germany similar claims were emerging among the first Romantic generation, such as Friedrich Schlegel, who claimed "Every good human being is always progressively becoming God" (1800). As for nature, it contains secrets, truths, sometimes even a personality, when approached by a reverential soul. Depth answers to depth, life to life. When we become a "living soul," as Wordsworth says in "Tintern Abbey," we see the "life" of nature. Enlightenment rationalism, and modern science, won the theological arguments but at the price of a dead universe. Romanticism rescues religious feeling, now no longer directed upward to God but outward to nature and inward to the soul, and it reanimates the one as it revives the other.

Perhaps the poem should have ended here, but, with an inevitable anticlimax, Wordsworth draws a conclusion from his profound vision, and goes on:

> Therefore am I still
> A lover of the meadows and the woods,
> And mountains; and of all that we behold
> From this green earth; of all the mighty world
> Of eye, and ear, both what they half create,
> And what perceive; well pleased to recognise
> In nature and the language of the sense,
> The anchor of my purest thoughts, the nurse,
> The guide, the guardian of my heart, and soul
> Of all my moral being.

(103–12)

The "half-creation" of the world, as we noted earlier, resembles the ambiguous mutual "impressing" of cliffs and thoughts in the opening section, but if we pause on this passage we may detect another interesting and somewhat uncertain idea. In the phrase "the mighty world / Of eye, and ear" the "of" is the most intriguing word. This is not *the* mighty world, it seems, the real world that we take in through eye and ear and that would exist whether we took it in or not. It seems rather to be the phenomenal world, the world as it appears to us through eye and ear, and it has two aspects or kinds of things, "what they [eye and ear] half create" and "what perceive." We might have expected Wordsworth to say we half create the phenomenal world and half perceive it, a respectable philosophical stance he seems to take elsewhere, but here he seems to bifurcate the world twice over, both in its sources (the senses versus "real" nature) and in its contents (some things are half the product of our senses and some things are just perceived entirely as they are). Wordsworth knew enough philosophy, and his friend Coleridge knew more than enough, to know that this question is bottomless. As with the vague "something" that rolls through all things, this passing stab at epistemology serves to evoke no more than a general idea, an intuition or feeling about how things are, and it gains its authority more from the sincerity and eloquence of the lines than from its logical cogency. He is writing a poem, after all, not a treatise, and it is a poem dramatizing a lived response to an occasion spoken to a particular person, as we soon find out. It is important to see, nonetheless, that Wordsworth again courts condemnation from pious Christians when he concludes this section by avowing that it is not God or the Bible that anchors his thoughts, or nurses, guides, and guards his heart, or animates his moral being, but nature and the language of the sense.

The final section, which begins with another little flourish of pointing words (*here*, *this*), is entirely addressed to his sister, who has been at his side, unknown to us, throughout.

> Nor perchance,
> If I were not thus taught, should I the more
> Suffer my genial spirits to decay:
> For thou art with me, here, upon the banks
> Of this fair river; thou my dearest Friend,
> My dear, dear Friend, and in thy voice I catch
> The language of my former heart, and read
> My former pleasures in the shooting lights
> Of thy wild eyes. Oh! yet a little while
> May I behold in thee what I was once,
> My dear, dear Sister!
>
> (112–22)

If nature and the language of the sense had not been his nurse and guide, he might still preserve his "genial spirits" because he can recapture them in his sister's voice and eyes. The phrase "genial spirits" repeats the phrase in Milton's *Samson Agonistes* (1671), where it means the spirits arising from one's "genius" or natural character. Because she is now what he was once, she can stand in for nature, almost as the spirit of this very place, the *genius loci*, at least to him. Her "wild" eyes are attuned to the "wild secluded scene" (6) and the "sportive wood run wild" (17) of the opening; he will return to her "wild eyes" (149) and to her "wild ecstasies" (139) in what follows. But just as he has changed in five years, he knows she will change too, as he reveals in what sounds like his last wish: "Oh! yet a little while[!]" This somewhat desperate note surfaces more quietly throughout the final section, and casts a somber light on both sister and brother, and on all humanity, as if it is ineluctably fated that we must all lose our genial spirits and shed our wild pleasures. Yet Nature still has power to redeem:

> And this prayer I make,
> Knowing that Nature never did betray
> The heart that loved her; 'tis her privilege,
> Through all the years of this our life, to lead
> From joy to joy: for she can so inform
> The mind that is within us, so impress
> With quietness and beauty, and so feed
> With lofty thoughts, that neither evil tongues,
> Rash judgments, nor the sneers of selfish men,
> Nor greetings where no kindness is, nor all

> The dreary intercourse of daily life,
> Shall e'er prevail against us, or disturb
> Our chearful faith, that all which we behold
> Is full of blessings.
>
> (122–35)

We hear again of the twofold gift of nature, "beauty" and sublimity ("lofty thoughts"), and hear a fuller account of just what these gifts protect us from. What was a general "din" and loneliness in cities (26–7), or a "fretful stir" and "fever of the world" (53–4), or perhaps the "still, sad music of humanity" (92), is now specified as selfishness and unkindness in speech, from evil speaking to cold greetings. We might have expected something worse, acts of violence or oppression, perhaps, but it is the routine experience of the city (the "world") that is uppermost in his fears, almost "daily life" itself, which threaten to wear us down, or drag us down, from our lofty inner citadel. And this daily life manifests itself in debased uses of language, which it is the calling of poets, of course, to combat.

In *The Autobiography of William Rutherford* (1881), William Hale White credited the lines "Knowing that Nature never did betray / The heart that loved her" with the beginning of his religious conversion, which he likens to that of Paul on the road to Damascus, but it was a conversion away from the narrow Calvinist theology he had studied, with its abstract "artificial" God which had "hardened into an idol," and toward "a new and living spirit."[9] A more religious vocabulary begins indeed to enter the poem at this point: a prayer is announced, Nature instills a "faith," all is "full of blessings." In fact "Nature" is capitalized for the first time and personified. In its three previous appearances (73, 90, 109) it was neutral, unmetaphorical, abstract; now she steps forward as a goddess who will not betray her disciples but lead them from joy to joy, while informing, impressing, and feeding their minds.

Now comes the prayer, still addressed to his sister but exhorting her to make Nature her companion.

> Therefore let the moon
> Shine on thee in thy solitary walk;
> And let the misty mountain winds be free
> To blow against thee: and, in after years,
> When these wild ecstasies shall be matured
> Into a sober pleasure; when thy mind
> Shall be a mansion for all lovely forms,
> Thy memory be as a dwelling-place
> For all sweet sounds and harmonies; Oh! then,
> If solitude, or fear, or pain, or grief,

Should be thy portion, with what healing thoughts
Of tender joy wilt thou remember me,
And these my exhortations! Nor, perchance,
If I should be, where I no more can hear
Thy voice, nor catch from thy wild eyes these gleams
Of past existence, wilt thou then forget
That on the banks of this delightful stream
We stood together; and that I, so long
A worshipper of Nature, hither came,
Unwearied in that service: rather say
With warmer love, oh! with far deeper zeal
Of holier love. Nor wilt thou then forget,
That after many wanderings, many years
Of absence, these steep woods and lofty cliffs,
And this green pastoral landscape, were to me
More dear, both for themselves, and for thy sake.

(135–60)

It is a lovely prayer, with the moon and winds, and his wish that her mind and memory become a "mansion" and "dwelling-place" of lovely and sweet forms, not just a reservoir, as perhaps his own has become, from which he draws sensations that console him in times of darkness and joyless daylight (52–3), but a permanent home for her spirit. If she nonetheless meets with "solitude, or fear, or pain, or grief," she will have the additional resource of the memory of this moment. His wish then turns somewhat anxious and mournful. Earlier Wordsworth looked forward to future remembrances of this second visit as providing spiritual food like that which had nourished him after his first, but now, fearing he may be separated from his sister, he asserts that, if Nature remains her companion, she will remember him and his exhortations. The place itself may not be enough. If he has made her for the moment almost into the spirit of the place, indeed almost into the now personified goddess Nature, he projects a time to come when she will take *him* to be its spirit, or rather the mediator of its spirit, its interpreter. Taken neat, as it were, her experience might be ecstatic, wild, full of dizzy raptures, but he does not let her take it neat: he dilutes it with his sermon about her inevitable sobering (140) and thus hastens the day when it will happen. His love for her is evident in many ways, and it is touching that he passes the torch to her, but he has half quenched that torch with his older-brother preaching. We should not be too hard on him, however, for he is groping with deep and unformulable intuitions into the power of nature, memories of unhappiness, fears of mortality, and separation from his beloved sister, all the while trying to give her the greatest gift he can.[10]

He is also writing a poem for the general public to read, and bringing it to a climax. The religious words grow more frequent and prominent: he is a "worshipper of Nature" (capitalized again), performing his "service" with "zeal" and "holier love." Nature, even this spot on the Wye, is his church now, and he is its priest. In 1815, learning that "worshipper of Nature" had caused offense to a right-minded reader, Wordsworth denied that he could fairly be so called. Only in "cold-heartedness" could a reader take literally and seriously "a passionate expression uttered incautiously in the Poem upon the Wye." He had grown more conservative, and more cautious, by 1815, and his disingenuous explanation does not carry conviction. Yet he goes on to say something more interesting. He denies that he looks upon God and Nature as the same thing, as Spinoza did. But he "does not indeed consider the Supreme Being as bearing the same relation to the universe as a watch-maker bears to a watch … there is nothing so injurious as the perpetually talking about making by God." He has taught his child the idea that God is "not like his flesh which he could touch; but more like his thoughts." If God is not the creator of the universe but more like its thoughts or mind, we are not far after all from the pantheism or serious nature worship of the poem. Wordsworth may have come to hold two beliefs, or outwardly professed one and inwardly held the other.

His other task as a poet was to bring this long and digression-prone poem into some sort of shape, and the simplest way to do so was to circle back to the opening scene. He had recurred to it twice before, with his deictics, but now it is more exact in phrasing, with "these steep woods and lofty cliffs" echoing "these steep and lofty cliffs" (5) and "this green pastoral landscape" restating "these pastoral farms / Green to the very door" (17–18). Coleridge called this sort of reprise a "rondo" in his discussion of his own poem "Frost at Midnight," which has much in common with Wordsworth's poem, for the reprise is clearest in music, but a sonata might be a better parallel than a rondo. The subjects of a sonata, after many developments and diversions, are recapitulated at the end. Something like this pattern is heard in the melody of "Tintern Abbey." We might add that Wordsworth's recapitulation is in a minor key, a sadder tone, and it modulates a late theme introduced two-thirds of the way through, by making his dear landscape dearer for the presence of his beloved sister.

And perhaps this almost elegiac ending, as if he is about to die and is bequeathing his dearest gift to his dearest friend, helps explain the long and awkward title with its date and groping attempt to locate the spot. To make sure she does not "forget / That on the banks of this delightful stream / We stood together" he makes an entry as if into her own journal, where time and place must be recorded.

In the 1980s, as "New Historicism" gained influence among literary scholars, along with a sophisticated Marxism, the title of the poem began to loom even larger than its length would seem to warrant, and it looked to some scholars as if it signaled a barely suppressed political or social reality that Wordsworth was trying to forget or flee. In a long and challenging essay Marjorie Levinson asks why Wordsworth, having evoked Tintern Abbey in the title, has nothing to say about it in the poem. The abbey is a conspicuous absence, she argues, an erasure that leaves a permeating smudge, "a visible darkness" that "precipitates and organizes" the text.[11] She also notes the multiple anniversaries evoked by the date – the eve of the ninth anniversary of the French Revolution, the exact eighth anniversary of Wordsworth's own arrival in France on a walking tour, and the fifth anniversary of the assassination of the French revolutionary leader Marat – but she discusses only the abbey, which Wordsworth and his sister Dorothy would have seen at least twice during their ramble and read about in a recent guidebook by William Gilpin that they carried with them. They would have seen, for instance, the homeless vagrants who were camping out in the abbey ruin, and the "poverty and wretchedness" (Gilpin's phrase) of the local people in and near the village of Tintern. The only mention of vagrants in the poem comes in the opening, where wreathes of smoke, "as might seem," suggest "vagrant dwellers in the houseless woods," or even a hermit sitting in his cave. That is as close as Wordsworth comes to registering a particular social fact; everything else he generalizes, blurs, and distances, transforming harsh social facts into aesthetic harmony, or replacing them with nature. The poem is a "palimpsest" (a page of ancient text scraped off and written on again), and "what the poem depicts is less interesting than the subject thereby overwritten" (34), the social or political subtext. "The primary poetic action is the suppression of the social" (37), and it is the duty of the critic to expose the cover-up.[12]

I have noted Wordsworth's tendency to generalize human suffering and distance himself from it, but it is quite a different thing to argue that this tendency, or any other features of the poem, can only be accounted for by some great force off stage that he refuses to confront. We might adopt Levinson's own distinction between explicating a poem, which she considers the easier task as well as the more "courteous" one, and explaining it.[13] I have been explicating the poem, I think, and I have been doing so largely by staying within the poem and pointing out meanings and relationships among parts; where I have gone outside the poem it has been to amplify the meanings of words and ideas, such as the sublime, that readers of Wordsworth's day would have known. Is that enough? Should we also "explain" a poem? That presumably means giving an account of its origin, what motivated it, as well as an account of certain details not well assimilated into its explicit argument structure, and to do those things we have to bring to bear what we know of Wordsworth's life. We noted, for example, the simile in Wordsworth's description of his state of mind five years earlier, when he followed "wherever nature led," but "more like a man / Flying from something that he dreads, than one / Who sought the thing he loved" (71–3). Within the poem itself, the only thing named that might be something to dread is the city, with its loneliness and heartlessness and din, but that may not seem satisfactory; an "explication" of the poem might not quite tie up that loose end. A kind of political psychoanalysis of the poem would "explain" that loose end by following it to its source outside the poem, and then, by using it to unravel other parts of the poem, to show the seams behind its apparently seamless texture.

What might Wordsworth have dreaded? Well, quite a bit, it turns out. Born in 1770, he was 19 and a student at Cambridge when the French Revolution began in July 1789. It is easy to forget how tremendous an event, or chain of events, the Revolution was, and how it roused the enthusiasm of large numbers of people, especially young people, throughout Europe. France was the largest, most populous, most powerful country in western Europe, its cultural center, and the ancient rival of Britain, just across the Channel. Almost overnight the near absolute monarchy of Louis XVI yielded to the demands of the Third Estate (the vast majority, who were not clergy or nobility) for a constitutional monarchy with a bill of rights. Many Britons felt that France was following Britain's lead (which had already a strong Parliament and anticourt traditions) or was going no further than enlightened reason and justice demanded. It seemed the beginning of the renovation of the world. "Bliss was it in that dawn to be alive," Wordsworth famously wrote, "But to be young was very heaven!" Everything seemed possible. Within exactly a year (less one day) of the storming of the Bastille Wordsworth landed in Calais for a tour of France with a friend. The next day was the anniversary Festival of the Federation, perhaps the happiest and most unified moment of the Revolutionary Era, where cities and villages across the nation celebrated in ceremonies and dances; Wordsworth danced with them, though he remained somewhat aloof from politics on this tour. He made another, much longer, visit a year later, where he saw much more, and followed events more closely: he was "pretty hot in it," as he later said, with friends among the revolutionaries. He also had an affair and fathered a child. But he left France in late 1792 on the eve of hostilities with Britain.

When the war broke out in early 1793, after the execution of the king (who had not cooperated with the new constitutions), Wordsworth was utterly out of sympathy with his own government, and with the majority of the British people, who had lost whatever sympathy they had felt with France. He grew more radical and explicitly "republican," drafted pamphlets, associated with political organizers and publishers. But he was also torn about the Revolution, which had been confiscated by the near dictatorship of Robespierre and lurched into the Terror for about a year. By 1793, too, British government censorship, prosecution of radical spokesmen for sedition or treason, and "Church and King" mobs made it dangerous for people like Wordsworth to speak out. That summer, when he made his first visit to Tintern Abbey and the Wye Valley, he might well have been in flight from something that he dreaded. By 1798, it is possible, he was fleeing again; his feelings about both France and Britain were still torturing him; he was soon to go to Germany for a year with Dorothy and Coleridge, perhaps to avoid the draft. There was also the first of several invasion scares that year, as rumors flew that French armies were amassing to invade Britain.

If we add to all this the poverty and wretchedness Wordsworth doubtless saw in and around Tintern Abbey on both visits, there are more than enough anxieties and conflicts that we may attribute to his mind and heart at the time he composed the poem. But are they in the poem? Are they so clamorous that Wordsworth could not set them aside as he wrote a poem about growing up and growing old and the consolations of nature, themes applicable to almost anyone at any time? He wrote forthrightly enough about France, war, poverty, and his troubled feelings about them on other occasions; if he had not, in fact, we would not be wondering why he left them out of this poem. He may have had a dozen other feelings and strong opinions rattling around in his mind as he composed the poem, all of which, rightly, we do not know anything about. The question is too complicated to be settled here, but a few points are worth taking in. A great deal of the historicist argument hangs on the title. If Wordsworth had left Tintern Abbey out of the title and located his dark sycamore some other way, it is fair to ask, would anyone have thought to argue that he was evading or suppressing the bitter social facts the abbey would have shown him? Is the abbey, as I proposed earlier, anything more than a convenient landmark for locating another place? As for the date, while July 13 may have been meaningful to Wordsworth, it could not possibly mean anything to a reader at the time; if Bastille Day passed through a reader's mind, it would also be dismissed, as 13 is not 14. In short, for all the history the New Historicists bring to bear on this poem, they are not historians enough, for they forget that much of the history they know, especially the history of Wordsworth's own involvement in social and political affairs in Britain and France, was unknown to readers at the time. Wordsworth's name was not attached to the first edition, and few people knew anything about him anyway. More to the point, perhaps, we do not know what else might have been troubling Wordsworth's soul at this time – he himself might not have known it – so it seems arbitrary to select out one or two things we do know something about and assume they were at work distorting the poem. And finally the New Historicists are not psychologists enough, for as they seek factors that "explain" a poem, as if a poem were a symptom, like an involuntary twitch, that must have a hidden cause, they pass over what is usually the prime motive behind any poet's poem: to compose a poem! Shelley was to say, "The poet & the man are two different natures: though they exist together they may be unconscious of each other, & incapable of deciding upon each other's powers & effects by any reflex act."[14] Byron was of the same opinion: "A man's poetry is a distinct faculty, or soul, and has no more to do with the every-day individual than the Inspiration with the Pythoness when removed from her tripod."[15]

I like to imagine Wordsworth today in the temple of fame, leaning down from time to time to pick up what people are saying about his poetry, and slapping his forehead as he learns of the kerfuffle scholars have recently made over the abbey at Tintern, which he happened to put in his title. If he could do it over again, I think, he might change the title to "Lines Written at 51° 45' N. Latitude, 2° 40' W. Longitude, or Thereabouts, On Revisiting the Banks of the Wye During a Tour, July 13, 1798."

To publish a poem is to enter into a kind of contract or understanding with readers that it is a public work accessible to them. A poem is not an everyday utterance or speech-act where slips of the tongue, say, might reveal something suppressed or repressed by the utterer; it is a formal and conventional imitation of a speech-act uttered by a persona created by the author, a work of craftsmanship the making of which takes many times longer than the internal time of the poem, or the time a reader takes to read it. Wordsworth spent four days composing the poem as he walked with his sister, then wrote it down, doubtless making little changes as he did; he later corrected proofs from the printer; several years later he made slight changes in the printed text, so there are two versions of the poem. We should remember, finally, that even if Wordsworth had felt that he should give full vent to his feelings and opinions about France and local vagrants and social injustice in general, however inappropriate to the subject of his poem, the political climate in 1798 was so reactionary that he would have been hard-pressed to get it published at all. As it was, he gave full vent to something else, his thoughts and emotions on returning to a dear place with his dear sister after a long time away.

Romantic odes

In his "NOTE to the Poem ON REVISITING THE WYE," in the 1800 *Lyrical Ballads*, Wordsworth writes, rather stuffily: "I have not ventured to call this Poem an Ode; but it was written with a hope that in the transitions, and the impassioned music of the versification would be found the principal requisites of that species of composition." Within two years Wordsworth was at work on his first and greatest ode, explicitly so-called; it was completed in 1804 and published in 1807 under the title "Ode." It was not until he reprinted it in 1815 that he gave it the subtitle by which it is known, another mouthful like the subtitle of the "Lines" on revisiting the Wye: "Intimations of Immortality from Recollections of Early Childhood." It is often reduced to the handier "Immortality Ode" or "Intimations Ode." As its theme, the loss of a gift he had in childhood and youth, and the compensation of a higher gift, resembles that of the earlier almost-ode, I will begin this chapter with a brief comparison of the two. I will then say something about odes in general, and lastly read closely two of the finest Romantic odes, one by Keats and one by Shelley.

Wordsworth's "Immortality Ode"

Though they are similar in length, the "Immortality Ode" and "Tintern Abbey" could hardly differ more in form. The 203 lines of the "Ode" are distributed into eleven stanzas of very uneven sizes, ranging from the eight lines of stanza six to the thirty-nine lines of stanza nine. Line lengths differ just as much, from the three syllables in line 30 ("Land and sea") to the fourteen in line 35 ("Shout round me, let me hear thy shouts, thou happy Shepherd-boy!"). The "Ode" is thoroughly rhymed, but under a scheme no more predictable than the stanza and line lengths. The twenty-three lines in stanza seven, for instance, rhyme like this: **abbabcdceecffdfggchhhii**. One would guess from this pattern that there would be a lot of couplets, but some rhymed lines are paired syntactically with ones before or after them, and some are of different lengths. And look how long it takes for the **d**-rhyme to find its mate – from line 7 ("life") to line 14 ("strife") – while the **c**-rhyme ("chart") finds its third counterpart ("part") seven lines after its second ("heart"). All these intricate but seemingly irregular formalities are a world apart from the much more regular but speechlike informality of the blank verse of "Tintern Abbey." And yet the "Ode" is meant to seem to be a spontaneous outpouring of thoughts and feelings.

The diction, for all that, is similar in the two poems, and in both it moves up and down in register somewhat as the emotional and rhetorical pressure rises and falls, though the ode is sustained on the whole at a higher pitch, as if the two great climaxes of "Tintern Abbey" were prolonged. There are a lot of direct addresses to various subjects ("Ye blessed Creatures," "Thou best Philosopher"), imperatives ("Shout round me," "Then sing, ye birds"), rhetorical questions ("Whither is fled the visionary gleam?"), and sixteen exclamation points, not all of them required by the imperatives. It is "impassioned music," to be sure, sometimes pressed to the breaking point. Though there are soft and meditative moments, even a light touch or two (as in the opening of stanza seven), the ode strives for sheer intensity of feeling, as if that will make up for the loss of the visionary gleam.

And that is the theme. The first two short stanzas are twins in structure, the first describing the time in the speaker's past when the world was clothed in a "celestial light" (4), the second describing the lovely and glorious natural things he still sees today, but both ending with a long line declaring his loss: "The things which I have seen I now can see no more" (8) and "there hath past away a glory from the earth" (17). This double rise and fall is repeated on a greater scale in the two longer stanzas that follow, where the speaker also reveals the occasion of his poem, a lovely May morning where children and lambs are frolicking as if on a holiday (32–3) or jubilee or festival (38–9). Though he promises no grief of his shall wrong the season (26), protests it would be a bad thing if he were "sullen" on such a day (42), and insists he feels in his heart the fullness of the bliss all around him (39–41), he nonetheless returns for the third time to the loss he announced in the first stanzas: "Where is it now, the glory and the dream?" (57).

The word "glory" has occurred three times already and will recur three times again, while "glorious" has appeared once and will reappear once. An unusual sense seems to be signaled here, something like "radiance" or "splendor" (for the noun), indeed the very "celestial light" or "visionary gleam" (56) that Wordsworth names. "Glory" trails with it a cloud of religious connotations, as "celestial" would suggest, from its use in such common phrases as "the glory of God" or "heavenly glory," and we are thus put on notice that the story of loss and possible recovery has serious spiritual implications, as if it were a classic religious autobiography like Augustine's or Bunyan's. The primary sense is visual, however: glory is a special kind of light, different from "the light of common day" (76), and when we are alert to that fact we can see the whole poem as permeated by the imagery of light of various kinds and from various directions.[1]

There is reason to believe that Wordsworth stopped work on the ode after the first four stanzas and let two years pass before resuming it. If so, why would this be? Is there a reason inferable from the poem itself? Certainly Wordsworth had other things on his mind in 1802, such as a visit to France (during the brief peace with Britain) to see his mistress Annette Vallon for the first time in nine years and to meet their daughter, and then to marry Mary Hutchinson and set up a new household, not to mention other literary work. Still, it is tempting to see the first four stanzas as a poignant statement of a problem that has no plausible solution – why do we have this glorious light when we are young, and why do we lose it? – and the remainder of the poem as a fresh start at finding one, both by giving a metaphysical explanation of the phenomenon and by offering a consolation for it.

In any case a new idea appears with stanza five:

> Our birth is but a sleep and a forgetting:
> The soul that rises with us, our life's Star,
>   Hath had elsewhere its setting,
>   And cometh from afar:
>   Not in entire forgetfulness,
>   And not in utter nakedness,
> But trailing clouds of glory do we come
>   From God, who is our home
>
> (58–65)

As he elaborates this idea it is clear that this is not proper Christianity but Platonism, the belief that our souls had a preexistence in heaven, or in the realm of the "Forms," before incarnating into our bodies. The usual Platonic view is that we forget our prenatal existence at birth or soon thereafter, but might recover some memory of it, or some of the knowledge we had in that realm as we gazed upon the Forms of things, through the discipline of philosophy and mathematics. As Wordsworth describes it, forgetfulness comes over us gradually as we grow up, for the light we bring with us at birth takes time to fade. Much of the poem explains this process by fleshing out the Platonic metaphor. So in stanza six we learn that the Earth, who is only our foster-mother, benevolently tries to make us forget the "glories" we knew in our "imperial palace" (83–4) and accept the "prison-house" (of stanza five) to which we are condemned, while in stanzas seven and eight we watch a child bring his own loss upon himself by "endless imitation" (107) of the doings of adulthood, the weddings, funerals, "business, love, or strife" (98) that fill our emptying lives, as if he deliberately tries to "provoke / The years to bring the inevitable yoke" earlier than it otherwise might (124–5). This sad picture of childhood perversity seems perverse itself in its refusal to appreciate the natural and imaginative purpose of imitative play, but this vivid and almost tragic scene – it would be fully tragic, perhaps, if the child knew what relentless fate was bearing down on him – certainly brings out the truth behind the Platonic myth that all adults must poignantly feel. Wordsworth does not mitigate its painfulness, moreover, by offering the usual Platonic recovery or "recollection" (*anamnesis*) of our preexistent knowledge provided by geometry and philosophy. The "recollection" in Wordsworth's subtitle is the adult's memory of early childhood, and what it gives us is the hint of immortality, perhaps even of reincarnation, though it is vague and uncertain. In this life there is no return of the light or celestial knowledge we have forgotten. Instead we can take cheer that "in our embers / Is something that doth live" (129–30) with the power to connect us, partially and fleetingly, to our childhood and to make us love the natural world with a deeper love. It is much the same moral that "Tintern Abbey" preaches, with its resigned farewell to his own youth and a passing of the torch to his younger sister, though the "Ode" is in a bleaker mood, more Stoic, in the end, than Platonic. Yet it teaches its lesson through so dazzling a variety of tones, lines, rhymes, images, and memorable phrases that it instills in some readers a feeling of grateful joy.

What odes are

If any single form is distinctive of British Romantic poetry, it is the ode. A good handful of the best-known poems have "ode" in their title: not only Wordsworth's "Ode" but Coleridge's "Dejection: An Ode," Shelley's "Ode to the West Wind," and several by Keats, notably "Ode to a Nightingale" and "Ode on a Grecian Urn." And to these we might add "Tintern Abbey," as Wordsworth himself suggested, as well as Byron's "Prometheus" and perhaps even Blake's "The Tyger," both of which are addressed to their subjects. It is obviously not their subjects that unite these poems. What are their "principal requisites," as Wordsworth put it? What makes them odes?

Our word "ode" comes to us from the Greek, via Latin and French. In Greek, an *aoidē* or *ōidē* meant simply "song," and could refer to anything sung, including the narrative tales performed by the bards (*aoidoi*) in Homer's *Odyssey* that we would certainly not call odes today. We use the term for the one surviving sizeable poem of Sappho, the "Ode to Aphrodite," and for the large collection of "Victory Odes" by Pindar, who celebrated the winners of athletic contests such as the Olympics, though Pindar's are much longer, grander, and more complicated than Sappho's. Pindar's, like Sappho's, are addressed to their subject, though Pindar's more elaborate odes may switch addressees from an athlete to a god, or from an ancestor to a city. His were designed to be sung and danced to by a chorus in a public square or theater; they come in triads of strophe, antistrophe, and epode, the first two words being dance terms meaning "turn" and "counterturn." Strophe and antistrophe had exactly the same meter, so the dance steps accompanying them would have been identical, or symmetrical. The earliest Pindaric ode in English, Ben Jonson's "To the Immortal Memory and Friendship of that Noble Pair, Sir Lucius Cary and Sir H. Morison" (published posthumously in 1640), labels its parts "The Turn," "The Counter-Turn," and "The Stand," though the last term is based on a theory of what dancers did rather than on the meaning of "epode," which means simply "after-song."

"Ode" in English, however, is also used for the *Carmina* or "songs" of the Latin poet Horace, which are much more like Sappho's example than Pindar's, but seldom invoke gods or heroes; indeed they are often urbane and self-deprecating reflections on such things as good wine or the pleasures of retirement to a farm. Horace explicitly claims, as we have seen, that he cannot soar like Pindar. That various English poems called "odes" were based on either the Pindaric or Horatian model has only bred confusion, made worse by incorporating features of two more forms, the hymn, also a classical term but with an inescapably Christian connotation, and the biblical psalm. The greatest Romantic poem called a hymn is Shelley's "Hymn to Intellectual Beauty," but it might well be titled an ode. (Calling it a hymn was perhaps meant to be cheeky, as it describes the opposite of a Christian conversion experience.) For the Romantic ode it is the Pindaric tradition that matters most.

Pindar, whose meter was misunderstood for centuries until modern scholars went to work on it, swamped as it seemed to be by "the impassioned music of the versification," and whose transitions from topic to topic were considered obscure even by the Greeks, gained a reputation for oracular depths or inspired heights beyond the ken of ordinary mortals, so odes of his sort, sometimes infused with biblical features, were adopted for serious or sublime subjects.

Both Thomas Gray (1716–71) and William Collins (1721–59) wrote Pindaric odes in triadic form, including two by Gray well known to the Romantic poets, "The Progress of Poesy" and "The Bard." But both these poets and many other odists wrote in regular stanzas as well, or in irregular but nontriadic schemes. English "Pindaricks" of the eighteenth century were often wildly irregular and unpredictable. By the time of the Romantic generations, triadic forms had been more or less abandoned, but almost anything else, regular or irregular, could be deployed in an "ode." Wordsworth's "Ode" and Coleridge's "Dejection: An Ode" both have highly varying but rhyming stanzas ("Dejection" has a stanza of eight lines, four of them short, and another of thirty-two lines, nearly all of them long), whereas Shelley's "Ode to the West Wind" and all of Keats's late odes are regular, except for slight shifts in the rhyme scheme in some of Keats's.[2]

Even though Pindar's own odes were strictly regular in their triadic struc-ture, the Romantics felt licensed by the English Pindaric tradition not only to play with stanza sizes and rhyme schemes but to make abrupt transitions between stanzas, regular or irregular, and sometimes even within stanzas. In the "Intimations" ode, as we have noted, Wordsworth leaves behind his state-ment and restatement of the loss of his "visionary gleam" that occupy the first four stanzas and begins the fifth with a new and startling metaphysical claim, "Our birth is but a sleep and a forgetting," that informs all the rest of the long-ish poem. In stanza two of "Ode to a Nightingale" Keats longs for a fine glass of wine, but then, after a melancholy survey of the miseries of human life in stanza three, he launches the fourth by exclaiming "Away! away! for I will fly to thee" – not by means of wine, however, but on wings of poetry. As for the impassioned music of the versification, we find it everywhere in Romantic odes, for the form required expressions of strong feelings, frequently in the state of rapture or visionary trance we discussed in Chapter 2, but all of it "contained" in meter and rhyme. Shelley's "Ode to the West Wind" is about as emotional as a poem can be – it is a desperate appeal to the god of the wind to transform him into its instrument of prophecy, a plea for a rapture – yet it is as intricately and tightly organized in structure, imagery, and stanza form as any poem of similar length in English.

Perhaps the most obvious feature of odes is that they are addressed to some-one – a person, a god, a bird, or a personified abstraction – who is not literally or physically present or capable of hearing the speaker. We call this kind of address "apostrophe," from a Greek word meaning "turning away," a turning away from the present audience to speak to someone or something elsewhere. Nearly all the poems of the Romantic era that are called "odes," however much they differ in theme and form, have such an addressee, or more than one. In several illuminating discussions of apostrophes, Jonathan Culler singles them out as distinctive features of lyric poetry in general, and not just odes, because in their strangeness they resist being reduced to an imitation of a real utterance, for "it is hard to imagine any nonpoetic or nonfictional utterance that would use them" other than "utterances by speakers who are waxing poetical" in the first place.[3] Certainly we can agree that the real John Keats may never have done anything so odd as to speak to a Greek urn, unless he was trying out his ode on it. Yet Culler may have drawn too firm a line between real-life utterances and this special feature of lyric speech. In a recent discussion Alan Richardson takes issue with Culler and shows the normalness of many sorts of apostrophe in ordinary speech.[4] We talk to babies and to dogs, for instance, knowing full well they glean very little from what we say. We talk to the dead. We encourage our car and curse our computer. We pray, and not always because we believe God or a saint is literally present. Very often we perform these speech-acts for the benefit of a third party, who "overhears" us, as readers "overhear" the speaker of a poem addressing someone or something else. (As far as that goes, addressing the reader, as in "Reader, I married him," is a kind of apostrophe.) Richardson makes a good case that there is a dense continuum of apostrophes between the perfectly normal (talking to babies) and the downright strange and "poetic" (addressing urns).

It is interesting to think about. As an introduction to Romantic poetry we could do worse than make a list of all the things we might or might not talk to in real life, and then work back from a list of addressees in poetry and ask what might bring us to speak to them outside the special poetic world. I would add two thoughts. Richardson grants that the normalness of certain kinds of apostrophe will vary from culture to culture and from time to time within one culture, but it is important to remember that poetry was conservative: it preserved as if in amber many conventions once normal but later extinct in everyday life, including apostrophes to various beings. If Pindar did it in ancient Greece, then it was acceptable for poets to do it in Britain in 1820. Secondly, it is one of the characteristic beliefs of Romanticism that, thanks to literal-minded scientific philosophy, and to commercial worldliness, we humans have lost the ability we once had to communicate with animals and inanimate things. When we fell from this blessed state, according to Blake, "A Rock a Cloud a Mountain / Were now not Vocal as in Climes of happy Eternity / Where the lamb replies to the infant voice & the lion to the man of years / Giving them sweet instructions" (*Four Zoas* VI, 71:4–7; E 348). Keats, in a passage Culler quotes, imagines a charioteer, the power of poetry, who "with wondrous gesture talks / To the trees and mountains" ("Sleep and Poetry" 136–7).[5] And it was a common lament among Romantics across Europe that we have lost the rich and satisfying pagan world of the Greeks, where every tree had a dryad, every mountain an oread, every stream a naiad. Everything had the ability to look at us and speak. Byron, Shelley, and Keats indulged this nostalgia for the Greeks, and so did Wordsworth occasionally, as in his sonnet "The world is too much with us" (to be discussed in Chapter 6).

Apostrophe implies personification: to speak to something not human is to anthropomorphize it, to endow it with a soul. Or perhaps, in keeping with the Romantic spirit, we should say it is to restore the soul that has fled from it – "At the mere touch of cold philosophy," as Keats puts it in "Lamia" (2.230). This may be hard to take seriously in some odes, which address abstract ideas. William Collins had written odes to Pity, Fear, Simplicity, Mercy, Liberty, Evening, and Peace, and all of these virtues or states of affairs were personified in detail, with emblematic clothing and props. They were all female, too: Pity is a "relenting maid," Simplicity a "decent maid," Fear a "mad nymph," Evening a "nymph reserved," Mercy a "smiling bride," and so on. In her "Ode to Despair" (1788) Charlotte Smith makes her addressee masculine, "Lord of the hopeless heart and hollow eye," though that is unusual. Mary Robinson seems to address an abstraction at first in her "Ode to Beauty" (1791), where other abstractions, such as Jealousy, Fame, Slander, and Flattery inhabit her sphere, though in the end "Beauty" sounds much like a real "beauty," a beautiful girl. Wordsworth makes Duty, in his ode to her, the "Stern Daughter of the Voice of God!" These are all little allegories, reaching far back into the literary tradition as well as into Renaissance paintings and emblem books. Such conventional gestures, fossilized in the poetic tradition, would not seem very imaginative or original or indeed Romantic, and by and large the Romantic poets avoided them. In his great ode Wordsworth speaks to nothing so nebulous as his subtitle, "Intimations of Immortality from Recollections of Early Childhood," but turns instead to children, lambs, and "Fountains, Meadows, Hills, and Groves." Coleridge does not speak to Dejection in his ode by that title, but to a "Lady" (in one version), to his "viper thoughts," and to the wind. Romantic apostrophe was most successful when the object addressed was a real object – a nightingale, an urn, the west wind – and when allegorical features were raised by a kind of poetic heat or pressure to something we tend to call symbolic or mythic, something more intense and intimate, in any case, than the traditional emblems.

How the poet creates a new symbolic character by means of apostrophe, then, is one of the processes we will keep in mind as we look closely at two odes, Keats's "Ode on a Grecian Urn" and Shelley's "Ode to the West Wind."

"Ode on a Grecian Urn"

Keats's ode ought to have been titled "Ode *to* a Grecian Urn," for its very first word is "Thou." Keats speaks *to* the urn, not just about it, and he speaks to several characters depicted on it, including trees, during all five stanzas. Then, at the end of the last stanza, after Keats calls it a "friend," the urn speaks to him, or to all of us, in reply, or, to state it more strictly, Keats projects or ventriloquizes on to the urn a final statement by it. (By "Keats," of course, I mean the speaker or "persona" of the poem, not John Keats the author.) Perhaps Keats thought "on" would avoid dismissal by urbane readers amused at the idea of talking to an urn, especially in a public museum, but if so he did not seem to worry about the absurdity of talking "to" a nightingale or autumn in other odes. The choice of preposition seems arbitrary.

In his opening two lines, in any case, Keats endows his urn with not only a soul but such particular human details as sex, age, and genealogy, and he inserts it into a little plot, very different from the routine allegories of many earlier odes:

> Thou still unravish'd bride of quietness,
>   Thou foster-child of silence and slow time,

These lines are astonishingly rich in meaning and sound.[6] After more than two thousand years the urn is still "unravish'd," still intact, still *virgo intacta*, a bride frozen at the moment between her wedding to Quietness and their nuptial night. Her bridegroom does not seem the type to ravish anyone; she has been left quietly alone for all these slow centuries. She has foster parents, surely Mother Silence and Father Time, who seem the perfect pair to have prepared her for this husband, but they seem not so much to have given her away at the wedding as to have assumed a fostering role thereafter. She is "still" by nature (the first printing had a comma after it), silent by upbringing, quiet by marriage. The metaphor invites the question: who were her real parents? The sculptor, no doubt, was her father, who gave her form; her mother might be the material (Latin *materia*, from *mater*, "mother"), that is, Marble (42), which he shaped. It was he who gave her away to Quietness and to the foster parents (perhaps they are her new in-laws), and they have been protecting her ever since from (it must be) noise.

Have we let our imagination wander too far into a little domestic story? It is difficult to know when to stop, for Keats teases us into thought, even though he tells us at the end that the urn teases us *out* of thought (44). He also loads a rich ore of sounds here, to use another metaphor he applied to poetry in one of his letters, not only sweet in their own music but peculiarly appropriate to their sense. The urn, as "bride," absorbed the long vowel of her title from her foster parents' "silence" and "time" while she was their "child"; that her husband has the same vowel expresses his fitness for her. Her foster parents were well suited to each other, too, as they shared not only the long vowel but the s, l, and t sounds ("silence" has a hidden t sound); they instilled these consonants in their "still" daughter and in her former title "foster child." We might note, too, how "slow time," two stressed syllables (a spondee), slows the time of the second line. This is rich and wonderful enough, but it carries over into the third line, which begins "Sylvan historian," a phrase that changes the metaphor but preserves most of the sounds of this still and fostered urn. Only now does this seam of sounds run out. This tour de force of compact meanings and phonemic correspondences bears out Culler's general point that lyric poems are not really very much like everyday speech, even though Wordsworth, as we saw, approaches the effect of natural speech in his blank verse and unstanzaic "Lines." If anyone ever addressed an urn, and even deployed these metaphors, he or she would never have chanted so gorgeous and intricate a tune.

> Sylvan historian, who canst thus express
>   A flowery tale more sweetly than our rhyme:

$$(3–4)$$

We may disagree that the urn can express anything more sweetly than the opening lines, but Keats modestly defers to her. Some readers have puzzled over what "thus" refers to,[7] but surely it means "by silence": it is by means of her silence that the urn can tell a tale so well – the first of several paradoxes or oxymora. She is "sylvan" because, as we will see, at least one of the scenes depicted on her, a "leaf-fring'd legend," takes place in the woods, and for the same reason her tale is "flowery." "Flowery," of course, is an ancient metaphor for a certain kind of speech, florid or ornate speech, which makes use of "the flowers of rhetoric." We might think, however, that a "historian" has no business resorting to such flowers, as her task is to recount the facts without embellishing them. An older, more or less poetic, sense of "historian" was available, however, as "story-teller," and indeed the words "history" and "story" have the same Greek origin. Keats has it both ways, but the usual sense of "historian" draws us right into the main issue the ode poses: do we seek historical knowledge or sweet expression, facts or flowery tales, truth or beauty?

The urn seems to fail at giving history lessons, for the speaker has no idea what tale she is expressing.

What leaf-fring'd legend haunts about thy shape
　Of deities or mortals, or of both,
　　In Tempe or the dales of Arcady?
　What men or gods are these? What maidens loth?
What mad pursuit? What struggle to escape?
　What pipes and timbrels? What wild ecstasy?

(5–10)

Some Greek ceramic vessels had identifying names written next to the deities
and mortals painted on them, but this is a marble urn and offers no such help.
With rising excitement and impatience the speaker asks seven "what" questions, almost as if he grows frightened at the orgy he is observing, shocked at
the contrast between the silent urn and the wild events sculpted on her, and
seeks to quiet his fears with some historical labels. His questions grow absurd,
for if it is reasonable to look for a label identifying the legend or myth, and the
locale, and the men, gods, and maidens, it is surely odd to ask "What struggle to escape?" or "What wild ecstasy?" as if the "identity" of such a struggle
or ecstasy depended on particular circumstances and were not the same at all
times and places. We can imagine that thought dawning on him as he asks the
last few questions, so as we begin the next stanza he seems to have caught his
breath and given up seeking facts: he enters empathetically into the scene.

Heard melodies are sweet, but those unheard
　Are sweeter: therefore, ye soft pipes, play on;
Not to the sensual ear, but, more endear'd,
　Pipe to the spirit ditties of no tone:
Fair youth, beneath the trees, thou canst not leave
　Thy song, nor ever can those trees be bare;
　　Bold lover, never, never canst thou kiss,
Though winning near the goal—yet, do not grieve;
　She cannot fade, though thou hast not thy bliss,
　　For ever wilt thou love, and she be fair!

(11–20)

　Since this is the first stanza we have quoted as a whole, we might pause to say
something about it as a form. Keats had written quite a few sonnets, constantly
experimenting with their patterns: sometimes Petrarchan or "legitimate,"
sometimes Shakespearean, sometimes mixtures of the two. He wrote a sonnet
about sonnets ("If by dull rhymes") that advocates more "interwoven" sounds
and practices what it preaches. He even wrote one in blank verse, with no
rhymes ("O thou whose face hath felt the Winter's wind"). Out of these experiments Keats seems to have hit upon the ten-line stanza he uses in four of his

great odes: a Shakespearean quatrain (rhyming **abab**) followed by a Petrarchan sestet (here **cdeced**, but with variations in other stanzas). This way he avoids what he called the "pouncing rhymes" of the couplets of the Petrarchan quatrains and the conclusion of the Shakespearean sonnet, and opens the stanza to various patterns of thought and syntax.[8] The two levels of indentation in the quatrain and the three in the sestet correspond to the rhymes, so your eye can readily pick out the pattern. (This is in contrast to Wordsworth's ode, where the indentations are not tied to rhyme but to line length.) The rhymes of the sestet are perfect, while in the quatrain, and occasionally elsewhere in later stanzas, the rhymes are slightly off, or "slant," though well within the range considered acceptable by readers at the time. Keats, as we have just seen, was committed to making his poems luxurious in sound and imagery. As he also seems committed to honesty about his experiences and feelings, you might say he has tried to embody in his poems, and especially the odes, the union of beauty and truth that his urn proclaims at the end.

In this second stanza he has left off his breathless questions and entered into the world shown on the urn in spirit. He does not, of course, entirely suspend his disbelief (to use Coleridge's famous phrase), for he is constantly aware that these engrossing pipers, lovers, and fair maidens are still fictional and motionless representations: even the "mad pursuit" is caught and stilled forever. Helen Vendler, in one of the finest recent interpretations of the ode, likens the speaker's response to the urn to the classic figure–ground dilemma that psychologists of visual perception study: we can see the rabbit, or we can see the duck, but we cannot see both at once.[9] Keats oscillates between taking the men and maidens as real, she says, and recognizing their unreality. And yet I think Keats also tries to project a compromise between these two mutually exclusive states, which are after all more complicated than the two perceptions of an optical illusion. He first claims that silent music, surely an oxymoron if we mean ordinary sensual music, appeals to "the spirit," which finds it sweeter than music the ear can hear. This might mean we can imagine, or hear in our head, the music of the piper, just as we can (it seems) summon up the "history" expressed by the silent urn, or it might mean something like the ancient idea of the music of the spheres, which we cannot hear on this earth but can recognize in the mathematical perfection of the celestial bodies and movements. We are reminded of Wordsworth's phrase, "the still, sad music of humanity" ("Tintern Abbey" 92), though Keats has not yet implied anything sad about the silent music or those who make it. If this contradiction has a resolution, however, the next one makes an almost fantastic assertion: that the figures on the urn can somehow learn from him that they will never leave their happy state. At first he suggests they might be saddened at the thought, but then he tells the lover, who is just about to win his kiss and his bliss from the maiden, not to grieve that he will never attain it, because he will never lose her either. Surely this state is impossible to sustain: it is a parallel universe where depictions of people, motionless only insofar as they are depictions, become conscious of being real people; or where the real people depicted, in full career, become conscious of being only depictions and thus unable to move. It is nonetheless a fascinating state to contemplate. Nor does Keats back down from it until (perhaps) at the end of the next stanza.

We should note the moment Keats chooses to celebrate. It is the "almost" moment, the instant before consummation or completion, before ravishment. As the urn herself is suspended in the hour before her deflowering, so the lover and his maid are hanging forever on the verge of their (or at least his) bliss. Many of my students, more experienced sexually than Keats, express skepticism about this choice of moment, and name other moments that they would prefer to be suspended in forever, notably orgasm. That moment strikes me as even harder to imagine as an eternal state than the "almost" moment, which even in real life is often prolonged. What if Keats found a pair of lovers in the act of copulating? At the opening of "Ode to Psyche" the speaker comes across Cupid and Psyche embracing, but asleep, as if they had just made love and would resume doing so when they awaken. That would be a good candidate for a suspended moment, though if you are asleep you might never appreciate it. These dizzying thoughts take us out of recognizable human life, where time rolls relentlessly on, where we succeed for moments or fail, and where our passions, as Keats says at the end of the third stanza, may leave us sorrowful and cloyed. The moment he chooses for the impossible suspension, then, is human in the end: the moment of longing, still filled with hope. That may well be our happiest state in the real world.

Vendler thinks there are three scenes on the urn, of which we have already viewed two: the orgy in stanza one and the "courtship" in stanza two. I have learned so much from Vendler that I hesitate to disagree, but I see only one scene in the first three stanzas. It is true the tone changes between these stanzas, in one of those abrupt transitions odes were known for, but tone in this ode is highly changeable; it changes again within the third stanza. Surely the pipes of line 10 are the same as in line 12, the "Bold lover" (17) is one of the men or gods in "mad pursuit" (9), and she who is fair and cannot fade (19–20) is one of the "maidens loth" (that is, reluctant) of line 8. Vendler goes on to develop three stances the speaker takes toward the realm of the urn, based on three aesthetic theories: (a) that art offers historical truth, (b) that art solicits sympathy with an idealized or archetypal state similar to our own, and (c) that art is a self-contained world that invites an empathic identification free of factual inquiry and self-interest.[10] As she elaborates these viewpoints they shed light on the attitudes that the speaker, and we, take up and drop, but I do not see them, as she does, as a three-phase progression toward a more thoughtful conclusion. It may be impossible to settle this question. I mention it to remind my readers that many good scholars disagree with each other and with me on many points. Different readers of the ode may visualize somewhat different scenes (perhaps the orgy scene is large enough to have less violent events in some of its corners) and hear somewhat different tones in the speaker, but it is a good rule of literary interpretation, as it is in the sciences, to choose the simplest reading that accounts for the evidence.

> Ah, happy, happy boughs! that cannot shed
>   Your leaves, nor ever bid the spring adieu;
> And, happy melodist, unwearied,
>   For ever piping songs for ever new;
> More happy love! more happy, happy love!
>   For ever warm and still to be enjoy'd,
>   For ever panting, and for ever young;
> All breathing human passion far above,
>   That leaves a heart high-sorrowful and cloy'd,
>   A burning forehead, and a parching tongue.

(21–30)

If the speaker was growing frantic with uncertainty at the end of stanza one, here he seems in the grip of another intense emotion, a rapture of envy, where for seven lines he can only repeat himself at a high pitch, with "happy" six times, "ever" six times, and three exclamation points. It is worth considering whether the ode would have been a better poem without this stanza, for it tells us nothing more about the urn itself and only something rather puzzling about human passion in its final lines, while the outburst of feeling is almost embarrassing to witness. We certainly would not suspect a gap in the poem if we went straight from the address to the lover that closes stanza two to the new scene, a sacrifice, in stanza four. If it fails to describe anything, what does this middle stanza do? It seems to enact a sheer intensity of feeling, a desire to stop time and preserve one's youth and be spared all "passion." It was risky of Keats to give such fevered expression to this feeling, which had been well enough implied in stanza two. But it reminds us, at least, of the unhappiness of our "breathing human" life, in contrast to the ideal figures on the silent and ageless urn. And that is important. We do not need to know about Keats's short life and his tuberculosis to appreciate this passage, but to acknowledge that all human lives are filled with misery, though it is an ancient commonplace, demands more of us than we expect to give while reading a poem about a Greek artifact. Keats asks it of us, and if we can enter into his feeling we will feel a greater gratitude for the urn as "friend to man" at the end.

The characters on the urn are "All breathing human passion far above." (The prepositional phrase is postponed; the normal reading would be "far above all breathing human passion.") And human passion "leaves a heart high-sorrowful and cloy'd, / A burning forehead, and a parching tongue." Why does Keats say so? We have been looking at "passion" as sexual desire, at least on the part of the male figures: Does sexual desire, consummated or not, leave our heart, forehead, and tongue so sad and sick? He seems to be generalizing here about "all" passion, not just sexual, and reverting to the oldest sense of the word, which is suffering or affliction. He leaves us with the uneasy impression that all intense feelings are disturbing and dangerous to our health. By contrast the cool and changeless urn stands for, and perhaps can instill, a calm and detached state of mind in its mortal viewers. And yet the scene the serene urn depicts is precisely the height of passion, and if we take the figures as men, not gods, it is human passion, even "breathing" human passion, a point underlined by "panting" in the line just before.

The next stanza introduces a new company:

> Who are these coming to the sacrifice?
>   To what green altar, O mysterious priest,
> Lead'st thou that heifer lowing at the skies,
>   And all her silken flanks with garlands drest?
> What little town by river or sea shore,
>   Or mountain-built with peaceful citadel,
>   Is emptied of this folk, this pious morn?
> And, little town, thy streets for evermore
>   Will silent be; and not a soul to tell
>   Why thou art desolate, can e'er return.

(31–40)

We readily imagine the speaker walking around the urn and finding another scene to contemplate. He asks three questions this time. He again wants to know the names of people and places, but he is in a much quieter and more thoughtful mood, and he already knows, somehow, that he sees a sacrificial procession coming to a green altar (presumably not depicted), that the animal is a heifer, an uncalved or "virgin" cow (not distinguishable in appearance from an older cow), and that it is morning. It is hard to say if he has progressed into a deeper or fuller understanding of art or history or the Greeks or anything; his calmer tone befits the sedate and "pious" procession. In contrast to the noisy orgy, with its pipes and timbrels and mad and wild action, this scene is silent, with the exception of the lowing of the heifer, while the town off stage is "silent" twice over: in the same way the orgy's music is unheard, and in a "real" way because no one is home.

The word "mysterious" is well chosen, not only because it resounds so well with "priest" but because the priest is both unidentified and, Keats seems to say, the leader of a Greek *mysterion*, a secret rite of initiation. (That seems unlikely, in fact, as the whole populace is in attendance.) It is also striking that six of the ten lines are about something else not visible on the urn, the little town, about whose location he can only speculate. The depicted scene prompts him to wander in his mind out of it altogether, into the invisible town, now deserted. He repeats the figure–ground compromise of the first scene, and imagines the town, which if it were real would be empty for a day, to be eternally "desolate," a very strong word. He has just been imagining the participants in the orgy as happy beyond all measure, the sorrowful note applying only to us breathing mortals, but now he finds the urn-world itself sorrowful. He might have felt some sadness for the heifer, soon to have its throat slit and its blood cast on the green altar – is it praying to the skies for deliverance? – but he reserves his sorrow for the empty town. It is as if he remembers that this imagined town, if it were not a generic fictional town to begin with, was inhabited twenty-three hundred years ago and might well be an abandoned ruin today. Time marches relentlessly on. But that is to violate the terms of the suspension of disbelief, I would suggest; it is surely to travel far to find something else to be sad about.

That thought, at any rate, pulls the speaker back a few steps, and he now contemplates the urn as a whole, and no longer as a bride or anything other than an artifact, though it is capable of speech at the end.

> O Attic shape! Fair attitude! with brede
>   Of marble men and maidens overwrought,
> With forest branches and the trodden weed;
>   Thou, silent form, dost tease us out of thought
> As doth eternity: Cold Pastoral!
>   When old age shall this generation waste,
>   Thou shalt remain, in midst of other woe
> Than ours, a friend to man, to whom thou say'st,
>   "Beauty is truth, truth beauty,"—that is all
>   Ye know on earth, and all ye need to know.

(41–50)

Not only in its opening lines but throughout the ode we have heard some intricately constructed sound effects, such as the repeated s sounds in stanza four, and what seems a pun in lines 39–40 with "soul" and "desolate," as if the little town were "de-souled" as well as solitary. In the opening lines of this final stanza the effects seem a little showier, wittier, less sincere: "Attic" and "attitude" are both a little *recherché* or precious, "Attic" referring to Attica, the peninsular region around Athens, and "attitude" in art criticism meaning the "disposition" or "posture" of a figure. Keats strikes an attitude himself here, and seems to signal that that is what he is doing; he is cooler for a moment, more detached, more conventional. He sounds superior to the urn, even condescending, in contrast with his rapt openness to her at the opening. He puns again perhaps, with "brede," which is a variant of "braid," something plaited or interwoven, and "breed," though probably not with "overwrought," which refers to the working of the marble and not to the state of mind of the men and maidens. He offers one last oxymoron, "Cold Pastoral." Tempe and Arcady (Arcadia), possible settings of the orgy, are traditional settings for pastoral poetry, which is poetry about shepherds, who often played pipes, sang ditties, and sought maidens, and by extension about rustic life in general.

But Keats soon grows more serious and candid, and the two most important and difficult passages have none of this studious cleverness. In the first of these, what does it mean to say, "Thou … dost tease us out of thought / As doth eternity"? It would seem that the urn has been teasing the speaker, and us, *into* thought all along. But "thought" may mean something more limited, systematic, and detached than the sort of associative musing or daydreaming that underlies some of the more interesting passages of the poem, such as the final three lines of the fourth stanza, which begin with an inconsequential "and," somewhat surprising after a question. "Thought" may have more to do with the search for information, for names and places and labels, that occupies stanzas one and four. I have been sparing in bringing in other texts so far, but a passage from one of Keats's letters is irresistible here, and commentators often cite it: "O for a Life of Sensations rather than of Thoughts!" (letter to Bailey, November 22, 1817). We might say, then, that Keats has been oscillating between thought (Who are these people? What rite is this?) and sensation (Play on, soft pipes! How happy to be forever young!): the urn first provokes thought, and then teases us out of it by the sweetness and evocativeness of its sculptures. It teases us as eternity does, for who can think consequentially about eternity? Indeed the urn is about as close a representative of eternity as a human product can be, being a foster daughter of slow time and now in her third millennium.

And that brings us to the final passage, the most frequently quoted lines of Romantic poetry and perhaps the most debated. What do they mean, and why do they conclude this poem? The first thing to try to get straight is who says what to whom. The version of the poem printed here, with quotation marks around "Beauty is truth, truth beauty," is the way it appeared in the volume of

Keats's poems called *Lamia, Isabella, The Eve of St. Agnes, and Other Poems* (1820). But the poem had appeared in a journal a few months earlier without the quotation marks (and with "Beauty" and "Truth" capitalized). We do not know if Keats authorized either punctuation; he may not have thought it important. Should we? The version with the quotation marks, which is how it is usually printed today, may hint that only the five quoted words are spoken by the urn; the remainder of the final two lines are spoken by someone else. But by whom, and to whom? Every possibility has been argued for. (a) The speaker of the whole poem turns from the urn and speaks the final line and a half to the reader. (b) The speaker speaks them to the urn. (c) The speaker speaks them to the figures on the urn. (d) The urn speaks them to the reader, that is, the urn speaks the entire two lines. The last choice might seem to privilege the first printed version, without the quotation marks, but no matter how it is punctuated the first five words may be taken as a quotation without implying that the speaker must change after it. The urn could be repeating a proverb or maxim, and then adding a comment on it; indeed some recent anthologies put quotation marks around the entire two lines, though there is no warrant for doing so in the earliest editions.

The first option, that the poem's speaker turns to the reader, seems a needless complication, for surely the urn is already speaking to the reader, subsumed under "man," and is quite capable of adding the last line and a half to the proverb-like saying about beauty and truth. It doesn't need the poet to endorse its teachings. This would be the first time, moreover, that the speaker turns to the reader; throughout the ode he has been speaking to the urn or to people and things depicted on it.

The second choice, that the speaker speaks to the urn, is easy to eliminate, for the urn cannot be addressed with "ye" (the plural); it has been correctly addressed with "thou" (the singular) throughout. It would be presumptuous and absurd, too, if the speaker, who has just heard the urn's maxim, were now to tell the urn that that is all it knows.

The third possibility, that the speaker addresses the figures on the urn, is free of that difficulty, but it seems odd for several reasons. The speaker has used "ye" of the "soft pipes" (12) and "your" of the "boughs" (22), while the humans or gods have always been in the singular, like the urn: the "youth" (15–16), the "lover" (17–20), the "melodist" (presumably the "youth") (23–4), "love," an abstraction connected with the "lover" (25–30), the "priest" (32–4), and the "town" (38–40); four of these six are addressed with "thou." To group all these together as one addressee seems forced and unmotivated. Since they are part of the urn world, moreover, they presumably already know what the urn knows, and do not need to be told it by the speaker; for his part, the speaker has just heard it for the first time, and to tell the urn figures that that is all they know would be almost as absurd and comical as to tell it to the urn itself (option b). Surely the decorum of the ode rules out such an anticlimactic turn.

The fourth option, that the urn speaks the last two lines, seems free of such problems. It is not quite right to say that the urn speaks to the "reader," however, for the "ye" seems addressed to the whole human race, "man," future generations of which, with their own woes, will visit the urn. One might object that "man" is singular and cannot be the antecedent of "ye," but "man" is surely plural in meaning if not form; the speaker, after all, who must be singular, says "our rhyme" to refer to *his* rhyme (4) and "other woe / Than ours" (47–8), though that could refer to back to "this generation" (46), another singular form with plural meaning. Nothing seems to prevent, and simplicity seems to demand, that the urn first quotes a truth and then tells us (us mortals) that that is the only thing we know on earth.[11]

How satisfying is this statement? Is it true, or at least plausible? Does the poem earn the right to conclude with it, that is, does it bring to a culmination the themes it has been dealing with all along? Some readers have found it disappointing, and have convinced themselves that Keats didn't endorse it. After all those questions from the speaker, they argue, the urn offers a cliché, pulled down from the Platonic skies, as if it hasn't really been listening to him and just repeats its little mantra. To claim that beauty and truth are identical, moreover, is on the face of it dubious. Are there no ugly truths, no beautiful lies? And what about the third great Platonic category, goodness?

I think the case is better than that. The urn has been listening to the speaker, I would argue, and tells him something he has been groping toward all along. It is the speaker, after all, who projects on to the urn what the urn "says," and what it says is the conclusion the speaker comes to from his questioning of it and his meditating on it. It might help to see this if one recites the five-word equation aloud with different emphases. We might think that when an urn speaks, it speaks out of context, as it were, with a marmoreal permanence and self-sufficiency, like the tables of the law, and hence it would pronounce these abstract nouns with an equal stress. But this urn is a "friend," and it is pleasing to think of it as giving friendly advice to the speaker, who has been asking questions, ten of them, first of the urn itself, then of the pipes, the youth, the lover, the boughs, the priest, the little town, and finally of the urn again. The urn feels called upon to reply. So its speech has a context, and that context should determine the way the words are stressed, the way their full meaning is made clear.

I suggest we stress the first "Beauty," and thereby imply that the urn is introducing beauty as a new topic, whereas "truth," unstressed, is the already existing topic. All those questions from the speaker were requests for information, for historical truth (names, places), even if a few of them in the first stanza were a little odd. After the seven questions of the first stanza the speaker yields to the inherent interest of the scenes on the urn and feels intensely moved by them. Then in the fourth stanza the questions come back, though in a calmer tone, and this time, in the final stanza, the urn replies. It seems to say: "You have been seeking after truth: give it up. *Beauty* is truth. You have already sensed this, as you felt drawn into the worlds on my surface without knowing any of the facts about them. My role is to tease you out of thought and into imaginative participation. My means of doing so is beauty." The ode would then have two similar movements, composed of the first three stanzas and the last two; in the first the speaker yields to beauty unawares, while in the second the urn makes him conscious of what he has done and states the lesson learned. The second part makes explicit what is implicit in the first.

There are other ways to stress the five words, of course, and my readers should try them out. One could note that beauty has also been a topic from the outset: the urn expresses a tale "more sweetly" than the speaker, the melodies are "sweet," the maiden is "fair," the "attitude" (an aesthetic term) is also "fair." Yet surely the burden of all the questions of stanzas one and four is truth. What is this legend? Who are these mortals or gods? Where are they? Who are these at the sacrifice? From what town? Why is it "desolate"? The speaker is *thinking* about the urn, not appreciating it; he wants to know things *about* it. But it turns out that all he "knows" is one truth about truth, that it is really beauty. If nonetheless the reader thinks that beauty and truth have both been themes all along, but oscillating in prominence, then he or she could read the equation by stressing the copula: "Beauty *is* truth." That reading would account better for the restatement, "truth [is] beauty," which is less well motivated under my first suggestion that we stress the first "Beauty." But I think putting the weight on "Beauty," as if it were now first introduced by the urn, which is after all a specialist in beauty, unites the poem into one conversation.

Real urns and marbles

Before turning to Shelley's ode, let me say something about historical contexts for this historian of an urn. Some interesting research into contemporary discussions among artists and art critics, some of whom Keats knew, may shed light on the meanings of "beauty" and "truth" and on the impact of Greek art on tastes and aesthetic standards, though in my view the research tells us more about how Keats was conversant with the debates of the day than it does about the meaning of the ode.[12] One historical project we can safely set aside, certainly, is the search for the "original" urn. Every few years an article appears with another candidate for *the* urn Keats "must have seen," but so far none of them has the two scenes (or three) that Keats's urn displays; some are not made of marble; some are not even Greek. I think this effort is a waste of time. Suppose we found a marble Athenian urn with pipers, males chasing maidens, trees with leaves, a sacrificial procession with a heifer, and all the rest of it. And suppose we could prove Keats saw it. Would it tell us anything about the poem we did not already know? Suppose we could determine just what leaf-fring'd legend was presented on the urn, and exactly who was coming to the sacrifice. Would that make a difference? The poem's speaker still would not know these things. Suppose there were a third (or fourth) scene, showing a wedding cere- mony. That might be pleasing, but would it add anything to our understanding of the first two lines? The urn of the poem, surely, exists only in the poem, and we can learn nothing more about it than what we can glean from the poem it- self. And the search for the "real" urn, for the "truth" behind the urn, seems to flout the lesson preached by the imaginary one.

We can, perhaps, gather something more about the urn by thinking about what urns are, that is, what the word "urn" (which admittedly appears only in the title) would mean to English readers in 1820, and that is something internal to the poem. A Greek urn might have had various uses, such as storing water, but its most prominent use, and the first meaning given in the *Oxford English Dictionary*, was to hold the ashes of the dead. A book better known to readers of Keats's day than it is to us was Sir Thomas Browne's *Hydriotaphia, or Urn- Burial* (1658), among other things a long meditation on death and oblivion. In the poem that was the best known and most loved in Keats's day, "Elegy Written in a Country Churchyard" (1751), Thomas Gray asks, "Can storied urn or animated bust / Back to its mansion call the fleeting breath?" (41–2). Keats seems almost to allude to the phrase "storied urn" with his "historian" urn. "Urn" in poetry was sometimes a metonym for "tomb." So it seems plaus- ible that the word "urn" would have brought to mind a particular kind of urn, the funerary or cinerary urn, or what the funeral business today calls the "cre- mation urn." If that is so, we must go back through Keats's ode to see what this connotation contributes to our understanding. It might send an extra shiver of feeling, for instance, into the speaker's exclamations over the immortality of the pictured figures, with all those repetitions of "for ever," and make more poignant his anticipation of his own death implicit in the line, "When old age shall this generation waste" (46). If the urn acts on us as eternity does (45), by teasing us out of thought and telling us that beauty and truth are one, does it thereby preserve our humanity as it preserves our ashes? As early as the phrase "slow time" (2) we might reflect, with Browne, that "Time, which antiquates antiquities, and hath an art to make dust of all things, hath yet spared these minor monuments" (chapter 5).

And yet Keats nowhere speaks of ashes or funerals; the urn's only function depends on its sculptured stories and its seeming timelessness. The lesson we learn from it, that beauty is truth, might have been taught as well by the Elgin marbles, the historical meaning of which is still hotly debated. We could certainly make a case that it is the antiquity of the urn, and its pristine state, that prompt thoughts about eternity and the wasting of human generations, and not its putative purpose in ancient Greece.

The Elgin marbles, indeed, provide another context in which to place the ode. In December 1798, Thomas Bruce, the earl of Elgin, was appointed ambassador to Selim I, the Ottoman sultan, and apparently obtained permission to remove some of the sculptures on the Parthenon and other buildings on the acropolis of Athens, then under Ottoman rule. By 1812 he had shipped back half the enormous frieze on the interior of the Parthenon and several statues from its pediments and metopes. He sold them to the British Museum, where the public flocked to see them. Keats saw them for the first time in 1817, and wrote a sonnet shortly afterwards called "On Seeing the Elgin Marbles." It begins:

> My spirit is too weak—mortality
> Weighs heavily on me like unwilling sleep,
> And each imagined pinnacle and steep
> Of godlike hardship tells me I must die
> Like a sick eagle looking at the sky.

He will begin his "Ode to a Nightingale" in a similar way, feeling oppressed, even drugged, by the contrast of a "godlike" power with his own mortality. The urn's effect is gentler, not surprisingly given the enormous scale of the Parthenon marbles, but like them, and like the nightingale, it evokes thoughts of mortal frailty. Yet the marbles reveal their own mortality, unlike the still unravished urn: Keats feels "a most dizzy pain, / That mingles Grecian grandeur with the rude / Wasting of old time." In the urn ode it is not the urn that "old age" will "waste" but "this generation." The similarities and differences between these two poems about Greek sculpture help us understand them both by bringing out certain features that we might not have dwelled on, such as the untouched perfection, and not just the great age, of the urn. The Elgin marbles are really ruins, and Keats's sonnet on them belongs among poems about ruins, such as the ruins of Rome, while "Ode on a Grecian Urn" is about something ancient that has, astonishingly, escaped the ravages and ravishment of time.

The most important context for more deeply reading "Ode on a Grecian Urn," of course, is the "Ode to a Nightingale," which was written at nearly the same time and published in the same art journal. Together they explore the domains of sight and sound – Keats emphasizes the invisibility of the nightingale as firmly as he does the inaudibility of the urn – and the arts of sculpture and music, the one representational, the other, though called a song, pure form, or vocalese; the one a man-made artifact, the other a natural act. I have found, even after going through the "Urn" with a fine-toothed comb, as I have done here, that a close reading of the "Nightingale" sends me back to the "Urn" with new insights, and vice versa.

"Ode to the West Wind"

Shelley's "Ode to the West Wind" also deals with death and human "woe," but the tone or mood of this desperate prayer to the wind god differs as much from that of Keats's ode as a howling wind differs from a silent urn. And yet for all the passionate pleading that permeates it, Shelley's ode is neatly, even elegantly, organized into five stanzas of four interwoven tercets and one couplet each.[13] Let's look at how the stanza works.

> O wild West Wind, thou breath of Autumn's being,
> Thou, from whose unseen presence the leaves dead
> Are driven, like ghosts from an enchanter fleeing,
>
> Yellow, and black, and pale, and hectic red,
> Pestilence-stricken multitudes: O thou,
> Who chariotest to their dark wintry bed
>
> The winged seeds, where they lie cold and low,
> Each like a corpse within its grave, until
> Thine azure sister of the Spring shall blow
>
> Her clarion o'er the dreaming earth, and fill   10
> (Driving sweet buds like flocks to feed in air)
> With living hues and odours plain and hill:
>
> Wild Spirit, which art moving everywhere;
> Destroyer and preserver; hear, O hear!

We noted earlier that Keats was led to the forms of his ode stanzas through his experimentations with the sonnet. Here Shelley seems to have simply invented a sonnet for the occasion. If it has fourteen lines, however, it is arranged like none of the standard forms, Petrarchan, Spenserian, or Shakespearean. It is somewhat like the Shakespearean sonnet in that it ends in a couplet, but Shakespeare always collected the preceding twelve lines into three quatrains, not the four tercets we have here. Noting the tercets, and the interlocking rhyme scheme (**aba bcb cdc ded ee**), we can scarcely miss the fact that Shelley has pressed the *terza rima* pattern of Dante into a sonnet. In the *Divine Comedy* Dante spun out his tercets into cantos of 150 lines or more, nor did he end them in the way Shelley does; they ended **wxw xyx yzyz**, so that the last rhyme of each canto, like the first, occurs only twice, but not in a couplet. The way the inner rhyme of one tercet becomes the outer rhyme of the next has been nicely captured by Earl Wasserman with the imagery of Shelley's first stanza: "each stanza [he means "tercet"] of the poem's *terza rima* contains an unused, unfulfilled line that, like a seed in the grave, upon the completion, or 'death,' of its own stanza gives birth to the rhyme of the next."[14] Perhaps Shelley had such an analogy in mind, but we may still ask why he takes the risk of invoking two such mighty predecessors as the greatest English poet and the greatest Italian poet.

As for Shakespeare, we can find a particular sonnet that may well have served as a seed of Shelley's imagery, Sonnet 73: "That time of year thou may'st in me behold / When yellow leaves, or none, or few, do hang / Upon those boughs which shake against the cold." Every major image of this sonnet – yellow leaves in autumn, the coming winter, sunset and night, fire and ashes – Shelley takes up in his wild lament over his premature aging and imminent death, as well as over the political torpor of humankind. As for Dante, stanza three depicts an Italian scene, though it goes on to describe the Atlantic. But more to the point, surely, is that Dante, exiled from Florence for political reasons, became a prophet, heralding the reunification of Italy (though it was not to take place for well over five hundred years, and after Shelley's day). At the end of his poem Shelley (or rather the speaker) will plead with the wind to make him its prophetic mouthpiece.

It is typical of Shelley's poetic technique to pile metaphor on metaphor, simile on simile, moving swiftly from one to another with little elaboration. The effect is to suggest both that the things of the world are filled with resemblances to one another and that no resemblance is exact: each unique thing or action can be defined only approximately by displaying one aspect after another through one lens after another. His images enrich our apprehension of the subject while suggesting that we cannot quite comprehend it. And they are often quite startling and original. To use his language in his *Defence of Poetry*, poets "unveil the permanent analogy of things by images"; poetry "purges from our inward sight the film of familiarity which obscures from us the wonder of our being." Shelley's metaphors have an "estranging" effect, inviting us to see the thing or deed as momentarily strange and new. That, as he says, is a function of all poetry – to present an old urn as a young bride caught in the moment before her nuptial bed is a fine defamiliarizing effect – but Shelley sometimes leaves his readers almost dizzy with the wonder of our being by administering an overdose of metaphor.

The West Wind in the first fourteen lines, for instance, is by turns a "breath," an invisible "enchanter," a charioteer, the brother of another Wind, and "Destroyer and preserver," while the sister Wind is a shepherdess, azure in color, who blows a "clarion." The leaves are "ghosts" stricken with disease, the seeds go to a "bed" and lie like corpses until awakened by the clarion's reveille, the buds are like a "flock" of sheep pasturing in air, and the earth dreams. The metaphors and similes fly thick and fast like leaves, seeds, or buds in the wind. They are not miscellaneous, however: Shelley has managed to organize the imagery of this stanza and the entire poem into one large scheme of analogies, undergirded by the natural pattern of seasonal phenomena, and the images in this stanza are indeed seeds of those in the following ones. One nice hint of the scheme comes from the word "Driving" (11), for it echoes "driven" (3) and thus helps us to see the parallel between the driving off of the dead leaves by the autumnal sorcerer and the gentle pasturing of the buds by his vernal sister, and then we note another parallel in the charioting (a kind of driving) of the seeds to their beds. Alert to analogies between the Wind siblings, we may ask what in the autumn corresponds to the clarion in the spring, and then it might occur to us that what an enchanter does is chant: he sings a spell to exorcize ghosts. One sort of music expels the dead, another rouses the seeming dead to new life. The "living hues" (12) of the buds makes us look again at the otherwise somewhat excessive list of leaf colors, for these are dead colors: no leaves are green, and the red ones, lest we entertain the thought of a healthy blush, have the "hectic" flush of consumption, the term then used for tuberculosis.[15] Spring and autumn are sister and brother, they do the same sort of thing, and they are complements rather than opposites.

The whole of the stanza, until the last three words, is one huge noun phrase governing the main verb, an imperative, "hear"; every other verb belongs to a subordinate clause. The result is an attempt to address and describe the god with his proper attributes. "O wild West Wind, thou ... / Thou ... // O thou, // Wild Spirit" – these invocations govern the descriptive clauses, and then, as if in hopes that they have been found acceptable to the god, Shelley asks it only to "hear" him. The next two stanzas are structured in the same way, ending with "hear," making three attempts to win the attention and favor of the unruly deity. Only then does Shelley state what he wants the Wind to hear, a prayer, a plea to do something for him. The poem is built like a classical ode or hymn, but since this is an unusual god there are no ritualistic formulas for invoking him, and Shelley must expand that part of the ode to huge proportions so we may hear just what power he is.[16]

> Thou on whose stream, 'mid the steep sky's commotion,
> Loose clouds like earth's decaying leaves are shed,
> Shook from the tangled boughs of Heaven and Ocean,
>
> Angels of rain and lightning: there are spread
> On the blue surface of thine aery surge,
> Like the bright hair uplifted from the head   20
>
> Of some fierce Maenad, even from the dim verge
> Of the horizon to the zenith's height,
> The locks of the approaching storm. Thou Dirge
>
> Of the dying year, to which this closing night
> Will be the dome of a vast sepulchre,
> Vaulted with all thy congregated might
>
> Of vapours, from whose solid atmosphere
> Black rain, and fire, and hail will burst: O, hear!

In the second stanza only one distinctive metaphor applies to the Wind, "Dirge / Of the dying year," which, whatever else it means, is an analogue of the chanting enchanter driving off the dead leaves. Beyond that, the wind has a "stream" or an "aery surge" and "vapours" or clouds that congregate – barely metaphors at all. But on the stream or surge are clouds that are presented in two striking similes, and the night is given a metaphor of apocalyptic grimness. The first cloud simile, "loose clouds like earth's decaying leaves" (16), links the stanza to the first, as if to say that what happens in the sky resembles what happens on earth, out of mutual "sympathy," perhaps, of the kind Shelley describes in a note to stanza three. This simile, based first on the similarity of clouds' shape, number, and speed in the wind to those of leaves, extends beyond the visible, I think, to something invisible, almost abstract. Commentators often mention waterspouts as the natural object behind "the tangled boughs of Heaven and Ocean" (17), and it is true that Shelley wrote elsewhere that a sculpture of dancing Maenads showed them as if in a whirlwind, like a waterspout, and their loose hair seemed caught in a tempest of their own making. The same cluster of images is present in the next simile, but in the poem itself we do not need to bring in a waterspout to account for the line. Heaven and Ocean, as if "tangled" together, produce clouds through evaporation, as Shelley knew perfectly well; the contribution of waterspouts is negligible. He wants to complete his parallel with leaves by describing the source of clouds in arboreal terms, and he pushes it past the limits of the visually imaginable.

His second effort with the clouds is extraordinary, and it brings the Wind close to a traditional Greek god, Dionysus, who was worshipped by Maenads or Bacchantes, women who danced ecstatically while filled with the god and the god's wine. The clouds rising from the western horizon to the zenith look like the loose hair blowing from such a Maenad. That would place her head just below the horizon, about to approach; she is a herald, an "Angel," of the coming "storm," an apt word for the effect of Dionysus when he visits a city. These "locks," moreover, are the right word for the cirrus clouds streaming overhead. Luke Howard had recently established the modern nomenclature for cloud types, and his term "cirrus" is simply Latin for "lock."

The transition to "Dirge" in line 23 is a bit abrupt, unless we are invited to think of Dionysus as bringing death and singing over it – the view, no doubt, of King Pentheus of Thebes in Euripides' *The Bacchae*, who refused to submit to the god and was destroyed by him. But the domain of the dirge is a church, where a requiem may be held, in this case for the dying year. The dirge not only resumes the image of the enchanter, but the "vast sepulchre" made by the night is connected to the dark graves of the seeds. Now we, beneath this "closing night" with its imminent rain and lightning and hail, are like the seeds in their tombs. If we felt confident that the seeds would rise or sprout from their "bed" (6), we might well feel a deep shudder of doubt that we will emerge alive from this bleak and seemingly sealed-off sepulchre. St. Paul likened us to seeds as he promised us the resurrection: "It is sown a natural body; it is raised a spiritual body" (I Corinthians 15.44). But this poem by Shelley the atheist does not offer us such comfort.

If comfort is to be had, we may find a little of it in the third stanza, the first half of which shows the West Wind in an apparently milder guise:

> Thou who didst waken from his summer dreams
> The blue Mediterranean, where he lay,   30
> Lulled by the coil of his chrystalline streams,
>
> Beside a pumice isle in Baiae's bay,
> And saw in sleep old palaces and towers
> Quivering within the wave's intenser day,
>
> All overgrown with azure moss and flowers
> So sweet, the sense faints picturing them! Thou
> For whose path the Atlantic's level powers
>
> Cleave themselves into chasms, while far below
> The sea-blooms and the oozy woods which wear
> The sapless foliage of the ocean, know   40

> Thy voice, and suddenly grow grey with fear,
> And tremble and despoil themselves: O, hear!

In waking the "blue Mediterranean" (30), which has "azure moss" (35), from his "summer dreams" (29), the West Wind resembles his "azure sister of the Spring" (9) who wakens earth from its winter dreams. We are not told what the earth dreams of – presumably spring – but here we learn that the Mediterranean dreams of "old palaces and towers," now, it seems, under water. They are the villas of Roman aristocrats who summered on Baiae's bay, west of Naples. That they are submerged means they are internal to the Mediterranean, part of him, as a dream is part of the dreamer and not outside him. Dreams, too, are fluid, watery. Yet there is something disquieting about this image of the sunken palaces (which the Shelleys saw on a visit in late 1818). It not only evokes the old moral suggested by Roman ruins – "O world's inconstancy! / That which is firm does flit and fall away, / And that is flitting, doth abide and stay," as Spenser had stated it in his translation of Du Bellay's "Ruins of Rome" – but the "pumice isle" reminds us that not far from this bay is Mount Vesuvius, which the poet Leopardi was soon to call "the Exterminator." Though the annual cycle from autumn to autumn via the renewal of spring consoles us for our losses and provides a model of Christian resurrection, nature also destroys life on longer and larger scales.

From the "sweet" scenes of the Mediterranean we pass to the Atlantic, whose surface, just now level, is transformed into chasms by the aroused West Wind. The Atlantic, too, has underwater blooms, woods, and foliage, like the flowers and moss of the Mediterranean, but if they were azure and thriving within the "wave's intenser day" (34), they have now grown "grey with fear" (41) and shed their leaves (that is "despoiled" themselves). Shelley's note explains that "The vegetation at the bottom of the sea, of rivers, and of lakes, sympathizes with that of the land in the change of seasons, and is consequently influenced by the winds which announce it." Marine biologists no longer think much of this idea, and in fact the poem does not really affirm it, for it is not out of sympathy with land vegetation that the sea foliage turns gray, but out of fear of the Wind, whose voice it knows. The poem's personifications have a logic different from anything science affirms, even the science of Shelley's day, though he believed there were deep connections between the human mind and such natural phenomena as electricity, magnetism, and certain chemical reactions. Something we might call "sympathy," in any case, pervades the poem through the intricate resemblances of land, air, and sea.

For the third stanza is about the sea and ocean as the first is about the land and the second the air or sky. In all three there are falling leaves, literal in the first and third, metaphorical (as clouds) in the second. The earth-centered first stanza speaks of "air" (11) where the bud-flocks feed; the air-centered second stanza speaks of a "stream" (15) and a "surge" (19), both mainly watery terms, and a "solid atmosphere" (27), which sounds earthy; while the third stanza gives much of its time to the plants growing on the floor of the earth below the waters. The fearsome "voice" of the Wind in the third stanza is heard as the enchanter in the first and the dirge of the second. It is as if the stanzas themselves sympathize with each other.

Up to now the speaker has said not a word about himself; it has all been rich descriptions of the Wind and his effects in the three realms of earth, air, and water, mostly violent and death-dealing, but with at least the promise of the reviving Wind of spring. Now, with the god fully described and implored three times to hear his prayer, the speaker tells us something of himself in the fourth stanza. He does not go right to his prayer, however, until its final four lines, for first he apologizes for the intrusion, indeed for having "striven / As thus with thee in prayer."

> If I were a dead leaf thou mightest bear;
> If I were a swift cloud to fly with thee;
> A wave to pant beneath thy power, and share
>
> The impulse of thy strength, only less free
> Than thou, O Uncontroulable! If even
> I were as in my boyhood, and could be
>
> The comrade of thy wanderings over Heaven,
> As then, when to outstrip thy skiey speed   50
> Scarce seemed a vision; I would ne'er have striven
>
> As thus with thee in prayer in my sore need.
> Oh! lift me as a wave, a leaf, a cloud!
> I fall upon the thorns of life! I bleed!
>
> A heavy weight of hours has chained and bowed
> One too like thee: tameless, and swift, and proud.

He begins this stanza by recapitulating the three previous stanzas in order, one line to each. If he were a leaf, a cloud, or a wave he would not have prayed to the Wind. If he were still a boy, he goes on, when he could fly (in his imagination) faster than the Wind himself, he would not have prayed. But he is neither an inanimate object nor an innocent child. He is in "sore need." Why? We do not know what griefs might lie behind "the thorns of life," but he seems mainly to be feeling old, bowed down by "A heavy weight of hours." That this should be his burden raises an interesting methodological question, of the sort we touched upon in our discussion of "Tintern Abbey." Shelley was 27 when he wrote the ode. In our time 27 seems young, and if we heard a poet of that age complaining like Shelley we would scarcely contain our patience, unless we knew of some particular suffering. Even in his time, when people had to grow up faster and diseases often carried people off at any age, 27 was not considered old. As it happens, Shelley was not well, and he felt old; his hair had turned white; he felt he had suffered physically and emotionally through many more years than the calendar indicated. The question is: is it important to know these facts? Is the speaker of the poem a burnt-out man of 27? You will decide this question yourself, but my own view is that the answer is "no": the poem, meant for the public, is to be interpreted with what the public can reasonably be expected to know, according to conventions then (and still) commonplace. Percy Shelley's life, though notorious in some circles at the time, is not a factor in the poem. The speaker of the poem is male, but that is about all we know of him at this point in the poem except that he feels old and weighed down by age and griefs.

A similar question arises with the line "I fall upon the thorns of life! I bleed!" Several current anthologies footnote the line with a reference to Christ's crown of thorns and thus imply that Shelley is comparing himself to Christ suffering on the cross. Is that right? The line says nothing about a crown, nor did Christ fall upon his. Surely the metaphor here belongs to the domain of leaves, the dominant image of the ode: Shelley feels like a fallen leaf. He is pleading to the Wind to lift him as it has lifted leaves and clouds and even waves, for he has fallen on to a thorn bush and is pierced by it. If we took the speaker as Christlike or (quite a different thing) *claiming* he is Christlike, what would it do to the ode? Surely it would diminish either the speaker or Christ, who never complained of old age, and it would invite a thousand thoughts about the life and death of Jesus, and his relationship to the Father, into a poem that is otherwise quite pagan, being about the relationship of the speaker to a god of nature.

The speaker, bent low by a heavy weight, has asked to be lifted up. In the final stanza he asks something more.

> Make me thy lyre, even as the forest is:
> What if my leaves are falling like its own!
> The tumult of thy mighty harmonies
>
> Will take from both a deep, autumnal tone,   60
> Sweet though in sadness. Be thou, Spirit fierce,
> My spirit! Be thou me, impetuous one!

Drive my dead thoughts over the universe
Like withered leaves to quicken a new birth!
And, by the incantation of this verse,

Scatter, as from an unextinguished hearth
Ashes and sparks, my words among mankind!
Be through my lips to unawaken'd Earth

The trumpet of a prophecy! O Wind,
If Winter comes, can Spring be far behind? 70

He asks to be made into an aeolian lyre (see page 28 above) for the Wind to play. He asks to share the Wind's "spirit." (We recall that Latin *spiritus* means "breath," the poem's first metaphor for the Wind; this is the wind of poetic inspiration.) He asks to *be* the Wind. He asks it to send his thoughts off like leaves and to scatter his words like ashes and sparks. And he asks it to be a trumpet of prophecy by blowing through his lips. That is a lot to ask, and it may seem at first to be a somewhat miscellaneous and inconsistent set of images. For the union with the Wind that he so desires, Shelley gives us another example of his characteristic rapid heaping up of alternative metaphors. But they are intricately interconnected, and just as tightly tied to the imagery of the first four stanzas. Indeed the imagery rounds back especially closely to that of the first stanza and thereby lends a satisfying sense of closure.

The stanza begins with a lyre and ends with a trumpet, both wind instruments. The lyre is likened to a forest in the autumn Wind, and that leads back to leaves again, though with a difference, for the speaker is no longer a leaf himself, blown about or fallen on thorns, but a tree that produces them for the Wind to take away. Between the lyre and tree images, the speaker asks the Wind to be his spirit, to be himself, so that, embodying the Wind, the speaker would blow his own thought-leaves over the universe and, through this very poem (65), scatter his words among mankind. Why "dead thoughts" (63)? They are like "withered leaves" (63), of course, and they echo the "leaves dead" of line 2, but has Shelley been compelled by his own imagistic scheme to say something inapposite to the manifest meaning? For surely his thoughts will be living, indeed rejuvenating; those who receive them will be revived by them, inspired by the same spirit. But we can nonetheless make some sense of "dead thoughts," I think, if we remember that leaves are also pages of a book and the speaker is a poet. We may think of the "Sibylline leaves," the scraps of prophecy written on palm leaves as they were uttered by the Cumaean Sibyl in her trance. Once the thoughts are written down, printed, bound, and "published" to the universe, they are dead; their author is no longer thinking them. That said, we note the speaker varies the image to ashes and sparks, something new in the poem. Ashes are an analogue of withered leaves, but sparks would correspond, surely, to seeds, which are living, if sometimes dormant or hibernating, sources of new life. Words have long been likened to seeds, notably in several of the parables of Jesus; we still "disseminate" knowledge in "seminars" (from Latin *semen*, "seed"). This reconsideration of "dead" thoughts by means of a new image lets Shelley recur to two of the three images of the opening, the leaves and seeds driven off by the autumnal Wind. As for the vernal sister Wind, we hear no more of buds, but the trumpet answers to her clarion and the "unawaken'd Earth" (68) corresponds to her "dreaming earth" in the spring (10). The speaker wants to be both Winds. He reminds us, too, of something we were not likely to think of in the first stanza, as the dead leaves are simply driven off, like ghosts, and that is that dead leaves do indeed serve new life. They "quicken a new birth" (64) as fertilizer or mulch! So do ashes. Yet, since the hearth is "unextinguished" (66), however burnt-out he feels, the speaker still has sparks that might incite mankind and ignite the change (left entirely unspecified) he desires. After a stanza each centered on earth, air, and water, we might have wondered where the fourth element is. Though "fire" (28) was to burst from the storm cloud of stanza two, it is only in the final lines that we learn the speaker has a few sparks left in him, amidst the ashes. It is enough, or will be enough if the Spirit fills him. And he will carry out his prophetic mission by means of this very poem, "by the incantation of this verse" (65) – yet another way he assumes the mantle of the Wind, who was an "enchanter" in the beginning. This ode, he prays to the god of inspirational wind, will turn into fertilizing leaves and ashes, incendiary sparks, a wakening trumpet for the renovation of the human race.

Yet it is all very vague. There is no prophecy in it, only a metaprophecy; it is a poem about becoming a poet-prophet, a poem about itself. And its final rhetorical question – "O Wind, / If Winter comes, can Spring be far behind?" – has struck many readers as both anticlimactic and oddly uncertain about the inexorable cycle of the seasons. "Winter," of course, symbolizes Shelley's own state of mind and, it seems, the state of "mankind," neither of which were certain to revive, but if you are going to conceive of personal or social processes in terms of seasons you cannot pretend they are not part of an inevitable and eternal succession. This poem has nonetheless inspired people, heartened them in their struggles for a better world. It has acted like a seed, whose intricate symmetries have kept it alive for readers and scattered it among mankind. Shelley made his social and political commitments plain enough elsewhere, after all, not least in the play *Prometheus Unbound*, which opened the volume (1820) that also contained "Ode to the West Wind." In this poem he faces the despair any reformer or revolutionary in Europe might have felt keenly in 1819, during the reaction that set in after the defeat of the French Revolution and Napoleon.

Addressing someone or something absent as if it were present – the gesture of apostrophe we find in all odes and many other poems – may be a sign of a larger absence or loss of something in the speaker's life and his or her effort to restore it, or bring it closer, or at least glimpse it. Keats yearns for a sustained moment of beauty to escape into from this world of "human passion" that makes him ill or leaves him desolate. Shelley longs to be possessed by the power of the wind not only so he can blow the prophetic trumpet but to rise from "the thorns of life." Both lament the inevitable passage of time: they envy the beautiful Greek figures "for ever young" or ache for their own boyhood when they felt at one with the wind. In this they both follow Wordsworth, whose "Ode" expresses his struggle to cope with the lost luminousness of childhood. All three poems, then, are elegies as well as odes. We might sum up by saying that the ode is a distinctly Romantic mode of elegy, a characteristic way of expressing, exploring, and controlling the grief and despair of mortal life.

Chapter 5

The French Revolution

Enlightenment and revelation   *106*

In April 1798 Coleridge published an ode of 105 lines about the French Revolution in the *Morning Post*. That fact alone, which would have struck no one at the time as remarkable, reminds us again of the importance of poetry two centuries ago as a medium for discussing any topic under the sun. It was far from the first of Coleridge's newspaper poems, and by 1798 he had acquired a reputation as a liberal reformer, and a man of "Jacobin" or pro-French sympathies, in a climate overwhelmingly hostile to such opinions. This poem, however, publically confessed his abandonment of the French Revolution and apologized for his earlier defense of it. Though in later reprintings he titled it "France: An Ode," in its first appearance he called it "The Recantation: An Ode." Much later he titled it "France: A Palinode," a word that evokes the famous *palinodia* or "back-ode" of the ancient Greek poet Stesichorus in which he retracts his attack on Helen. It is a "recantation" in the original sense of that word, a "back-song" or song of retraction for songs sung earlier. From the beginning, he writes, despite British opposition to it, "Unawed I sang" in favor of the Revolution (27), and even when Britain went to war against France "my voice, unaltered, sang defeat" to her enemies (36). But now he sings a new tune.

Though it is not one of the greatest Romantic odes, it repays close attention, and to come to it after reading Shelley's "Ode to the West Wind" lends it further interest, for Shelley's ode could be read as a kind of reply to it, a "back-song" to those of an earlier generation who have recanted their youthful revolutionary commitments. We dwell on it here, however, in a separate chapter, as an occasion to talk about the French Revolution itself, for it is impossible to understand the body of Romantic poetry as a whole without appreciating the cataclysmic events in France and everywhere in Europe after 1789, the enthusiasm they roused at first among what Wordsworth called "disingenuous youth" in Britain, and the bitter despair that arose when the ideals of the Revolution were confiscated and betrayed by the revolutionary French government itself. Even poetry that seems to be purely about the beauty or sublimity or healing power of nature takes on an extra charge when set against the political tumult of the day, and the censorship imposed on certain opinions about it, as we saw argued in a certain reading of "Tintern Abbey." Indeed the "retreat" into nature of which Wordsworth has been accused is explicitly acknowledged, and celebrated, in Coleridge's ode of the same year.

Here is the first of its five stanzas:

> Ye Clouds! that far above me float and pause,
>   Whose pathless march no mortal may control!
>   Ye Ocean-Waves! that, wheresoe'er ye roll,
> Yield homage only to eternal laws!
> Ye Woods! that listen to the night-birds singing,
>   Midway the smooth and perilous slope reclined,
> Save when your own imperious branches swinging,
>   Have made a solemn music of the wind!
> Where, like a man beloved of God,
> Through glooms, which never woodman trod,   10
>   How oft, pursuing fancies holy,
> My moonlight way o'er flowering weeds I wound,
>   Inspired, beyond the guess of folly,
> By each rude shape and wild unconquerable sound!
> O ye loud Waves! and O ye Forests high!
>   And O ye Clouds that far above me soared!
> Thou rising Sun! thou blue rejoicing Sky!
>   Yea, every thing that is and will be free!
>   Bear witness for me, wheresoe'er ye be,
> With what deep worship I have still adored   20
>   The spirit of divinest Liberty.

Coleridge is at pains to establish that he has always been dedicated to liberty, so that when he comes to his retraction proper he can claim he has been consistent in his principles and mistaken only in where he looked to see them embodied. Hence his strained attempt to show that such natural things as clouds, waves, and the swinging branches of trees are "free." He must be aware that such things are utterly dependent on the wind, which in turn depends on temperature differences on the earth, which are themselves determined by natural laws in an endless chain, but he contrives to present clouds, waves, and woods as free in one or another metaphorical respect. The clouds follow no predetermined path, he says, and no mortal can control them; the waves do indeed obey "eternal laws," but only after they "Yield homage" to them, as if they are feudal vassals who might freely choose to do otherwise; and the branches, which are manifestly helpless before the wind, are made to seem creative by turning the wind into music, like an aeolian harp, and they are "imperious," too, an adjective as unconvincing as it is surreptitiously political, as if, far above mere voluntary vassals, they are emperors. These personifications, of course, are enabled in part by the opening gesture common to odes, apostrophe, as Coleridge pretends that clouds, waves, woods, sun, and sky can all hear him and freely grant what he requests.

Though it is easy to see the delusory wishfulness of the imagery imposed on clouds, waves, and trees, we must grant that Coleridge is nonetheless on to something here. Compared to us mortals, these large natural things and processes, including the great sun itself, may indeed *seem* free: they do their own thing, and they impose on us, who can only admire and defer to them. Perhaps they seem free because they don't try to do things they can't do, "unnatural" deeds (such as those the French would try to do); by obeying the natural laws that seem so suited to them they seem not to "obey" them at all but consent to them out of an inner affinity. Coleridge nonetheless speaks as if he can compel them to "bear witness" for him that he has always worshipped liberty (a command repeated in stanza two). He speaks as if he is on trial and needs to prove that he has never advocated tyranny even though he endorsed the French Revolution, now grown tyrannous. Rather than enter his own earlier published poems and sermons into evidence, he quite unnecessarily paints himself into an awkward corner by suggesting that all his songs were sung privately, while he was wandering in the woods, and so he can call only the woods and the other natural objects as witnesses. (Shelley was to do the same thing in "Hymn to Intellectual Beauty.") Coleridge risks this absurdity, surely, because it is so important to assert his deep kinship with nature itself.

He also wants to show the jury that he has always been religious, and religiously attached to liberty. Hence the simile for himself in line 9, "like a man beloved of God," as if he had a special divine calling, like a prophet's or monk's. As he wanders through untrodden glooms, like the "pathless march" of the clouds, he pursues "holy" fancies and is "inspired" by what he sees and hears; at the end he claims that it is with "deep worship" that he has always "adored" "divinest" liberty. This religious language seems gratuitously thick, as if he feels vulnerable on that flank. As we shall see, it is France's irreligion and blasphemy as much as her tyranny and aggression that have brought about his recantation.

We should note here the very regular verse form of this ode, in contrast to Coleridge's "Dejection," which resembles Wordsworth's "Intimations" ode in its striking and unpredictable variations in stanza. The stanzas of "France" are identical in length (twenty-one lines) and its rhyme scheme is constant and not very unusual throughout (ten rhyme sounds, so only one is used three times). The lines are nearly all pentameters; only a few are shortened by one foot. It seems fair to say that Coleridge was establishing a steady, predictable, and not very adventurous form here to underscore his claim of consistency, of discipline, even of sobriety, in his political commitments. Certainly a form as wildly irregular as that of "Dejection" would have defeated his purpose.

The second stanza begins the recent story of France, interrupted by his protests of loyalty, and it is a "magic" story out of a medieval romance:

> When France in wrath her giant-limbs upreared,
> And with that oath, which smote air, earth and sea,
> Stamped her strong foot and said she would be free,
> Bear witness for me, how I hoped and feared!
> With what a joy my lofty gratulation
> Unawed I sang, amid a slavish band:
> And when to whelm the disenchanted nation,
> Like fiends embattled by a wizard's wand,
>   The Monarchs marched in evil day,   30
>   And Britain join'd the dire array;
> Though dear her shores and circling ocean,
> Though many friendships, many youthful loves
> Had swol'n the patriot emotion
> And flung a magic light o'er all her hills and groves;
> Yet still my voice, unaltered, sang defeat
> To all that braved the tyrant-quelling lance,
> And shame too long delayed and vain retreat!
> For ne'er, O Liberty! with partial aim
> I dimmed thy light or damped thy holy flame;   40
> But blessed the paeans of delivered France,
> And hung my head and wept at Britain's name.

The typical romance plot might have a damsel in distress, emprisoned or "enchanted" by a wizard who commands giants or dragons with his wand; she must be rescued by a knight with a lance. Here it is she who is a giant, and she who frees herself from the enchantment (28) simply by swearing an oath and stamping her foot. (The oath seems to refer to the "Tennis Court Oath" of June 20, 1789, when the members of the bourgeois Third Estate, who had proclaimed that they rightly represented the country as a whole, refused to disperse when the king ordered their usual meeting room closed and betook themselves to a tennis court where they vowed to remain in session until they established a new national constitution.) Soon monarchs (Prussian and Austrian) are invading France, as if *they* are enchanted, "Like fiends embattled [forced into battle] by a wizard's wand," but France brings her "tyrant-quelling lance" to bear against them, like a knight. Coleridge's rewriting of the romance plot to fit the historical facts is almost feminist: here is *la France*, a new Joan of Arc, rising on her own and defending herself against male wizards and monarchs. He wants us to admire her, I think, but the drastic departure from traditional romance may also be meant to make us uneasy, to sense something unnatural about it all. And isn't there a touch of the absurd about the line "Stamped her strong foot and said she would be free" (24)? The *OED* does not record an instance of the phrase "she put her foot down" until late in the nineteenth century, but it is hard to dispel an image of a spoiled and petulant young girl demanding her independence. And the oath, the historical version of which Coleridge certainly supported, when it smites air, earth, and sea (23), seems to be doing something violently unnatural to those natural things he celebrates in stanza one. It is slippery imagery, and it may have eluded Coleridge's full control, since his focus is on his own defense. At any rate, through the first years of the Revolution and the wars it provoked, while confessing his shame and dismay at Britain's bloody part in them, Coleridge insists again that he has remained a loyal worshipper of liberty.

The third stanza tells how he coped with two new motives to renounce France, "Blasphemy" and bloody warfare beyond the implicitly defensive measures taken against invading tyrants.

> "And what," I said, "though Blasphemy's loud scream
>   With that sweet music of deliverance strove!
>   Though all the fierce and drunken passions wove
> A dance more wild than e'er was maniac's dream!
>   Ye storms, that round the dawning east assembled,
> The Sun was rising, though ye hid his light!"
>   And when, to soothe my soul, that hoped and trembled,
> The dissonance ceased, and all seemed calm and bright;   50
>   When France her front deep-scarr'd and gory
>   Concealed with clustering wreaths of glory;
>   When, insupportably advancing,
>   Her arm made mockery of the warrior's ramp;
>   While timid looks of fury glancing,
>   Domestic treason, crushed beneath her fatal stamp,
> Writhed like a wounded dragon in his gore;
>   Then I reproached my fears that would not flee;
> "And soon," I said, "shall Wisdom teach her lore
> In the low huts of them that toil and groan!   60
> And, conquering by her happiness alone,

> Shall France compel the nations to be free,
> Till Love and Joy look round, and call the Earth their own."

Coleridge, as a Dissenter, indeed a Unitarian, was no friend of "Priestcraft" (95), and was not likely to have lamented the measures the revolutionary agencies took against the Roman Catholic Church, though they were severe and provoked violent resistance among peasants in western France and, later, in occupied Belgium and Italy. The blasphemy that sounded so loud in his ears must have been the brief experiments with state-sanctioned atheism, such as the Cult of Reason, which culminated in a Festival of Liberty at Notre Dame in Paris in November 1793, where a young girl dressed as the Goddess of Reason was "worshipped" by an enthusiastic crowd of radicals. Meanwhile our heroine France has acquired something beyond her bloodless tyrant-quelling lance, for her "front" (forehead) is now "deep-scarr'd and gory" from the wars, defensive, offensive, and domestic, which have marked the Revolution since early 1792. Warriors flee before her, and domestic treason writhes like a dragon, slain not by a knight on a rescue mission but crushed, in an echo of her stamping foot in stanza two (24), under her own "fatal stamp" (56). During the quieter periods, when moderates took control of the ever-changing governments, Coleridge could feel hopeful: the sun was still rising through morning storms, and soon Wisdom would spread among the rural masses ill prepared for liberty. He ends this stanza with a version of Rousseau's famous paradox, "On le forcera d'être libre": "He will be forced to be free." This was often invoked by French politicians justifying invasions of monarchies nearby, but here Coleridge reconceives it as the contagious example of nonviolent education and benevolence that his utopian imagination still conjured up, despite everything.[1]

But now it is too late, and the fourth stanza marks the turning point, when he can no longer defend France and liberty together. What causes him to break? The last straw is the invasion of Switzerland ("Helvetia") by French armies in March 1798. It was a complicated affair, as Switzerland was not a country but rather a loose congeries of cantons of widely different political types, some of which welcomed the French at first. Napoleon had crossed the Alps in 1796 to defeat the Austrians in northern Italy, and from then onwards needed to secure the Alpine passes to protect his northern flank. Whatever its justification, the invasion of Switzerland stood out against the invasions of other lands, which had either attacked France or were territories held by monarchs and feudal lords. The Swiss had not provoked France, and their cantons were republics! Though France had already shown that it put its national interests above the cause of liberty in the lands it dominated, it seemed particularly outrageous to exploit the Swiss and even suppress their own liberty-loving "patriots."

Forgive me, Freedom! O forgive those dreams!
  I hear thy voice, I hear thy loud lament,
  From bleak Helvetia's icy caverns sent—
I hear thy groans upon her blood-stained streams!
  Heroes, that for your peaceful country perished,
And ye that, fleeing, spot your mountain-snows
  With bleeding wounds; forgive me, that I cherished   70
One thought that ever blessed your cruel foes!
  To scatter rage and traitorous guilt
  Where Peace her jealous home had built;
    A patriot-race to disinherit
Of all that made their stormy wilds so dear;
    And with inexpiable spirit
To taint the bloodless freedom of the mountaineer—
O France, that mockest Heaven, adulterous, blind,
  And patriot only in pernicious toils!
Are these thy boasts, Champion of human kind?   80
  To mix with Kings in the low lust of sway,
Yell in the hunt, and share the murderous prey;
To insult the shrine of Liberty with spoils
  From freemen torn; to tempt and to betray?

Not only was "Switzerland" a federation of republics but it had acquired the reputation as a "free" land because of its long struggle against the Austrians, going back at least to the legendary fourteenth-century hero William Tell (who was, ironically, adopted by the French as a symbol of its new client state, the Helvetic Republic). Now the French have not only shed the blood of these free mountaineers but have been cutting deals with the Austrians in Italy, turning over independent Venice to them, for instance – another republic. The French revolutionaries had once claimed to be "patriots," those who, from well before 1789, put their country (*patrie*) before king and court, but now the French leaders have been in bed with kings "in the low lust of sway," while they went on hunts, like aristocrats, for Swiss patriots. In the face of all this, Coleridge turns against France; he runs out of excuses, or "dreams" of better times; and he asks Liberty for forgiveness.

Coleridge's "recantation," we noted, is a song, an ode, meant to unsing his earlier songs (27, 36). But his references to his songs make up only a part of the larger theme of music. The woods he first addresses listen to the "night-birds singing" (5) when they are not making their own "solemn music" out of the wind (8). Himself a kind of night-bird, wandering as he is by moonlight, he imagines that the trees listen to him as well as to the birds, while for his part he is inspired by each "unconquerable sound" (14). The oath that smites nature

(23) might be a harsh sound, but he makes nothing of it, and by the end of the second stanza he is blessing "the paeans of delivered France" (41), paeans being songs of thanksgiving, originally addressed to Apollo for deliverance from disease. Then this "sweet music of deliverance" is interrupted by "Blasphemy's loud scream" (43–4), but only for a time, after which "The dissonance ceased" (50). Now, finally, the "loud lament" and "groans" from Helvetia reach his ears (65–7), along with the shouts of the French conquerors, yelling in the hunt (82). The last reference to sound in this stanza is loud and dissonant, in contrast to the sweet sounds of liberty and the solemn music of nature. Is it too much to say that by bringing out this theme Coleridge is implying in some way that his own song, this one, must make musical amends for the dissonance of his earlier ones, which were out of harmony with nature and natural liberty?

He withdraws, at any rate, from the pursuit of political liberty and takes refuge in the realm of winds and waves.

> The Sensual and the Dark rebel in vain,
>   Slaves by their own compulsion! In mad game
>   They burst their manacles and wear the name
>   Of Freedom, graven on a heavier chain!
>   O Liberty! with profitless endeavour
> Have I pursued thee, many a weary hour;   90
>   But thou nor swell'st the victor's strain, nor ever
> Didst breathe thy soul in forms of human power.
>   Alike from all, howe'er they praise thee,
>   (Nor prayer, nor boastful name delays thee)
>   Alike from Priestcraft's harpy minions,
>   And factious Blasphemy's obscener slaves,
>   Thou speedest on thy subtle pinions,
> The guide of homeless winds, and playmate of the waves!
> And there I felt thee!—on that sea-cliff's verge,
>   Whose pines, scarce travelled by the breeze above,   100
> Had made one murmur with the distant surge!
> Yes, while I stood and gazed, my temples bare,
> And shot my being through earth, sea and air,
>   Possessing all things with intensest love,
>   O Liberty! my spirit felt thee there.

Coleridge has already given a plausible, if simplistic, diagnosis of the political ills of France – that the French people are too "sensual" (bound by their senses, seeing no further than their narrow circumstances) and too "dark" (unenlightened) to govern themselves, so their rebellion against feudal monarchy and priestcraft only brought about a worse tyranny. Those who live in low huts need to learn the lore of Wisdom (59–60) before they try to overthrow their government. Such a gradualist view need not entail a rejection of politics altogether, and indeed resembles that of several parties in France itself, not to mention reformers in Britain. So it seems an abrupt non sequitur to dismiss political liberty as hopeless. We might agree that liberty does not accompany "the victor's strain" (a final reference to music), but surely it is strange to claim that it cannot be found "in forms of human power" (91–2). Where else can it be found? In stanza one we heard Coleridge talking himself into believing that trees and waves are free, and as he circles back to the opening scene we can only expect him to reaffirm it, but now we see the consequences of his initial myth. Coleridge is recanting not just his misplaced faith in France but his belief that *any* political change might improve the lot of the hut dwellers and enlarge the scope of liberty. The liberty he imagines alone on the sea-cliff's verge is rather like the old idea of "Christian liberty," an inner state entirely disconnected from the social or political world. A reviewer of the poem, indeed, asked what connection Coleridge's "Liberty" has with "civil freedom." In a private note Coleridge replied, "surely the object of this stanza is to show, that true political Freedom can only arise out of moral Freedom."[2] But even if we can bring ourselves to agree to that proposition – the French themselves, after all, constantly harped on about citizenly "virtue" as a precondition of political liberty – the poem says something very different. Coleridge's state of mind or mood is one with which we can well sympathize, and it is as ancient as the Roman poetry of retirement or retreat from the futility, vanity, corruption, and violence of the city into the welcome solitude of the farm where one can cultivate one's vines and one's leisure. As a statement about liberty, however, it is surely a shallow myth, and one that Coleridge himself did not even try to sustain, for he returned again and again to British and European politics. His political opinions changed, but he did not suddenly become apolitical. One could argue, in fact, that he no longer supported liberty in Britain or anywhere else, but stability, authority, and deference to tradition. But that is another story.

This ode is an apology in two senses of the word: he asks for forgiveness for his former mistake, and he offers an *apologia*, a defense, of his loyalty. For he insists that his mistake was not one of the heart – he has always been a steadfast worshipper of liberty – but of the mind or sense – as he thought liberty might be incarnated in a revolutionary nation. And while he also says it cannot be embodied in any nation, it is still telling that the nature where he finds it, the "there" where his spirit felt it (105), is in England.

What also comes through clearly in this poem is Coleridge's depth of feeling, his hopes and fears, defiance and despair, over the endlessly varying struggles within France and between France and Britain. It is hard, after more than two centuries, to enter into the enormous excitement, the religious enthusi-asm, that the French Revolution roused throughout Europe, and especially among young people. "Few persons but those who have lived in it," Robert Southey wrote years later, "can conceive or comprehend what the memory of the French Revolution was, nor what a visionary world seemed to open upon those who were just entering it. Old things seemed passing away, and nothing was dreamt of but the regeneration of the human race."[3] The classic statement of this state of mind is Wordsworth's, a passage from *The Prelude* that first appeared in Coleridge's journal *The Friend* in 1809:

> Oh! pleasant exercise of hope and joy!
> For mighty were the auxiliars which then stood
> Upon our side, we who were strong in love!
> Bliss was it in that dawn to be alive,
> But to be young was very heaven! oh! times,
> In which the meagre stale forbidding ways
> Of custom, law, and statute, took at once
> The attraction of a country in Romance!
> When Reason seem'd the most to assert her rights,
> When most intent on making of herself
> A prime Enchanter to assist the work,
> Which then was going forward in her name!
> Not favour'd spots alone, but the whole earth,
> The beauty wore of promise—that which sets
> (To take an image which was felt no doubt
> Among the bowers of paradise itself)
> The budding rose above the rose full blown.
> What temper at the prospect did not wake
> To happiness unthought of? The inert
> Were rous'd, and lively natures rapt away![4]

Wordsworth makes explicit here what is implicit in the plot of Coleridge's ode, the literary inspiration – "Romance" – of the attraction France held for young people, or for "lively natures," and he brings out the religious beliefs the Revolution mobilized, for the idea that paradise had returned, Southey's "regeneration of the human race," was not just another literary allusion.

As we noted in Chapter 3, France was the largest country in western Europe, twice as populous as Great Britain, and a powerful centralized state whose armies usually dictated the borders and alliances of the Continent. Its cul-ture dominated even where its armies did not: the French language was spo-ken, sometimes even as a first language, by the aristocracy of every nation and most of their educated classes, and French monuments in art, literature, and architecture were emulated everywhere. The revolution in America had been an inspiration, but America was far away and its population small; the revolution in France was a thunderbolt striking at the center of the world. Everything now seemed possible. The great parliamentarian Charles James Fox exclaimed, "How much the greatest event it is that ever happened in the world! and how much the best!"[5] And then, as France lurched from constitutional monarchy to republic, with a king guillotined in 1793; swayed left and then right, through defensive warfare to invasions, counterrevolution, and terror; and finally yielded to an emperor more powerful than any king, all in less than a decade; the unprecedented joy and hope of many Britons yielded by fits and starts to demoralization, dereliction, and dismay (or in a few cases stubborn defiance), not to mention government censorship and repression. In this decade Romanticism was born.

Enlightenment and revelation

Two poems of 1792 by prominent women poets well display the hopes, dreams, and fears of British well-wishers who saw in the French Revolution the fulfillment of the Enlightenment ideal. The year 1792 was crucial (though every year seemed crucial as they came and went): France went to war with Austria and Prussia, declared itself a republic, and abolished the monarchy; it was also the year of the "September Massacres," the first great wave of the Terror, when over a thousand prisoners were murdered by "patriotic" soldiers and other Parisians who feared they might reverse the gains of the Revolution if they escaped or were set free. France seemed on the verge of epochal greatness, against which the mob attacks would soon shrink to a small blemish, as much the fault of Austria and Prussia as of unruly *citoyens*, but equally she seemed on the brink of collapsing into irredeemable chaos and violence.

Anna Laetitia Barbauld's nine-quatrain poem, "On the Expected General Rising of the French Nation in 1792," falls into two equal parts, first a call for France to rise up and deal a mighty blow against the "royal vultures" now invading her, then a call for generosity and forgiveness.[6] It begins:

> Rise, mighty nation, in thy strength,
> And deal thy dreadful vengeance round—
> Let thy great spirit, roused at length,
> Strike hordes of despots to the ground!

She imagines an enormous rush to the colors by every able-bodied man (the first modern *levée en masse*, or mass conscription, was ordered a year later):

"in millions pour thy generous bands, / And end a warfare by a blow!" If this picture of a sudden and final end to hostilities sounds unrealistic, her vision in the second half of the poem is a wishful dream: "Then wash with sad repentant tears / Each deed that clouds thy glory's page." She calls on France to welcome back her "outcasts" (the *émigrés* who have fled the country), honor the fallen who opposed the Revolution, and furl her conquering banners. Nothing like this was to happen for a century or more. Yet it would be unfair, I think, if we condescendingly dismissed Barbauld's dreams, which were shared by Coleridge, Wordsworth, and many others – we who have the advantage over them of two centuries of revolutions to ponder. How many cynical "realists," after all, predicted the "velvet" revolutions in eastern Europe of 1989? In any case, Barbauld ends her poem with the same hope Coleridge had entertained ("conquering by her happiness alone"): "Obey the laws thyself hast made, / And rise the model of the world!" She nicely returns to the verb of the opening line, and suggests a spiritual transformation or sublimation of "rising." It was controversial in the Britain of 1792, and dangerous a year or two later, to propose France as a model of the world, which would imply that Britain, whose dominant order smugly thought *Britain* was the model of political liberty (as indeed in 1789 some French revolutionaries themselves thought it was), should now imitate France and let London shopkeepers dictate terms to the king. But at least Barbauld remains true to her Enlightenment heritage as she envisages the spreading of social renovation by precept and example rather than by violence.

Even more securely in the Enlightenment mode is a passage from Helen Maria Williams' verse-epistle "To Dr. Moore," where enlightenment literally dawns on the common people of France:

> For now on Gallia's plains the peasant knows
> Those equal rights impartial Heaven bestows.
> He now, by Freedom's ray illumined, taught
> Some self-respect, some energy of thought,
> Discerns the blessings that to all belong,
> And lives to guard his humble shed from wrong.

The enemies of the Revolution hide like moles from "the spreading light," hoping "their eloquence, with taper-ray / Can dim the blaze of philosophic day." Like Coleridge's rising sun (48), this day of enlightenment is inevitable. When it comes, Williams goes on to say, it will shake to the ground the "gothic piles" that feudal governments resemble, with their labyrinths, towers, drawbridges, and dungeons. She is alluding perhaps to the Bastille, demolished within months of its storming on July 14; that prison was not only a metaphor for the intricate and secret ways of the Old Regime but also a very literal extension of its arbitrary power. In its stead will arise a "temple" "Of fair proportions, and simple grace, / A mansion worthy of the human race," of an architectural style, we cannot help thinking, called Neoclassical, the favorite style of the Enlightenment. The French revolutionaries, like the Americans before them, adopted the language and imagery of the Roman republic, with its senates and tribunes and various ceremonial objects, as if they were leaping back over all the dark "gothic" centuries since the fall of Rome. But for most of the century the Neoclassical style in building had appealed widely to landowners who considered themselves enlightened or at least up to date.

These two poems show one side of the response to the Revolution, one continuous with the traditions that inspired it in the first place. But another strand was at least as important for the Romantics, the tradition of Christian millenarianism or apocalypticism. Particularly among Dissenters the events in America and Europe seemed to fulfill the prophecies of Isaiah, Ezekiel, Daniel, and Revelation. Joseph Price and Joseph Priestley, for instance, both Unitarian ministers, preached in several chapels that the Revolution was a sign of the Second Coming of Christ, to the fury of Edmund Burke, whose long reply to Price, *Reflections on the Revolution in France* (1790), was the first and greatest of the anti-Revolution tracts. After the war had begun Priestley published *The Present State of Europe Compared with Antient Prophecies* (1794), where he identified the Revolution with events in Revelation. Just as today, especially in America, the credulous scan the Bible or Nostradamus or the Mayan calendar for clues to the 9–11 attacks, tsunamis, or global warming, many latter-day prophets in pubs and pulpits ransacked the Scriptures for explanations of what seemed unprecedented political cataclysms.[7]

William Blake, who said that the Bible is the "Eternal Vision or Imagination of All that Exists" (*Vision of the Last Judgment*), and who made nearly two hundred illustrations of scenes from it, instinctively borrowed apocalyptic imagery for his poems about France and America. *The French Revolution* (1791), the first book of which was set up in type but apparently never published, recounts the early events: the gathering of the Estates General; the king's dismissal of Necker, his financial minister; fierce debates among the nobles about what to do; and Lafayette's ordering the army out of Paris (not historically correct). This might be interesting enough, but what strikes the reader is the sheer portentousness of it all, with clouds and flames and other omens at every turn, from the first line ("The dead brood over Europe, the cloud and vision descends over chearful France") to the final scene ("And the bottoms of the world were open'd, and the graves of arch-angels unseal'd"). Great meteorological and astronomical omens also permeate *America: A Prophecy* (1793), which Blake engraved in his "illuminated" manner on copper plate, but the most biblical moment comes when the American revolutionary spirit, embodied in a fiery young male named Orc, rises over the Atlantic to the terror of Albion, after which we are given an apocalyptic vision of American independence in terms of the general resurrection:

> The morning comes, the night decays, the watchmen leave their
>   stations;
> The grave is burst, the spices shed, the linen wrapped up;
> The bones of death, the cov'ring clay, the sinews shrunk & dry'd.
> Reviving shake, inspiring move, breathing! awakening!
> Spring like redeemed captives when their bonds & bars are burst;
> Let the slave grinding at the mill, run out into the field:
> …
> Singing. The Sun has left his blackness, & has found a fresher morning
> And the fair Moon rejoices in the clear & cloudless night;
> For Empire is no more, and now the Lion & Wolf shall cease.
>
> (6:1–6, 13–15)

And so it is with nearly all of Blake's works. He did not recant his early sympathies as Coleridge did, but reconsidered the agency of social renovation, hoping less from the revolutionary force symbolized by Orc and more from a kind of spiritual transformation embodied in Jesus, a widening of the imagination and embracing of human brotherhood. While there is little of the blood-drenched imagery of Revelation in his epic works *Milton* (1804–*c*. 1810) and *Jerusalem* (1800–*c*. 1815), there is much about resurrection, transfiguration, and the dawning of a new age without war and accusations of sin. On the allegorical level of both poems, Albion represents Britain, so when he awakens from a long sleep at the end of the poem his transformation resembles both a conversion experience in an individual soul and a revolution in a nation.

As for Coleridge, apocalyptic imagery and millenarian dreaming are muted in "France: An Ode," but they are loud and plentiful in several earlier poems, such as "Religious Musings" (1794–6). That poem, which made a deep impression on many readers, is thoroughly imbued with Christian belief, from the nonviolent meekness that shines "When heedless of himself the scourged Saint / Mourns for the oppressor" (13–14) to the "day of retribution" (303) which is soon to come. That day will avenge the suffering ones of the earth – the slaves, the wretched, the aged women kept just sufficiently alive through charity that their slow death does not seem murder (287–9), the soldiers "Forced or ensnared" into the army and slaughtered on the battlefield (293–5), and their widows, wracked with nightmares, trying to care for a "screaming baby" in a miserable cottage (296–300). For now

> The Lamb of God hath opened the fifth seal:
> And upward rush on swiftest wing of fire
> The innumerable multitude of Wrongs
> By man on man inflicted! Rest awhile,
> Children of wretchedness! The hour is nigh;
> And lo! the great, the rich, the mighty Men,
> The Kings and the chief Captains of the World,
> With all that fixed on high like stars of Heaven
> Shot baleful influence, shall be cast to earth,
> Vile and down-trodden, as the untimely fruit
> Shook from the fig-tree by a sudden storm.

(304–14)

It is not quite right to equate the sudden storm with the French Revolution, for the range of the poem is greater, but the Revolution and the wars it provoked are surely parts of the storm, behind which is Christ himself, now not as he appeared as the meek sufferer on the cross but the character in the Book of Revelation who not only opens seals but rides on horseback with a sword in his mouth. As events soured Coleridge on France, he grew ambivalent about "Religious Musings." In "France: An Ode" he implicitly recants his harnessing of such tremendous biblical imagery to the events of the day. But until 1798, at least, Coleridge cherished visions of the apocalypse and the millennium, and they helped make him a poet.

We have already seen the religious touches in Wordsworth's account of the joy his generation felt at the news of the French Revolution ("very heaven," "bowers of paradise"). These might seem mere extravagances, but Wordsworth, though less insistently than Coleridge (as he was less religious than Coleridge), also resorted to the language of Revelation and other prophecies when he wrote first of the French Revolution and then of personal encounters with nature. It is not always easy to distinguish them from his "spots of time" when "huge and mighty Forms" moved through his mind (to quote from *The Prelude*), but when he describes in detail his year in France (1791/2) and his alienation from his own country, which went to war with France shortly after his return home (1805 *Prelude* Books 9, 10, and 11), his language sometimes shifts to a religious register. When he learned that Robespierre had fallen, he tells us, he sang a hymn of triumph: "Come now, ye golden times / … / … as the morning comes / Out of the bosom of the night, come ye" (10.541–4). He had already identified with the biblical prophets:

> But as the ancient prophets were enflamed,
> Nor wanted consolations of their own
> And majesty of mind, when they denounced

On towns and cities, wallowing in the abyss
Of their offences, punishment to come;
Or saw like other men with bodily eyes
Before them in some desolated place
The consummation of the wrath of Heaven;
So did some portion of that spirit fall
In me to uphold me in those evil times,
And in their rage and dog-day heat I found
Something to glory in

(10.401–12)

In assuming their mantle, or a portion of it, Wordsworth like Coleridge grew into his mission as a poet, of the sort we considered in Chapter 2.

The most famous apocalypse in *The Prelude*, however, in a passage that uses the very word for the only time, is not about revolution or politics but about the sublimity of nature and its relation to the imagination. He was walking with a friend across the Alps (in 1790, a year before his long stay in France):

The immeasurable height
Of woods decaying, never to be decayed,
The stationary blasts of waterfalls,
And everywhere along the hollow rent
Winds thwarting winds, bewildered and forlorn,
The torrents shooting from the clear blue sky,
The rocks that muttered close upon our ears—
Black drizzling crags that spake by the wayside
As if a voice were in them—the sick sight
And giddy prospect of the raving stream,
The unfettered clouds and region of the heavens,
Tumult and peace, the darkness and the light,
Were all like workings of one mind, the features
Of the same face, blossoms upon one tree,
Characters of the great apocalypse,
The types and symbols of eternity,
Of first, and last, and midst, and without end.

(6.556–72)

Though it takes place before the revolutionary period both in chronology and its placement in the poem, this mighty passage – one long sentence, a two-part list that unites woods, waterfalls, winds, rocks, stream, and clouds with an ultimate symbolic revelation – stands out as more central to Wordsworth's poetic world than the scenes, also vividly described, of tumultuous France. The most powerful visionary passage in all of Wordsworth, many readers feel, and one of the most steeped in religious language, is about nature seen as a mind – yet not necessarily as the product of the Creator. The mind seems indwelling, the soul of those impressive natural things, and might even be the human mind, at least when exalted by the imagination. We are near to the state of mind Coleridge was in at the end of "France: An Ode" (the "unfettered clouds" might have floated out of that poem into Wordsworth's), though without a recantation, of course, since there was nothing as yet to recant. By 1798, when he returned to the banks of the Wye with his sister, as we saw, he might have been retreating from political commitments both dangerous and disillusioning. If so, he retained his visionary faculty and his prophetic calling well after that time.

The younger generation of Romantics, coming of age well after the glorious onset of the Revolution, was less disillusioned by its failure and could draw lessons from it with more detachment. Shelley, however, born in 1792, seems to have recapitulated much of the intellectual and emotional process that Wordsworth, Coleridge, and Southey, and to a degree even Blake, underwent during the exciting and harrowing events themselves. Shelley immersed himself in the eighteenth-century Enlightenment authors whose works prepared the way for the Revolution, and he learned as much as he could about its history. One lesson he drew, a rather obvious one but one he thought through in detail, is that the *next* revolution had better be nonviolent. Tyrannical governments fall when their subjects cease to obey them, indeed cease to regard them, and the virtues we need to shrug them off are courage, patience, and self-sacrifice – the very virtues soldiers in an army are presumed to possess. In his early epic *Laon and Cythna* (1817), Shelley reimagines the French Revolution, holding it to a higher standard, where its leaders show forgiveness and restraint when they succeed. Nonetheless the enemy counterattacks, forcing the revolutionaries to strictly defensive violence; when that proves inadequate and the revolution is defeated its two leaders, the lovers Laon and Cythna, are transported to a spiritual realm which, however tragically their own movement was crushed, will inspire future ones in a way the badly conducted French Revolution cannot. In his "The Mask of Anarchy" (1819), a ballad-like poem "written on the occasion of the massacre at Manchester" (as his subtitle puts it), soon known as the "Peterloo" massacre, where a large and nonviolent rally of reformers was brutally dispersed by cavalrymen, Shelley restages the rally: this time the huge crowd does not flee in panic before troops, artillery, bayonets, and whatever else "the tyrants pour around" (303) but remains still, standing "with folded arms" (321) as the cavalrymen "Slash, and stab, and maim, and hew" (342). He thinks the troops will return home with shame, scorned and shunned by the women of the land as well as by "true warriors" (356) who would not be so base as to attack unarmed civilians. The nation will awaken from its slumber and shake off its chains. If all that sounds naïve, it inspired Mahatma Gandhi, who on at least one occasion read "The Mask of Anarchy" aloud to his followers in India, and with real impact practiced what it preached.

These are two of Shelley's reprises of the failed French Revolution; another is his great play *Prometheus Unbound*, which we will consider in Chapter 10. Though Shelley was a son (or grandson) of the Enlightenment and called himself an atheist, all three works are rich in apocalyptic and millenarian imagery drawn mainly from the Bible. In "The Mask of Anarchy" the imagery begins in a satirical mode. The speaker of this poem observes a masque or procession of maskers, or reverse-maskers, where an allegorical figure dresses up as a real person: Murder, for example, with seven bloodhounds (the mystic number in Revelation), wore a mask like Castlereagh, the Foreign Secretary and leader of the reactionary Holy Alliance in post-Napoleonic Europe. Climaxing the parade is Anarchy himself, satirically named, since the despots of Britain and Europe all claimed to be pillars of order and guardians against revolutionary chaos; "he rode / On a white horse, splashed with blood; / He was pale even to the lips, / Like Death in the Apocalypse" (30–3), an invocation of one of the four horsemen, Death, riding a pale horse (Revelation 6.8). After Shelley recounts the destruction these figures wreak on the people of the earth, the satire falls away, and he imagines a "maniac maid" named Hope who lies down before the horses, whereupon a great quasi-biblical event takes place: a mist rises between her and Murder, Anarchy, and the others, turning into a giant warrior with the morning star on his helmet. He passes overhead, and Anarchy and his henchmen fall dead or flee. He plays a role much like the Lamb of God in Revelation, though it is telling that it is Hope who inspires the vision, not Christian Faith. Wherever he passes "Thoughts sprung" (125) from the prostrate masses, thoughts that tell them they share a hope for a new society and, sharing it, have the power together to bring it about. At this point a voice arises as if from the earth, and it sings a long song about freedom, calling on the people of England to "Rise like Lions after slumber" (151). The voice describes the particular act that the masses must perform, and it is most unlionlike: a restaging of the Peterloo rally, but this time with no panic and certainly no retaliation. It is much in the spirit of *Laon and Cythna*, which is a reprise of the French Revolution but without its spiraling violence, but unlike that poem, which ends only with hope sequestered in another realm, the "Mask" lays out a path to success – idealistic, to be sure, but down to earth, a path people could follow, and have followed, to overthrow tyranny.

It was widely understood that the French Revolution was brought about by people who had read the great Enlightenment intellectuals or *philosophes* and held firm beliefs about reason in government and the rights of man and citizen. Like the American Revolution a few years earlier, the Enlightenment seemed to embody itself in political deeds. It was just this feature that Edmund Burke excoriated in his *Reflections on the Revolution in France* (1790): abstract ideas, infesting the brains of "sophisters" and lawyers, led them to abolish all the traditions, customs, and heart-satisfying rituals of France, and the consequences would be dire.

Two or three decades later, when many of these consequences had come to pass, the Romantics were tempted to abandon politics and public advocacy, as we have seen. But they never really did. Their hopes that France would renovate the world were dashed, but they did not give up their self-appointed role as prophet and sage. They preached a new sermon, perhaps – Wordsworth and Coleridge sounding more like Burke the traditionalist, Shelley sounding like a revolutionary on a higher plane – but preach they did. That intellectuals, even poets and artists, had played a part in the Revolution was not forgotten, even if that part was rescripted in the light of catastrophic events. Poets, better informed now about feelings as well as ideas, felt summoned to lead the British people, or at least counsel its leaders. Wordsworth became "The Sage of Rydal Mount," while Coleridge wrote such treatises as *On the Constitution of Church and State* (1830). Byron and Shelley became darlings of the labor movement, their poems appearing frequently in the journals of the Chartists of the 1840s. Tennyson, Robert Browning, and many other poets of the Victorian era were looked to for guidance in an age of waning religious belief and rapid social change. It was not until the end of the century that the role and image of the poet began to change decisively into what we still think of as the Romantic mode: a retreat into art-for-art's-sake aestheticism, an anti-bourgeois Bohemianism or "decadence," and a pseudo-politics of extravagant gesture conscious of its ineffectualness. We are wrong, however, to call this sort of thing Romantic. It is a later, post-Romantic phase, though continuous with earlier Romanticism. In its first high and heroic days, Romanticism answered a call to change the world.

Chapter 6

Romantic sonnets

When we think of the English sonnet we inevitably think first of Shakespeare, Spenser, Sidney, Donne, and other poets of the Renaissance, but the second great age of the sonnet was the Romantic era. "English Romanticism," Harold Bloom memorably put it, "was a renaissance of the Renaissance," and one of the distinctive features of this second renaissance was a revival of lyric forms, among which the sonnet had pride of place.[1] A convenient way to review its history before Romanticism is to look at one of Wordsworth's, a sonnet on the sonnet, published in 1827:

> Scorn not the Sonnet; Critic, you have frowned,
> Mindless of its just honours; with this key
> Shakespeare unlocked his heart; the melody
> Of this small lute gave ease to Petrarch's wound;
> A thousand times this pipe did Tasso sound;   5
> With it Camoëns soothed an exile's grief;
> The Sonnet glittered a gay myrtle leaf
> Amid the cypress with which Dante crowned
> His visionary brow; a glow-worm lamp,
> It cheered mild Spenser, called from Faery-land   10
> To struggle through dark ways; and when a damp
> Fell round the path of Milton, in his hand
> The Thing became a trumpet; whence he blew
> Soul-animating strains—alas, too few!

This is a fairly comprehensive history of the sonnet, naming seven of its greatest creators, three Italian, three English, and one Portuguese (Camoëns), and in all but one case offering a distinctive image for what the sonnet became in their hands. Three of the images are musical instruments, culminating in

Milton's trumpet, the traditional instrument of the epic. It omits Ronsard, Lope de Vega, and other French and Spanish Renaissance sonneteers, but Wordsworth would have had to write at least two sonnets to get everybody in. This one, appropriately enough, is a cross between the Italian or Petrarchan form, which is divided into an octave of two identically rhymed quatrains (**abba abba**) followed by a sestet (**cdecde** or some variation), and the Shakespearean form, which falls into three quatrains followed by a couplet (**abab cdcd efef gg**). The syntax, moreover, sometimes straddles the quatrain structure: "with which Dante crowned / His visionary brow" runs right across the most important break point in the Petrarchan pattern, where there was usually a *volta* or "turn," while Milton occupies not just the final couplet but a line and a half before it. It is not the greatest of Wordsworth's sonnets, but it is something of a tour de force, with some tidbit to chew on about each poet.[2]

After Milton's too few sonnets, sonnets in English grew even fewer and further between for nearly a century. Pope and Dryden were not interested in them; Collins and Goldsmith wrote none. A new start was made when Thomas Edwards published thirteen of them in 1748, but they made little impression. Thomas Gray wrote only one, an elegy on the death of Richard West (published in 1775), but it had a large influence, offering the sonnet as a vehicle for melancholy meditation, as opposed to the themes of love and religious faith that prevailed during the Renaissance or the public and political themes Milton trumpeted. Thomas Warton, Jr., soon followed with a set of sonnets (1777); and then Smith, Bowles, Cowper, Coleridge, Lamb, and Wordsworth made the sonnet the central form it has remained until now. Shelley and Keats wrote great ones, and even Byron, who despised the form, wrote two; of the canonical Romantic poets only Blake never showed any interest in them.[3]

Two sonnets of the early revival

Charlotte Smith deserves much of the credit for the sonnet revival. Enlarging the mode of Gray's one sonnet, her *Elegiac Sonnets* (1784, with many later expanded editions) were widely appreciated for their mournful and contemplative mood, brought on by a grief never identified. Smith is usually considered a poet of Sensibility rather than Romanticism – she appeals in her "Preface" to readers who have "sensibility of heart" – but especially in Romanticism's early days it is difficult to separate them. Here is one of her best sonnets:

Written in the Church-yard at Middleton in Sussex

Press'd by the Moon, mute arbitress of tides,
    While the loud equinox its power combines,
    The sea no more its swelling surge confines,
But o'er the shrinking land sublimely rides.
The wild blast, rising from the Western cave,   5
    Drives the huge billows from their heaving bed;
    Tears from their grassy tombs the village dead,
And breaks the silent sabbath of the grave!
With shells and sea-weed mingled, on the shore
    Lo! their bones whiten in the frequent wave;   10
    But vain to them the winds and waters rave;
They hear the warring elements no more:
While I am doom'd—by life's long storm opprest,
To gaze with envy on their gloomy rest.

This is Shakespearean in form, with three quatrains and the "turn" of thought placed before the final couplet, but it gestures toward the tighter rhyme scheme of the Petrarchan type by repeating the outer rhyme of the second quatrain ("cave," "grave") in the inner rhyme of the third ("wave," "rave"). We are in a country churchyard, like the setting of Gray's celebrated "Elegy," but here it seems to be night, if the moon is visible and full, as it would have to be to make for the highest tide, the "spring" tide, when sun and moon pull the seas from opposite sides. The high tide is pushed ashore by an "equinox," that is, an equinoctial gale, a gale at the beginning of spring or fall. Surely it is now fall; this wild west wind, like Shelley's, is the breath of autumn, and like his wind it brings destruction and an almost "gothic" apocalypse of death. Indeed if the spring west wind, as Shelley tells us, raises the "dead" seeds to life from their beds, this fall west wind raises the dead, all too literally, while they remain corpses, their bones whitening in the waves. It is the waves that are driven from their "heaving bed" (6), victims as well as agents of destruction. The scene is vividly described for twelve lines before the turn inward, where the "I" of the final couplet contrasts herself with the dead: they are turned out of their graves, but feel nothing, while she feels "life's long storm" and wishes she were one of them.

The poem reflects the standard eighteenth-century poetic style in its frequent use of adjectives, as if it were a settled conviction that a naked noun, lacking the decent drapery of an adjective, does not belong in decorous verse. So "swelling" (3), "wild" (5), "huge" (6), "frequent" (10), and "gloomy" (14) are colorless and almost redundant. As Goldsmith said of Gray's "Elegy," the sonnet is "overloaded with epithets."[4] But there are some fine lines, such as

"But o'er the shrinking land sublimely rides" (4), and especially "And breaks the silent sabbath of the grave!" (8), which has a nesting sound structure, with "break" and "grave" sharing their long vowel and r sound and "silent sabbath" alliterating. Sabbaths should be silent, and days of rest. This line, prominently placed at the end of the second quatrain, makes it a little easier to sympathize with the speaker's longing for "rest" at the end, despite the noisy havoc the storm has made amidst the resting place.[5]

In her preface Smith states that the sonnet is "no improper vehicle for a single Sentiment." A single sentiment, presumably, like the feeling of envy for the peace of death, occupies only a moment of time. The storm may have raged for a whole night, but its single-minded work can be described in a few lines, after which a mere couplet can capture the speaker's emotion. This brevity and this focus on one scene, one thought, or one feeling have come to seem the distinctive virtue of the sonnet. "A Sonnet is a moment's monument," Dante Gabriel Rossetti was to write (in 1881), "Memorial from the Soul's eternity / To one dead deathless hour." In this lies much of its appeal to Romantic poets, not only in Britain but on the Continent, for one of the characteristics of Romanticism is the celebration of the "moment," the moment of intense feeling or insight. Lyrical forms other than the sonnet, of course, can convey such a moment, but it is interesting that even longer forms used for narrative, as we will see in Chapter 9, had a tendency to crystallize around moments or static scenes.

Renaissance sonnets, beginning with Petrarch, were often published as parts of a loosely connected sequence or cycle. In Shakespeare's set of 154 sonnets, for example, various subsets can be discerned, focused on similar themes or addressees, though four hundred years of critical ingenuity have not come up with a single overarching story. In the Romantic era there were attempts to enlist the sonnet almost as stanzas in a narrative poem. Why not? The Spenserian stanza, though it has nine lines instead of fourteen, closes itself off with its long last line in a way similar to the conclusion of a sonnet, and it was created in the first place to tell a long story at a leisurely pace, *The Faerie Queene*. Mary Tighe, Byron, Shelley, and Keats all managed the Spenserians with skill. An interesting experiment in telling a story through sonnets was Mary Robinson's *Sappho and Phaon: In a Series of Legitimate Sonnets* (1796), which retells in forty-four Petrarchan ("legitimate") sonnets the fatal love story of Sappho, told by Ovid in his *Heroides* and freely translated by Pope in 1712, as we noted in Chapter 2: abandoned by her lover Phaon, she travels far to find him, is spurned again, and leaps to her death off the Leucadian cliff. These sonnets, too, have a "momentary" quality, and it is fair to ask how much each sonnet requires the knowledge of the preceding ones. The story is well enough known in any case, but some of the sonnets could stand alone, even if Sappho's tale were unknown.

XXIV. Her Address to the Moon

O THOU! meek Orb! that stealing o'er the dale
Cheer'st with thy modest beams the noon of night!
On the smooth lake diffusing silv'ry light,
Sublimely still, and beautifully pale!
What can thy cool and placid eye avail,
Where fierce despair absorbs the mental sight,
While inbred glooms the vagrant thoughts invite,
To tempt the gulph where howling fiends assail?
O, Night! all nature owns thy temper'd pow'r;
Thy solemn pause, thy dews, thy pensive beam;
Thy sweet breath whisp'ring in the moonlight bow'r,
While fainting flow'rets kiss the wand'ring stream!
Yet, vain is ev'ry charm! and vain the hour,
That brings to madd'ning love, no soothing dream!

Poems to or about evening and night, and especially to the moon, were a staple of the poetry of Sensibility and Romanticism.[6] The moon was more "poetic" than the sun or what Byron called "gaudy day," and had long been associated with the imagination. It was symbolically malleable enough either to absorb the projected state of mind of the poet or to resist it as a contrast. Smith's moon is "mute arbitress of tides" while the speaker cannot command her feelings; the sea is "press'd" by the moon while she is "opprest" by her "life's long storm." Sappho's moon is "meek," with "modest beams" and "cool and placid eye," while Sappho is maddened with love and "fierce despair." The moon cheers, tempers, sweetens, and soothes "all nature," but not Sappho, who is wracked with "inbred glooms." In the one line that links this sonnet to the others we learn she is contemplating suicide, "To tempt the gulph," and she will indeed plunge into the sea at the end of the sequence. Is this sonnet a monument to a moment? It seems more diffuse, like the moonlight on the lake, and slow, like the "solemn pause" of night. It is a monument to an hour, perhaps, a vain one, that brings no solace to Sappho.

Even more than Smith's, Robinson's sonnet obeys the convention that nouns need adjectives: of twenty-four nouns, sixteen are preceded by an adjective, and one by two adjectives. The two detached adjectives of line 4 are each preceded by an adverb! This habit feels too much like padding, and saps some of the poem's power. But the basic strategy is effective enough: the serene natural scene, presided over by the "sublimely still" moon, not only cannot soothe the distraught speaker but seems to make her condition worse, or at least more poignantly felt by the reader, on whom the sweet scene might not have made much of an impression had it not been described by this poet who can no longer share its blessings.

Two sonnets by Wordsworth

Wordsworth turned to the sonnet almost twenty years after Smith, but after he did there was no stopping him: he published over five hundred of them on every imaginable subject from sleep ("To Sleep" is the title of three of them) to the abolition of the slave trade, including series of sonnets on, for example, the River Duddon and the history of the Church of England. Not surprisingly quite a few of them seem slack, dutiful, unimaginative, but several are among the most admired in the language. Here is one of his great Petrarchan sonnets:

Composed upon Westminster Bridge, 3 September 1802

Earth has not any thing to shew more fair:
Dull would he be of soul who could pass by
A sight so touching in its majesty.
This city now doth like a garment wear
The beauty of the morning—silent, bare,   5
Ships, towers, domes, theatres, and temples lie
Open unto the fields, and to the sky,
All bright and glittering in the smokeless air.
Never did sun more beautifully steep
In his first splendour valley, rock, and hill;   10
Ne'er saw I, never felt, a calm so deep.
The river glideth at his own sweet will—
Dear God! the very houses seem asleep;
And all that mighty heart is lying still.

Westminster Bridge[7] runs east and west, for the Thames flows northward at that point. If you stand on the bridge and look west to Westminster and northeast to the City, the scene will be flooded with the light of the morning sun behind you. That is, if the weather is unusually clear and it is early enough and warm enough that the city's fires are not yet lit. Wordsworth has been lucky to be granted a rare sight, memorable enough to date (as he dated "Tintern Abbey" four years earlier), a moment when the city is "smokeless." The beauty of it catches his breath.

Or is it the sublimity of it? It is a "silent" and "calm" moment; the sight is "fair" and "touching"; the city wears the morning's "beauty" and the sun steeps it "beautifully." We easily imagine the city as female, as cities are traditionally described, donning a beautiful garment presented her by her paramour the sun, presented as male (*his* splendour in line 10). Yet the sight has "majesty," however touching, and a "mighty heart," not yet up and doing. I would suggest that much of the power of the poem rests in the hint that something gigantic and even frightening has, for a miraculous moment, shown itself as graceful and even vulnerable, the sublime condescending to be beautiful. London did not always seem sublime to Wordsworth; sometimes he hated it for its worldly bustle and noise, the anonymity of its crowds, its sheer size. In this morning light, however, the ships, towers, domes, theaters, and temples, which by some lights might be sublime, are made beautiful by being naturalized, as they lie open unto the fields and sky, steeped like the valleys, rocks, and hills of Wordsworth's Lake District.

In two ways the city looks like a utopian vision. That it is bathed in the sun's "first splendour" suggests not only the "glorious" light of dawn (as we find it described in the "Intimations" ode) but the light of the first day of creation, before the fall and alienation of humankind. Its connection with field and sky, valley and hill, bring it to kinship with the primordial garden. That we see "domes, theatres, and temples," somewhat surprisingly for a short list of sights in the London of 1802, evokes a classical city, Athens or Rome perhaps, republics of equal citizens.[8] Whatever suggestions are in play here, it is only for a moment. Soon a hundred thousand fires will be lit, and the roar of getting and spending will rise with the smoke.

"Getting and spending," of course, is lifted from another of Wordsworth's sonnets, "The world is too much with us," written between 1802 and 1804 and published in 1807:

> The world is too much with us; late and soon,
> Getting and spending, we lay waste our powers:
> Little we see in nature that is ours;
> We have given our hearts away, a sordid boon!
> The Sea that bares her bosom to the moon;   5
> The Winds that will be howling at all hours,
> And are up-gathered now like sleeping flowers;
> For this, for everything, we are out of tune;
> It moves us not.—Great God! I'd rather be
> A Pagan suckled in a creed outworn;   10
> So might I, standing on this pleasant lea,
> Have glimpses that would make me less forlorn;
> Have sight of Proteus rising from the sea;
> Or hear old Triton blow his wreathed horn.

It is interesting that the first word of "Westminster Bridge" is "Earth" while the first two words of this sonnet are "The world." Struck by the momentary beauty of London, Wordsworth assimilates it into nature, the earth, but the usual pursuits of London are unnatural and worldly. In the King James Bible "world" (or "this world") contrasts with the kingdom of God or the spirit, and "worldly lusts" are denounced, such as the pursuit of "filthy lucre" (Titus 2.12, 1.7), while in Wordsworth's poetry "world" contrasts with "earth," "nature," and the visionary power of our imagination. In or out of London we destroy this power by giving our hearts to getting money and spending it, by the business of living in the world; as a result our hearts are hardly worth giving away, and we grow blind to nature, or to our kinship with it.

Having summarized our condition in general terms in the first quatrain, the speaker now does something startling in the next three lines. He himself apparently has not altogether lost the power to see something in nature that is his. His imagination is engaged, and metaphors, similes, even myths flood into his sight. The Sea reveals herself like a lover to the moon (not unlike the city lying open to the sky), while the Winds, also personified, having howled for hours, are now asleep, "up-gathered" like the closing petals of flowers at night. As they depict this hushed and lovely moment ("now") these lines enact what we have lost the power to do. They give us a glorious glimpse of the realm for which we are out of tune. There is some loss of logic here, for if the speaker were out of tune and unmoved like the rest of us he would be incapable of these magical visions, but the poem gains greatly from them by making us feel the loss.

In the sestet he turns to the ancient Greeks as a culture where such imaginative myths about the sea, moon, and winds were still believed in. It is an unusual move for Wordsworth, who tended to find more spiritual food in the Middle Ages than in Antiquity, but this "Romantic Hellenism" was common among the great German poets Goethe, Schiller, and Hölderlin, and would soon be taken up by the younger British Romantics Byron, Shelley, and Keats. Here, for a moment, Wordsworth would rather have been nursed with pagan beliefs (there was really no Greek "creed") if they could make him feel less abandoned by nature and could grant him the sight and sound of the sea gods Proteus and Triton. His claim is meant to shock, I think: the exclamation "Great God!" indicates his surprise at his own audacious wish, while at the same time reminding readers that he does not, in the end, believe in the outworn Greek deities. Or perhaps he is addressing God directly, telling him that the gods He supplanted had their virtues.[9] Wordsworth does not, of course, blame God for the loss he feels (as Schiller did in "The Gods of Greece"), for, as we have seen, his stance resembles that of the New Testament in its warnings against worldliness. Much of the interest of this sonnet lies in this "Christian" paganism.

We cannot safely generalize about style from a handful of instances, but compared to the sonnets by Smith and Robinson, the two by Wordsworth have strikingly fewer adjective–noun pairs: just three each in "Westminster Bridge" and "The world is too much with us." The semantic weight lies more in the nouns and other parts of speech; there is less conventional or decorative filler, and thus greater density and intensity of meaning.

Keats and Chapman's Homer

"Intensity" is a word we associate with Keats, who invoked it as the highest virtue of literature and art. It is something he felt one night in 1816 as he looked over a folio of George Chapman's translation of Homer's *Odyssey* with his friend Charles Clarke. Chapman's version was exactly two centuries old, and Keats had never seen it. The Homer he knew was Alexander Pope's standard translation of 1726, because Keats could not read Greek, for all his love of Greek culture. Both English versions are in rhymed couplets, unlike the original, and both are fond of alliteration, also un-Homeric, but Chapman's version is usually simpler in diction, less polished, and more "intense" than Pope's.

Here is Pope's account of Odysseus staggering ashore at the land of the Phaeacians at the end of Book 5 of the *Odyssey*:

> That moment, fainting as he touch'd the shore,
> He dropp'd his sinewy arms: his knees no more
> Perform'd their office, or his weight upheld:
> His swoln heart heaved; his bloated body swell'd:
> From mouth and nose the briny torrent ran;
> And lost in lassitude lay all the man,
> Deprived of voice, of motion, and of breath;
> The soul scarce waking in the arms of death.

We see here, as we saw in the sonnets by Smith and Robinson, the eighteenth-century habit of pasting adjectives on to nouns, sometimes with unintentionally comic effect, as with the "briny torrent" flowing from Odysseus' mouth and nose. Intensity is seriously sapped, too, by abstract nouns, as in the equally comic "his knees no more / Perform'd their office," and "lost in lassitude." This same passage Chapman renders with much greater vigor:

> Then forth he came, his both knees falt'ring, both
> His strong hands hanging down, and all with froth
> His cheeks and nosthrils flowing, voice and breath

Spent to all use, and down he sunk to death.
The sea had soak'd his heart through; all his veins
His toils had rack'd t' a labouring woman's pains.
Dead weary was he.

The briny torrent is now a vivid "froth," in final position for emphasis and in alliteration with three other words. No more unperformed "office": Odysseus' knees simply falter. No more "lassitude" in which to be lost: Odysseus sinks to death. No more "arms of death" (did Pope mean to contrast them with Odysseus' "sinewy arms"?): instead the tersely final "Dead weary was he."

To Keats this was a revelation. He stayed until six in the morning reading Chapman, then he hurried home, wrote a Petrarchan sonnet, and delivered it to Clarke's breakfast table by ten. It was, of course, "On First Looking into Chapman's Homer":

Much have I travell'd in the realms of gold,
  And many goodly states and kingdoms seen;
  Round many western islands have I been
Which bards in fealty to Apollo hold.
Oft of one wide expanse had I been told   5
  That deep-brow'd Homer ruled as his demesne;
  Yet did I never breathe its pure serene
Till I heard Chapman speak out loud and bold:
Then felt I like some watcher of the skies
  When a new planet swims into his ken;   10
Or like stout Cortez when with eagle eyes
  He star'd at the Pacific—and all his men
Look'd at each other with a wild surmise—
  Silent, upon a peak in Darien.

Keats is an armchair traveler, a reader of books of golden poetry. The realms, states, kingdoms, and islands are the worlds created by different bards, vassals of Apollo. The medieval or feudal terms – "fealty," "demesne" – are anachronistic, since Chapman is from the late Renaissance and Homer is, of course, premedieval, though the tale of Odysseus was about reclaiming a demesne (on a western island) and testing the fealty of family and servants. It is a pretty conceit, if not terribly original. More interesting is the shift from seeing to hearing, which allows Keats to contrast being told *of* Homer (by Pope) with hearing Homer directly, that is, getting him "pure" through Chapman, who lets Keats breathe him in by speaking him out loud and bold. Breathing Homer's air is to be "inspired" by his "spirit" (Latin *spirare*, "breathe"). Then, in the sestet, Keats reverts to sight for his similes for how he felt: a watcher of the skies, an explorer with eagle eyes. He also makes good on his opening metaphor of literary travels by citing a literal explorer who sailed around many western islands on the way to Panama and the Pacific, where he was seeking realms of literal gold. The astronomer discovers a new world (William Herschel had discovered the first new planet with his telescope in 1781), and the explorer Cortez explores *the* New World (though Balboa, not Cortez, was the first European to see the Pacific from its eastern shore).[10] The "wide expanse" of Homer's demesne is itself a world, greater than the states and kingdoms Keats had known, the works of lesser poets, all secondary and subordinate to the father of western poetry. After two and a half thousand years a young Englishman feels he has gone back to the source, and the West's oldest literature seems completely new.

Shelley and Ozymandias' ruin

Even if we count the five sonnet-like stanzas (in *terza rima*) of "Ode to the West Wind" and the translations of two sonnets by Cavalcante, Shelley composed fewer than two dozen sonnets, and half of them never left his notebook in his lifetime. One of his most interesting is "To Wordsworth," published in 1816, which mourns the loss of Wordsworth's former glory, when he was "as a lone star, whose light did shine / On some frail bark in winter's midnight roar." It displays Shelley's command of the form and its recent history: the grieving tone of this Wordsworthian sonnet conceals a barbed inverse homage, for the lone star alludes to the star in Wordsworth's own sonnet to Milton, "London, 1802," which begins "Milton! thou should'st be living at this hour" and goes on to say "Thy soul was like a star and dwelt apart." Shelley implies that if Wordsworth had maintained his lonely vigil in "honored poverty," instead of selling out to the local gentry, as Shelley believed he had, his star would still be guiding us and we would not be grieving over him as if he had "ceased to be." Wordsworth should be living at this hour.

  Shelley's greatest sonnet, certainly the one chosen most often for anthologies, is "Ozymandias" (1818):

> I met a traveller from an antique land,
> Who said—"Two vast and trunkless legs of stone
> Stand in the desert ... near them, on the sand,
> Half sunk a shattered visage lies, whose frown,
> And wrinkled lip, and sneer of cold command,
> Tell that its sculptor well those passions read
> Which yet survive, stamped on these lifeless things,
> The hand that mocked them, and the heart that fed;
> And on the pedestal these words appear:

> My name is Ozymandias, King of Kings,
> Look on my Works ye Mighty, and despair!
> Nothing beside remains. Round the decay
> Of that colossal Wreck, boundless and bare
> The lone and level sands stretch far away."—

Ozymandias is the Greek name of the Egyptian pharaoh we know as Rameses II (*c.* 1304–1237 BCE), one of the most powerful of pharaohs, a warrior who enlarged the Egyptian empire and a builder of monuments to himself. "King of Kings" was a title of diplomatic precision, applicable at that time to the Egyptian and Hittite rulers and perhaps one or two others; lesser rulers were merely "Kings." He was as vainglorious as any tyrant after him, stamping his name and likeness everywhere during his long reign and siring a hundred children.[11]

Shelley makes unusual shifts in the sonnet form. There is a syntactic break between the octave and sestet, but not a "turn" of the usual sort: the speaker (the "traveller") reports what he saw without passing judgment from beginning to end, except in his praise of the sculptor in line 6. But of course there is an extraordinary turn in meaning, and it is here that the greatness of the poem resides. It emerges in Ozymandias' command (11) as an irony that detonates the meaning he intended. Addressed to mere "Kings" in his own day or soon thereafter, Ozymandias' words are meant to make them despair over emulating his might or glory, but the ravaging hand of time has rewritten their context, so the kings of kings today cannot escape a more devastating truth: this is what their works will come to in the end. The even, reportorial tone, which has been likened to "a careful, almost itemized procedure of surveying and noting, distantly suggesting the style of British Levantine topographical and early archaeological writings,"[12] and which thus seems unaware of the irony it reports, is supported by a rhyme scheme that has no couplets and no sequence that quite rounds itself out until the end. The opening quatrain's **abab** pattern is certainly conventional, but the second quatrain, tightly knitted syntactically to the first, rhymes **acdc**, the a-rhyme underscoring the continuity, and then offering, in a way most unusual in traditional sonnets of any form, a rhyme word ("things") that will reach across to the sestet to find its mate ("Kings"). The sestet is made of two *terza rima* tercets, with the middle rhyme of the first the mate to the detached rhyme of the octave. These rhymes also knit the octave and sestet together, but they have a more striking function: by standing out from the firm norms of sonnet rhyming they call more attention to themselves than we might pay to the other rhyming words. To pair them is to compare them: kings are lifeless things, even while they are alive.

Beyond the rhymes, it is obvious, Shelley gave a good deal of thought to the sounds of his poem. The alliterating pairs are the most prominent – **cold command** (5), **hand** and **heart** (8), **boundless and bare** (13), and **lone and level** (14); they stand out as if they were proverbial expressions, and they signal to us that we are meant to hear this poem as a piece of meaningful music as well as see its scenery, follow its argument, and appreciate its tone of voice. There are sound patterns that encompass the entire sonnet, such as the st- cluster that rings loudest in **stone / Stand** (2–3) but also resonates in **vast** (2), **stamped** (7), **pedestal** (9), and **stretch** (14), and more subtly in **its sculptor** (6) and **yet survive** (7). And there are more local effects, such as the alliterative link between **traveller** (1) and **trunkless** (2), the similarity of **trunkless** to **sunk** (4), **wrinkled** (5), and **sculptor** (6), and the assonance of **wrinkled lip** (5), not to mention the s sounds that pervade lines 2 through 7. (Although there are eight pairings of adjective and noun, most of them are striking and indispensable.)

The most interesting theme of this meaningful music rests on the salience of the syllable -and- in the octave. It sounds in the first end word (**land**), which rhymes twice (**sand, command**); it is in **antique** (1), **Stand** (3), **hand** (8), and, almost, **stamped** (7); and its vowel is echoed in the stressed vowels of **traveller** (1), **vast** (2), **half** (4), **shattered** (4), and **passions** (6). When in line 10 the name **Ozymandias** is finally pronounced, it is as if the all the preceding sounds, like trumpets, have been heralding his arrival – most closely, and tellingly, in **command** (5). But after that the syllable falls silent, with nothing but a weak **that** echoing its vowel (13), until in the final line we hear what the once commanding sound of **Ozymandias** has dwindled down to: **sands**.

The only thing that "stands" from the once vast empire of Ozymandias is a pair of "vast" legs that now support nothing. All the rest is broken in fragments half sunk in sand – the sand of the desert that stretches far away but also the "sands of time" that have flowed for three thousand years. In describing the "frown, / And wrinkled lip, and sneer of cold command" still extant on the shattered face, Shelley has taken liberties with Egyptian art, which invariably presented pharaohs with impassive and utterly typical faces. He might have made his point just as well by saying that there is nothing to distinguish this visage from those of a thousand other male Egyptians: all tyrants are alike, and equally forgettable. Instead, Shelley brings out the idea that this broken stone colossus was once connected to a real human being, while naming only those attributes and "passions" that are in fact utterly typical of tyrants. In doing so he also makes room for the artist, who read his royal subject well.

The syntax of lines 6 to 8 is a bit perplexing until one sees that "survive" is a transitive verb that takes "hand" and "heart" as its objects. Transposed into normal word order, the long period would be this: "Near them, on the sand, Half sunk a shattered visage lies, whose frown, And wrinkled lip, and sneer of cold command, Tell that its sculptor read well those passions which, stamped on these lifeless things, yet survive The hand that mocked them, and the heart that fed [them]." We see that the king's passions are still alive, para-doxically, in that they are stamped on "lifeless things," the stone fragments of the face. Both the sculptor, whose hand "mocked" or imitated the passions, and Ozymandias himself, whose heart fed those passions, are long dead. So are the "works" of the pharaoh, but this work by a nameless sculptor still remains, however fragmented, as both a testament of tyranny's shattered glory and of the sculptor's great skill. If anyone deserves immortality, it is he, not his sneer-ing commander.

The colorful and fanciful description of the facial expressions, and the praise of the sculptor who preserved them, depart from the otherwise low-key expository manner of the traveler's report. Shelley the poet, a fellow craftsman, signals here his recognition that poets have had a similar mission, and that this very poem may be an instance of it. For is it not a further irony, and one brought about by time no less than the irony in the pharaoh's words, that the name Ozymandias might well have been forgotten except by classical scholars had Shelley not written so memorable a sonnet about him? Everest also finds it ironic that "Ozymandias's statue in fact exists for us now only within the rhet-oric of Shelley's poem."[13] But Shelley could reply that what he has preserved in his poem is not the statue of Ozymandias but the shattered ruins of the statue, a very different thing. He is no doubt implicitly evoking the long trad-ition among poets that their work will outlast monuments of stone or brass, a tradition abundantly confirmed in the very fact that we know about it, and in the poets' very words. He is Horace's heir, the Horace who names the phar-aohs' pyramids as more susceptible to time's destruction than the monument he has written (*Odes* 3.30). The one feature of Ozymandias' monument that has survived intact is the "words" on the pedestal. It is true that many poets have served tyrants and burnished their reputations, but many others, such as Milton and (for a time) Wordsworth, have stood up to them, and it is these poets who will have the last word.

It is hard to see how this sonnet, unlike the others we have been considering, could be called a moment's monument. It is a monument's monument. And the monument that is its subject has been around for some three thousand years. Yet time, a long succession of moments, has ruined it, as it deserved to be ruined. It was a ruin in Roman times, whereas Horace, who urged us to "seize the day," is still intact and alive.

To readers who recognized that Ozymandias was an Egyptian pharaoh, an allusion to Napoleon might have hovered over the poem. Napoleon conquered

Egypt in 1798, but in 1818, the date the sonnet appeared, he had been empris-oned on the island of St. Helena for over two years. This king of kings had made all Europe tremble, but now "thou and France are in the dust," as Shelley had written in his sonnet "On the Fall of Bonaparte" (1816). Another irony: it was Napoleon's invasion of Egypt that led to the decipherment of hiero-glyphics by Champollion, so that, one might fancy, Napoleon could read the inscriptions on the pedestals of the fallen pharaohs. What did he learn from them? Perhaps he remembered them later during those long days on that bleak island. Britain, in any case, learned nothing, for in 1882 it invaded Egypt and incorporated it into the Empire – an empire that would last little longer than the life span of Ozymandias himself.

Chapter 7

Romantic love lyrics

A large share of Romantic lyric poetry, and a large share of the best of it, does not fall under such well-defined categories as "sonnet" or even the looser genre called "ode." Wordsworth and Coleridge, as we saw, wrote poems of various lengths called "Lines" (usually with a descriptive subtitle), Coleridge wrote "Monodies," Shelley wrote "Stanzas," several poets wrote deliberate fragments, and so on. Many Romantic poems were called "songs" and were even set to music, but songs come in many shapes and sizes. Some poems are very short – a couplet or quatrain – while others, such as Coleridge's "conversation" poems or Wordsworth's "Tintern Abbey," are fairly long. They may or may not come grouped into stanzas or graced with rhyme. The main reason we call all of them "lyric" is merely genealogical, as we trace their ancestry back to songs sung by Greeks to the lyre, and that fact is of little help in categorizing them in 1800 or today. A good handbook of literary terms defines "lyric" as "A brief subjective poem strongly marked by imagination, melody, and emotion, and creating a single, unified impression."[1] I have no better definition to offer, and yet I have sometimes come across poems that I would like to call "lyric" but that do not strike me as very imaginative, melodious, emotional, or even subjective. It might be simpler, then, to retain "lyric" as the residual category after we separate out narrative and dramatic verse, which are more readily defined, or to enumerate its subgenres with a miscellaneous addendum: "lyric poems include odes, sonnets, and the like." Neither approach is very satisfactory, but they needn't trouble us as long as we have a rough idea of what we are talking about.

An impressive effort to define a distinctively Romantic kind of lyric poem was mounted by M. H. Abrams in his 1965 essay "Structure and Style in the Greater Romantic Lyric."[2] He includes several of the "conversation" poems of Coleridge ("Eolian Harp," "Frost at Midnight," "Fears in Solitude," and "Dejection: An Ode"), Wordsworth's "Tintern Abbey" and "Ode: Intimations of Immortality," Shelley's "Ode to the West Wind" and "Stanzas Written in Dejection," and Keats's "Ode to a Nightingale" as the paradigms for this as yet unnamed genre. These poems

present a determinate speaker in a particularized, and usually a
localized, outdoor setting, whom we overhear as he carries on, in
a fluent vernacular which rises easily to a more formal speech, a
sustained colloquy, sometimes with himself or with the outer scene,
but more frequently with a silent human auditor, present or absent.
The speaker begins with a description of the landscape; an aspect or
change of aspect in the landscape evokes a varied but integral process
of memory, thought, anticipation, and feeling which remains closely
intervolved with the outer scene. In the course of this meditation the
lyric speaker achieves an insight, faces up to a tragic loss, comes to a
moral decision, or resolves an emotional problem. Often the poem
rounds upon itself to end where it began, at the outer scene, but with
an altered mood and deeper understanding which is the result of the
intervening meditation.

This model, which displaced the Pindaric ode as the favored longer lyric form,
Abrams christens "the greater Romantic lyric." As I have already discussed
"Tintern Abbey" and "Ode to the West Wind" at length I will leave it to my
readers to apply his description to them, and to keep it in mind as they explore
the other examples he cites. We might add Coleridge's "France: An Ode" to
Abrams' short list. It begins, as we saw in Chapter 5, with a description of a
natural scene, though it is not very particularized; its embodiment of "liberty" provokes the memory of the speaker's failed and painful attempt to find
it embodied in France; at the end he rounds back to nature again and confesses
his changed and chastened convictions. A "fluent vernacular" is less in evidence in this more formal, even forensic, ode, and there does not seem to be
an implied human auditor (it is addressed, like a good ode, to natural things
and then to Liberty), but it has some of the features of Abrams' type. We could
certainly call it a characteristically Romantic sort of ode. It does not detract
from Abrams' proposal – it may enhance it – that there are ambiguous cases;
his idea lights up many poems even if, in the end, they seem to be poems of a
different sort.

   In this chapter, faced with thousands of lyric poems, I will single out a few
that I am tempted to call "the lesser Romantic lyric," but I cannot claim that
they fall into a pattern as coherent as the one Abrams presents. In contrast to
his group, they are all short. To give the chapter some coherence I have chosen
poems that for one reason or another can be called "love poems." One or two
are love poems in the strict sense, that is, poems addressed to one's beloved;
others are about a loved one, or the meaning of love itself. Several of them
are also about death: death caused by love, or the death of love, or love that
survives or transcends death. Though the word "romantic" today is closely

wedded to "love," the Romantics wrote less love poetry than one might expect, even in the broad sense, but what they wrote is often beautiful and poignant.

One of William Blake's most haunting and elusive lyrics is "The SICK ROSE," from *Songs of Experience* (1794):

> O Rose thou art sick.
> The invisible worm,
> That flies in the night
> In the howling storm:
>
> Has found out thy bed
> Of crimson joy:
> And his dark secret love
> Does thy life destroy.

This poem, like nearly all of Blake's poems long and short, was published only on copperplate, with the text engraved alongside illustrations, or what Blake scholars often call "illuminations," and with watercolor added by hand. It was never in his lifetime printed in the ordinary fashion by a publisher; had it been, his odd punctuation would have been cleaned up. Text and design, then, always appeared together. In fact it was often hard to distinguish them, for Blake liked to add flourishes to his script and even insert little figures of people or birds among the lines. In this plate, the "The" of the title has a swirling T that echoes the coiling vegetation. Whether the rest of the design elements, such as the drooping females on the upper tendrils or the many thorns throughout, alter the way we interpret the text, is a subtle question. Blake, in any case, meant his poems and designs to make up one composite work. They were meant to be triply composite, in fact, for there are reports that Blake sang his "Songs" to melodies of his own devising, but we have no musical notations in his hand.

These two short quatrains, rhyming **abcb**, and with two stresses in each line, tell a condensed little story about a "secret love" of a (male) worm for a (female) rose. It is not only secret but the lover is invisible and flies under cover of night to his goal, the rose's "bed." Such a "love" leads only to sickness, not lovesickness but what sounds like venereal disease. The literal story here is obvious enough: the speaker walks into a garden in the morning after a stormy night and finds a rose or rosebud blighted by a canker-worm. He is shocked; he knows it will die. Of course roses have been emblematic since the Greeks of beauty and beauty's brevity, but it seems particularly tragic here that this rose should be blasted in the bud. Since the Greeks, too, roses have stood for girlhood, also brief, and for girls' virginity before they are "deflowered." The sexual symbolism in Blake's poem is also obvious, but we are left wondering just what has gone wrong and why. Is this a rape? Were rose and worm secret lovers? If her bed is of "crimson joy," was it her joy too, or just the worm's? If it had been open love, carried on in the sunshine (which Blake elsewhere celebrates), would she have been spared her fatal sickness? Is secrecy itself a sickness? Commentators have found this little poem bottomless in its suggestiveness, and capable of sustaining any number of implicit plots.

Whatever story we conjure up, we must not minimize the dramatic scene, where the surprised speaker comes upon the wilting rose and speaks to her. If the poem shows what is wrong with "secret love," there is another kind of love expressed by the speaker himself, or if not love then at least a pitying affection. The scene seems to evoke the moment in Milton's *Paradise Lost* when Adam learns that Eve has been seduced by the serpent into eating the forbidden fruit. He has been making her a garland, and when he hears the news it "Down dropped, and all the faded roses shed." Shocked, and knowing that she is now doomed, Adam speaks to her: "How art thou lost, how on a sudden lost, / Defaced, deflowered, and now to death devote?" (9.893, 900–1).[3] It may be too much to ask this little poem to bear such archetypal weight, but Blake seems to be implying that every abrupt and violent transition from innocence to experience, however commonplace (and there are three infected roses in the design to remind us how commonplace it is), recreates our original loss of the Garden of Eden. Just before they were expelled from it, Adam and Eve felt ashamed of their nakedness. As Blake asserts elsewhere, their sense of shame *was* the fall.

If "The SICK ROSE" presents a sick kind of love, what kind of love is healthy or good? In another brief poem of *Experience* Blake weighs two contrasting kinds:

The Clod & the Pebble

Love seeketh not Itself to please,
Nor for itself hath any care;
But for another gives its ease,
And builds a Heaven in Hells despair.

So sang a little Clod of Clay,
Trodden with the cattles feet:
But a Pebble of the brook,
Warbled out these metres meet.

Love seeketh only Self to please,
To bind another to its delight;
Joys in anothers loss of ease,
And builds a Hell in Heavens despite.

It is not one of Blake's most accomplished poems, if only because "Warbled out these metres meet" is insufferably precious and vacuous, but with clarity and brevity the poem states the contraries that concerned Blake throughout his career: innocence and experience, love and jealousy, forgiveness and resentment, expression and suppression of desire, and what he called "the annihilation of Selfhood" and its opposite, pride and self-aggrandizement. The Clod of Clay seems the perfect Christian, who has no concern for itself but cheerfully sacrifices its "ease" for another, building a heaven where it can. The Pebble is the opposite, selfish, controlling, even cruel, building a hell in its wake, much like the invisible worm. One would think this is an open and shut case: the Clod is Blake's mouthpiece and the Pebble stands for everything Blake campaigned against all his life. Yet more than one good Blake scholar has defended the Pebble as at least realistic and worldly and has criticized the Clod as naïve and life-denying. To be trodden by the cattle's feet has seemed the well-deserved and ignominious fate of one so simple. Most scholars, unhappy with the Clod, still cannot bring themselves to endorse the Pebble, so they end up arguing that Blake has presented a stalemate between two positions, neither of which is his own, which is a synthesis of some kind, a Clobble.

I think these interpreters have projected on to Blake their own discomfort with the Clod's self-sacrificing ethic. While the two creatures get the same amount of space, and the Pebble gets the last word, I think it is clear that the Clod is Blake's exemplar of genuine love. To say that the Pebble has answered the Clod is like saying that the Crucifixion has answered the Sermon on the Mount. To a genuine Christian, Jesus meant what he said and knew what he did, however difficult it is to follow him; besides, the Resurrection has answered the Crucifixion. Blake places the poem early in the *Songs of Experience*, so he lets the Pebble close the door on the malleable and resilient state of Innocence and usher us into the impermeable and stony-hearted state of Experience. I admit the poem is a bit clumsy, and the speaker of the middle stanza passes no judgment (unless "metres meet" implies one). But it is important, here and in every poem, not to confuse your own opinions with the poet's. You may disagree with the Sermon on the Mount, to be sure, but you may not pretend that Jesus wasn't sincere.[4]

One of Robert Burns's most beloved love songs, a love song in the strict sense, addressed to the beloved, is "Ae Fond Kiss" (1791),[5] sent in a letter to Nancy McLehose on the eve of her departure for Jamaica to rejoin her estranged husband:

> Ae fond kiss, and then we sever;
> Ae fareweel, and then for ever!

Deep in heart-wrung tears I'll pledge thee,
Warring sighs and groans I'll wage thee.

Who shall say that Fortune grieves him,
While the star of hope she leaves him?
Me, nae cheerful twinkle lights me;
Dark despair around benights me.

I'll ne'er blame my partial fancy,
Naething could resist my Nancy: 10
But to see her was to love her;
Love but her, and love for ever.

Had we never lov'd sae kindly,
Had we never lov'd sae blindly,
Never met—or never parted,
We had ne'er been broken-hearted.

Fare-thee-weel, thou first and fairest!
Fare-thee-weel, thou best and dearest!
Thine be ilka joy and treasure,
Peace, Enjoyment, Love and Pleasure!   20

Ae fond kiss, and then we sever!
Ae fareweel, Alas, for ever!
Deep in heart-wrung tears I'll pledge thee,
Warring sighs and groans I'll wage thee.

Burns wrote poems in (a) standard literary English, in (b) a Scots English (or "Doric") so Scottish as to be almost opaque to non-Scots, and in (c) various compromises between them. This song is perfectly intelligible to non-Scots except for a couple of words: "ae" means "one" and is pronounced "ay" (as in "day"), and "ilka" (19) means "every."

It has seemed a perfect an expression of love and love's grief. Walter Scott in 1809 wrote of the fourth "exquisitely affecting" stanza that it "contains the essence of a thousand love tales," while nearly two centuries later the Irish poet Seamus Heaney quoted three stanzas as evidence that Burns had achieved "the melody of inwardness."[6] As opposed to Scott we might find the fifth stanza the most affecting as it is the least self-regarding: he wishes her every happiness, even love. It suits, perhaps, the restraint implicit in the title phrase, as it is only *ae* kiss that he asks for. The second half of the opening (and closing) stanza, however, sounds stagey, artificial, and self-indulgent, lacking the fresh simplicity of several of the other lines, and thus a poor choice for the end of the poem. That the speaker shifts his stance a little, it is true, lends the poem more psychological interest. After two stanzas about tears, groans, and despair he movingly exonerates his fancy for incurring them, for Nancy was irresistible: "But to see her was to love her; / Love but her, and love for ever." ("But" in both places means "only.") The stanza that Scott praised seems almost a complaint, as if it says "if only we had never loved, or even met!" But that sentiment seems out of keeping with the hint that loving her was worth it after all, and with the gently self-effacing next stanza. If it is not a complaint then it is little more than an obvious tautology: if we hadn't met, or we hadn't parted, then we wouldn't be broken-hearted.

But to notice these inconsistencies and absurdities seems almost beside the point, so aptly does this poem bespeak the griefs in a thousand lives, indeed in *ilka* life. Who has not sunk into self-pity while struggling to be noble in facing such loss? Who has not contrived heart-wringing appeals to the beloved about to depart while acknowledging their futility? And who has not, having heard a thousand love songs, resorted to literary clichés to express the grief of lost love? That Burns evades as many clichés as he does and still expresses the warring feelings so fully is to his everlasting credit. We should remember, too, that just as Blake's poems came inseparably with their designs, this song, like virtually all of Burns's, is meant to be sung.[7] After having felt a little superior to it as I read it in print, I confess I was moved to tears when I first heard it performed.

Thomas Moore's *Irish Melodies*, appearing in ten parts from 1808 to 1834, holds a place in Irish culture much like that of Burns's *Poems, Chiefly in the Scottish Dialect* (first edition 1786) in Scottish culture; Burns and Moore became their countries' "national poets." More often and more explicitly than Burns, Moore laments the oppressed state of his homeland, though usually in a mood of wistful regret rather than anger or exhortation. But he began as a love poet, and one of his love poems, published in the first volume of *Irish Melodies*, has become famous.

> 'Tis the last rose of summer
>   Left blooming alone;
> All her lovely companions
>   Are faded and gone;
> No flower of her kindred,
>   No rose-bud is nigh,
> To reflect back her blushes,
>   To give sigh for sigh.
>
> I'll not leave thee, thou lone one!
>   To pine on the stem;   10
> Since the lovely are sleeping,
>   Go, sleep thou with them.

Thus kindly I scatter,
  Thy leaves o'er the bed,
Where thy mates of the garden
  Lie scentless and dead.

So soon may *I* follow,
  When friendships decay,
From Love's shining circle
  The gems drop away.   20
When true hearts lie withered
  And fond ones are flown,
Oh! who would inhabit
  This bleak world alone?

This is a farewell poem, in a sense, like Burns's "Ae Fond Kiss." It also reminds us of Blake's sick rose, but where that rose was destroyed by a worm, this one is seemingly healthy, not yet "faded" like the others, and where Blake's speaker reacts with shock when he comes upon her, Moore's speaker sadly but calmly commits euthanasia to put her out of her emotional misery. She is alone; no companions still live to share her joys or griefs. The speaker scatters her petals "kindly," he claims, but it is difficult to suppress a shiver at what is, given the personification of the rose, a murder, worse than the involuntary homicide in Blake's poem. We are asked, however, to take as serious the claim that living friendless is worse than death, and take as sincere the speaker's wish to die as soon as friendship and love drop away. However sentimental the sentiment, and however redundantly it is expressed, with love and friendship decaying, dropping away, withering, and flying off, there is no reason to question it. The poem is as dearly loved as it is because it speaks of a sadness universally felt as one grows older.

Am I right to call it a love poem? I would not argue that the speaker loves the rose, even as much as we might surmise Blake's speaker loves *his* rose. It is an office of friendship or compassion to scatter her leaves, just as he hopes that God or nature will carry him away when he is no longer a link in "Love's shining circle," but the rose does not stand for his love or for his beloved. The rose stands for him: the poem is an extended simile. The rose also stands for love itself, or the capacity to love, which must be reciprocated among friends and lovers or it will die of loneliness. This is a poem, then, about love in all its forms as the most important thing in life, and the only thing that saves us from the bleakness of the world.

"The Last Rose of Summer" is well known as a song in a setting by John Stevenson; the score appeared with the text in its first printings. It gained a new popularity throughout Europe from a version of it in Friedrich von Flotow's opera *Martha* (1847), which remains in the repertory today, though it is not often mounted. Much better known now are recordings by Sarah Brightman, Charlotte Church, and the "Three Irish Tenors."

"My heart is like the failing hearth," by Letitia Elizabeth Landon (1827), courts cliché but evades it sufficiently to touch us by its simplicity of diction and resigned tone.

> My heart is like the failing hearth
>   Now by my side,
> One by one its bursts of flame
>   Have burnt and died.
> There are none to watch the sinking blaze,
>   And none to care,
> Or if it kindle into strength,
>   Or waste in air.
> My fate is as yon faded wreath
>   Of summer flowers;   10
> They've spent their store of fragrant health
>   On sunny hours,
> Which reck'd them not, which heeded not
>   When they were dead;
> Other flowers, unwarn'd by them,
>   Will spring instead.
> And my own heart is as the lute
>   I am now waking;
> Wound to too fine and high a pitch,
>   They both are breaking.   20
> And of their song what memory
>   Will stay behind?
> An echo, like a passing thought,
>   Upon the wind.
> Silence, forgetfulness, and rust,
>   Lute, are for thee:
> And such my lot; neglect, the grave,
>   These are for me.

This song (it was so labeled as part of a medley called "The Golden Violet") has several subtle musical effects beyond the rhymes, which themselves seem unusually prominent because the lines are short. Landon contrives internal rhymes, off-rhymes, and various clusters of assonant and consonant sounds. She begins in a somewhat showy way with "heart" and "hearth," whose deep sonic kinship has long been exploited in poetry, but she continues to pair words like these more quietly through most of the poem: "failing" and "flame," "bursts" and "burnt," "watch" and "waste," "sinking" and "kindle," "faded" and "fragrant," "summer" and "sunny," "Lute" and "neglect," with perhaps a triplet in "waking," "Wound," and "wind." These sound similarities have the effect, aside from the sensual pleasure they afford, of making many of the phrases seem inevitable and right.

The poem is lucidly constructed out of three similes: two quatrains for the first, two for the second, and three for the third. The first relies on the ancient metaphor of love as a fire, a metaphor at least as old as Sappho, but in making it a hearth fire Landon brings it home, as it were, to a woman's sphere. More strikingly, the hearth is "by my side" (2), a phrase that belongs naturally to the language of human love or friendship. While she watches the sinking fire, there are "none" by *her* side to watch her heart, none to care whether it may kindle again in love or "waste in air" (8), a phrase that anticipates the third simile.

Though the second simile is a figure for her "fate" rather than her "heart," as the first and third are, the comparison to flowers ineluctably evokes love as well. She could almost be Moore's last rose of summer, blooming (or fading) alone. More precisely, she is a wreath of summer flowers, with perhaps the hint that she has had more than one love, as the "bursts of flame" suggest in the first simile. It is now well past summer, and past the hours of sunshine; those hours correspond to the plural "none" (5): none watch or care as the hearth sinks now, no hours recked or heeded as the flowers died. The next lines are perhaps the most heart-breakingly bitter: "Other flowers, unwarn'd by them, / Will spring instead" (15–16). Looking on the inevitable return of spring, and the inevitable blooming of young girls' love, Landon rises to nearly the distance William Butler Yeats achieves in his poem "Sailing to Byzantium" as he reduces a summer scene of young lovers to "Those dying generations," but she entertains the futile thought that the new flowers, had they known what last summer's flowers came to, might choose not to love, or not to live. Yet life will go on in an endless cycle, love will go on, and hearts will break.

It might seem a consolation that the speaker-singer has wakened her lute, the third simile, but the song the lute shares with her heart (it is "their song" in 21) will be short-lived; it is nearing the end now, and will amount to no more than an echo or thought "Upon the wind" (24), as fleeting as the hearth that may "waste in air" (8). No memory of it will remain (a prophecy happily untrue). Even worse, the lute itself will rust as the singer will cease playing it; she will neglect it as all lovers have neglected her. All that remains is the grave, and she lacks even the kind assistance Moore gives to summer's last rose.

Wordsworth is not known for love poetry, but a series of subtle and moving poems now labeled "the Lucy poems" are about a beloved girl or young woman. They are also, like several we have just considered, about death, for the salient fact about "Lucy" is that she has died.[8] Scholars, of course, have speculated endlessly about who Lucy was, but it seems hopeless, and thankfully needless, to find out the original. Coleridge wrote, "Some months ago Wordsworth transmitted to me a most sublime Epitaph / whether it had any reality, I cannot say.—Most probably, in some gloomier moment he had fancied the moment in which his sister might die."[9] Or maybe not. Biographical footnotes would only interfere with the poem, in my opinion, and Wordsworth surely felt the same way.

The "most sublime Epitaph" is "A slumber did my spirit seal."

> A slumber did my spirit seal,
>   I had no human fears:
> She seemed a thing that could not feel
>   The touch of earthly years.
>
> No motion has she now, no force[;]
>   She neither hears nor sees[;]
> Rolled round in earth's diurnal course
>   With rocks, and stones, and trees!

It is brief, like an epitaph; we could imagine it inscribed on her tombstone. (Wordsworth was very interested in epitaphs, and wrote three essays on them in 1809–10.) It is in the "common meter" of church hymns, quatrains of two couplets of alternating lines of four and three feet, rhyming **abab**, and in simple diction: only the word "diurnal" is a little erudite, and it harmonizes so well with the rest of its line as to feel inevitable. These features may lend the poem some gravity or solemnity beyond what the theme itself solicits. The basic meaning also seems simple enough, as it states the essence of any mourner's grief: she was alive then and seemed immune to death, but now she is dead and has joined the realm of dead things.

Yet almost every line is rich in implication and even ambiguity. For good reason, then, more critical ingenuity has been devoted to this poem, line for line, than to any other poem of Wordsworth's.[10] We might at first read the opening line, for instance, as meaning that *her* slumber (that is, her death) sealed his spirit as if in a tomb, that he died when she did, but the next line makes us abandon this deep if common sentiment, for it implies that he had no human fears during the time his spirit was sealed. The slumber, then, was *his* slumber, and it sealed his spirit while she was still alive.[11] He was unconscious, it would seem, of her vulnerability to "The touch of earthly years."

The speaker sees that in retrospect he had "no human fears." What are they? Does the line mean the speaker was not human himself, being immune to the fears any human might have? Does it mean he had no fear for *her* as a human, that is, as a mortal, subject like all mortals to time and death? The latter seems more plausible though a little less likely syntactically. Many readers envisage her as a young girl, with an air of eternal youth, who had charmed the speaker into a suspension of worldly common sense, as if he were dreaming about her. Yet "The touch of earthly years" might well mean growing older, not necessarily dying, though we know she has died. We could envisage a much older woman who has suddenly died, though she seemed ageless.

Most striking is the word "thing." It is hard to know how much weight to give it. At first it may seem to carry a little more resonance than "someone": "She seemed to be someone who could not feel the touch of earthly years." Yet when we have read the second stanza, where she is indeed numbered among such real *things* as "rocks, and stones, and trees," we understand "thing" differently. The speaker suggests that she seemed a thing then, while she is really a thing now. The old use of "thing" in such phrases as "young thing," referring to a girl, or "poor thing," also usually about a girl, seems in play here as well. It is a puzzling, even uncanny, word in this context.

If we step back a little from the second stanza and keep in mind that this is a kind of epitaph or elegy, it is surprising that there is no consolatory thought about an afterlife, no expression of faith that she is now in heaven or even that she lives on in our remembrance. If the stanza offers any consolation, it is of a "pantheistic" or materialistic sort: she is now at peace, unconscious, absorbed into the natural world, into the earth her mother, who calmly rolls her round each day. Once she could not feel the touch of "earthly years," it seemed, while now she cannot feel the touch of earthly days, "earth's diurnal course." It is hard to say what solace her present state offers to the speaker, for his tone is so difficult to interpret. The exclamation point at the end may suggest the speaker's shock at his discovery that she is now just another thing rotating with the earth, though that sits poorly with the otherwise calm and stately language; perhaps it suggests a kind of relief or happy recognition that the earth has reclaimed her as part of herself.

So many parts of this little poem are so uncertain in meaning and mood that we could make a case that it is a failure, yet nearly all readers who have commented on it have found it deep, even "most sublime," in Coleridge's phrase, haunting, touching, and hard to dislodge from their mind. Edgar Allan Poe wrote that the death of a beautiful woman is the most poetical of all topics, and that topic is almost the topic of this poem, or it is the topic we readily project on to it. We take it as a love poem, and yet it enters another terrain, both dreamlike and detached, floating somewhere between melancholy paralysis and cosmic reconciliation. It conjures many thoughts and feelings about life and death, and without sorting them out it seems to lay them quietly to rest.

We shall conclude this chapter with a much admired poem by Byron from 1815.

She Walks in Beauty

She walks in beauty, like the night
Of cloudless climes and starry skies;
And all that's best of dark and bright
Meet in her aspect and her eyes:
Thus mellow'd to that tender light
Which heaven to gaudy day denies.

One shade the more, one ray the less,
Had half impair'd the nameless grace
Which waves in every raven tress,
Or softly lightens o'er her face;   10
Where thoughts serenely sweet express
How pure, how dear their dwelling-place.

And on that cheek, and o'er that brow,
So soft, so calm, yet eloquent,
The smiles that win, the tints that glow,
But tell of days in goodness spent,
A mind at peace with all below,
A heart whose love is innocent!

We are told virtually nothing "about" her except that she has black hair (9) and that she is beautiful. It is her beauty that is characterized, but in a way hard to visualize: a perfect balance between "dark and bright" and with a soft heavenly light that falls on her like grace. Her beauty is internal as well, as her face expresses her goodness and her heart's innocent love. The description teeters on the edge of the indescribable or the "nameless," and much of its effect depends, I would suggest, on the sincere admiration of the poem's speaker, which comes across more clearly than the picture he paints, perhaps all the more clearly for its lack of concrete detail. He is dazzled, he is rapt, but he is detached: he wants nothing from her: he is not wooing her, lamenting his loss of her, envying her lover, or anything of the sort. If we came to this poem after reading a good deal of Byron, who has much to say about women and his many affairs with them, we might find this stance of distant admiration surprising. Equally surprising, and troubling to some readers, is the speaker's ready assumption that he can read her heart through her face. Her heart may or may not really be innocent, but his own seems to be, if he can make so naïve an extrapolation from her smiles and glowing blushes on her cheeks.

Led by such worldly thoughts, some readers have wanted to know who she "really" was. The consensus among biographers is that "she" refers to a Mrs. Anne Wilmot, the wife of Byron's first cousin, whom Byron saw dressed in mourning (for whom is not known, but evidently not for her husband) at a party. She wore black but apparently scandalized some of the ladies present by wearing dark spangles as well. The poem, then, is Byron's defense of the beautiful Mrs. Wilmot.

I think Mrs. Wilmot is another of the many red herrings dragged across Romantic poetry by scholars who think everything involved in the inception or composition of a poem is thereby *in* the poem. Some anthologies add a footnote about Mrs. Wilmot's spangles and soon the unwary reader thinks there are references to spangles in the poem, that the woman's dress and not only her tress is raven, that she is in mourning, that she is causing a scandal, and so on. None of these "facts," however, is in the poem. With all respect to the beautiful Mrs. Wilmot, this poem is not about her.

In the poem itself perhaps the first thing that strikes us is the air of effortless skill behind these lovely lines about this lovely woman. Even when he recycles such off-the-shelf alliterative phrases as "cloudless climes" and "starry skies," the speaker induces us to accept them among his fresher phrases by his admiration for the woman and the syntactic and rhythmic patterns that govern all three stanzas. The sound patterns, too, are rich beyond the somewhat gaudy alliteration in line 2. The end rhymes of the first two stanzas, for example, are closer than the **ababab** scheme requires, for the long i sound governs all six end words in stanza one while the two sets of rhymes in stanza two are closely related slant rhymes.[12] Indeed in stanza two there are several instances of what we might call "rich slant rhymes": whereas "rich rhyme" (from *rime riche* in French poetry, where it is common) includes a "support" consonant before the rhyme syllable (such as **knight** and **night**, or **lake** and **slake**), "rich slant rhyme" enlists such a consonant even where the rhyme syllables are slightly mismatched: **grace, tress, -press; less, place;** even **-press, place.** There is a tour de force of assonance in the second stanza: **shade, ray, impair'd, nameless, grace, waves, raven,** and **face.** More subtle is the set **mellow'd, tender,** and **heaven** in stanza one. The phrase **serenely sweet** is assonant as well as alliterative. If the descriptive force of the language remains vague or abstract, Byron has compensated for it by offering a kind of musical equivalent of her ineffable beauty.

Byron risks (but somehow avoids) a "sing-song" effect by making his iambic tetrameter lines perfectly regular except for the inversion in the opening foot of line 4 ("Meet in"). We might think line 6 has nine syllables, but "heaven" was conventionally compressed into one syllable, as we still find in hymnals today (see Appendix, page 228). Thoughout the poem are pairings and parallels: "cloudless climes and starry skies"; "dark and bright"; "her aspect and her eyes"; "One shade the more, one ray the less"; "How pure, how dear"; "on that cheek, and o'er that brow"; and so on. Some of these phrases verge on feeling like filler ("One shade the more" means almost the same thing as "one ray the less"), but their near redundancy expresses the inadequacy of all phrases before this beauty, and the pairings perhaps catch the trick of "dark and bright," as if they embody the spirit of that perfect union of opposites.

The opening clause, "She walks in beauty," has the freshness and suggestibility of the subject herself. Beauty seems to be an aura that surrounds her, that moves as she moves; beauty is not so much a quality she has as a quality she is in. It is perhaps the tender light of heaven that follows her around, but it would be more appropriate to say she generates her own aura. A phrase of Shelley's sounds like an explication: "A lovely lady garmented in light / From her own beauty" ("The Witch of Atlas" 81–2). To say she "walks" in it is not to say that she walks beautifully, though no doubt she does, but that to be in beauty is her accustomed or innate state; it has a biblical ring, as when one "walks with God." The gently religious touches open the way to the transition from beauty to goodness that has bothered some readers. No doubt Byron, the real Byron, had opinions as cynical as one could wish about real women and their capacities for deception, but the real Byron is not the speaker of these lines.[13] It is a fictional voice that captures the state of being captured by a woman who seems, nay who is, an ideal undivided spirit. She is a "beautiful soul" in the sense that such writers as Shaftesbury and Schiller gave it as they explored the role of beauty in nurturing moral character. We may be skeptical of this ideal, if we feel comfortably superior to Shaftesbury and Schiller, but we may not deny that "she" is what he says she is.

Is it a love poem? I think it is, and perhaps the greatest of those we have looked at in this chapter. We hear of *her* love, at least, in the final line, but surely we sense his love, too, innocent like hers, captivated by her but serene and unpossessive. The grace that falls on her she in turn sheds all around her, making us, during the moment we drop our worldly knowingness, better souls, more capable of innocent love ourselves.

Love secret and sick or open and well, love selfish or selfless, a lost beloved, friends lost, life loveless and neglected, loss accepted, and the sheer wonder of a loving heart in a lovely woman – the themes in this little selection of

Romantic lyrical poems show such variety that they defy reduction to any notion of "Romantic Love." By the same token, there is no common notion of the "Romantic Self," though some accounts of Romanticism have made much of it. For every assertion of self there is an effort at selflessness; for every expression of the "egotistical sublime" (in Keats's phrase for Wordsworth's stance) there is one of "negative capability," an uncritical openness to experience; for every interior journey there is an encounter with real people and events. Blake put it most sharply in "The Clod & the Pebble," but the relationship between the self and the capacity for genuine love is arguably the central concern of all the poets. Faith and Hope, for most of them, had to be reconsidered, for they could not accept the orthodox Christian scheme of salvation, but they would agree with St. Paul that the greatest virtue is Love.

Chapter 8

Romantic ballads

The volume of poems that contains "Tintern Abbey" is entitled *Lyrical Ballads, with A Few Other Poems*, and at least twelve of its twenty-three poems, including the longest by far, are ballads. To the second edition (1800) so many more "other" poems are added (and only a handful of new ballads) that *A Few* is dropped from the subtitle, but the title remains the same: the ballads get top billing. Though "Tintern Abbey," the "Lucy" poems, "Michael," and "The Old Cumberland Beggar" are all to be found in it, poems we think of as far greater than all but one of the ballads (the one by Coleridge), Wordsworth evidently still expected his readers to find ballads most attractive, perhaps out of curiosity as to what "lyrical" ballads might be. Ballads were in vogue, and Wordsworth and Coleridge were riding the wave.

Found throughout Europe and beyond, folk ballads, or traditional ballads, are very old, probably many millennia old. They are fairly short oral narrative poems sung by illiterate men or women, often with a repeated refrain sung by a group, the "chorus." In many places they seem to have been danced to, at least during the refrains, as the very word suggests: it comes from Old French *ballade*, from Provençal *balada*, which meant "song accompanied by dance," from *balar*, "dance," from Latin *ballare*, from Greek *ballizein*. Our words "ball" and "ballet" are from the same Latin source. They tell a story, often about love or war, and usually enter it near the climax or most dramatic moment. There is little background or context setting, characters are generic types and thinly sketched, the narrator's voice is impersonal, and the diction is simple and unembellished. Most oral ballads were divided into stanzas or strophes, with rhyme or other sound effects; in English the typical "ballad stanza" had alternating four-beat and three-beat lines, four lines to a stanza, and rhymed **abab** or **abcb**.

Scholars have disputed whether traditional ballads were composed by "the people" collectively as they sang and danced them, or were composed by individuals, who may or may not have been professional minstrels, and then altered over the years as successive generations performed them. This may be a distinction without a difference, as even during a group composition session surely some individuals will contribute more bits than others, and a single singer may take the new song to another community, altering it a little in the process, while even among the guild of professional ballad-bards a great deal of borrowing and reworking of traditional material must have been common. At any rate, by the late eighteenth century literary scholars had "discovered" the ballads and begun to collect them, recording their words (and sometimes music) in anthologies such as Thomas Percy's *Reliques of Ancient English Poetry* (1765), which launched the "ballad revival," and Walter Scott's *Minstrelsy of the Scottish Border* (1802).

Inspired by Percy, Germany saw a similar vogue for collecting ballads, and that in turn led to the writing of a new sort of ballad by literate and educated poets, the *Kunstballade* or "art ballad." In 1771 Gottfried August Bürger published a long *Kunstballade* called "Lenore," based on a much shorter ballad in Percy's *Reliques*, and it caused a sensation. In an eight-line stanza rhyming **ababccdd**, with additional internal rhymes, it tells the spooky tale of young Lenore, distraught at the failure of her lover to return from the wars and dismissive of her mother's pleas to pray for solace; her lover comes for her after all and takes her for a wild ride through the night on a black horse. Lenore believes until the end that he is taking her to their nuptial bed:

> "And where is then thy house, and home,
>   And bridal bed so meet?"
> "'Tis narrow, silent, chilly, low,
>   Six planks, one shrouding sheet."
>
> "And is there any room for me,
>   Wherein that I may creepe?"
> "There's room enough for thee and me,
>   Wherein that we may sleepe."

They ride past a funeral procession and other sights until they enter an iron gate into a graveyard, whereupon Lenore's lover turns into a skeleton and the horse vanishes into smoke, and she dies.

I have quoted from a translation by William Taylor, which divided the unusual stanzas of the original into the more familiar quatrains. His was one of five translations published in 1796, the last of which was by Walter Scott, who later said that translating "Lenore" and another ballad by Bürger made him into a poet. Another version of that year, by J. T. Stanley, appeared with three plates designed by William Blake. On reading Taylor's version in a journal, Charles Lamb wrote to Coleridge, "Have you read the Ballad called 'Leonora' in the second Number of the 'Monthly Magazine'? If you have!!!!!!!!!!!!!!!" (that's fourteen exclamation points).[1] Soon Coleridge and Wordsworth were reading Bürger in various translations and then two years later in the original during their sojourn in Germany. Almost every young poet was taken with "Lenore" when he or she first encountered it. Felicia Hemans found it enthralling. By the 1820s Victor Hugo in France and Alexander Pushkin in Russia, among many others, were writing ballads inspired by it.

Bürger's emphasis on the psychological state of Lenore, and his prolonging of the wild ride to elicit every gothic shudder, probably encouraged Wordsworth and Coleridge in their "experiments" in the "lyrical" ballad.[2] In his preface to the 1800 edition Wordsworth says the main purpose of all the poems, including the ballads, is "to illustrate the manner in which our feelings and ideas are associated in a state of excitement." It is "to follow the fluxes and refluxes of the mind when agitated by the great and simple affections of our nature." Traditional ballads often focused on dramatic moments, during which the main characters might reveal something of their psyches; Wordsworth and Coleridge are pushing the ballad further along that path until it arrives at a state common to lyric poetry, where the tale recedes and a moment of insight or feeling emerges as the main subject.

Lyrical ballads

Though it is not his most successful ballad, Wordsworth's "Simon Lee, The Old Huntsman" shows clearly what the experiments were driving at. Its subtitle, "with an incident in which he was concerned," signals its two-part structure, which first tells how the aged huntsman, who once worked for a master now long dead, must labor in his field for a scanty living, and then recounts an "incident" in which the narrator played a key part. The "incident" is so slight a thing compared to wars or tragic loves that it hardly seems a tale at all, but it is Wordsworth's point that it really is a tale if we will take it as one.

The eight-line stanza is reminiscent of Bürger's innovation, but with a different rhyme scheme:

> In the sweet shire of Cardigan,
> Not far from pleasant Ivor-hall,
> An old man dwells, a little man,
> I've heard he once was tall.

> Of years he has upon his back,   5
> No doubt, a burden weighty;
> He says he is three score and ten,
> But others say he's eighty.

The **ababcded** pattern has a distinctive touch: the d-rhyme, in the most prominent place of the stanza, is always dissyllabic. That is unusual, and unfortunate, for such rhymes tend to be funny, or witty, and often feel contrived (notice the inversion in line 6 to prepare for the rhyme), effects quite out of place in a poem meant to wring mournful thoughts out of the reader. Perhaps we can justify the narrator's tactless jauntiness by taking the first and longer part – up to midway through the ninth stanza – as confessing his thoughtlessness before his transformational encounter with the old man, but such a reading would elevate the encounter to a plane too high for it to sustain; the whole poem, moreover, is told by the narrator *after* the encounter, and there is nothing in the first sixty-eight lines to suggest that they no longer represent his present state of mind.

After the account of Simon Lee's life and current plight, the narrator grows self-conscious:

> My gentle reader, I perceive
> How patiently you've waited,   70
> And now I fear that you expect
> Some tale will be related.
>
> O reader! had you in your mind
> Such stores as silent thought can bring,
> O gentle reader! you would find
> A tale in every thing.
> What more I have to say is short,
> And you must kindly take it;
> It is no tale; but should you think,
> Perhaps a tale you'll make it.   80

There is something arch if not silly in the idea that the narrator can perceive the patience of the reader, but the author who is constructing the narrator might well assume that any reader who has made it to line 69 must be about to run out of it, "gentle" though he or she may be. The repeated appeals to the reader might themselves try the reader's patience. Yet the tone changes with the fine line "Such stores as silent thought can bring," which might have come from "Tintern Abbey" or one of the other "other" poems in the volume. And we are invited, in the spirit of "Tintern Abbey," to half create the tale. It seems to me the poem redeems itself with the "incident," and the silent thought at the end of it.

One summer-day I chanced to see
This old man doing all he could
About the root of an old tree,
A stump of rotten wood.
The mattock totter'd in his hand;
So vain was his endeavour
That at the root of the old tree
He might have worked for ever.

"You're overtasked, good Simon Lee,
Give me your tool" to him I said;   90
And at the word right gladly he
Received my proffer'd aid.
I struck, and with a single blow
The tangled root I sever'd,
At which the poor old man so long
And vainly had endeavour'd.

The tears into his eyes were brought,
And thanks and praises seemed to run
So fast out of his heart, I thought
They never would have done.   100
—I've heard of hearts unkind, kind deeds
With coldness still returning.
Alas! the gratitude of men
Hath oftner left me mourning.

The stark contrast between the hopeless efforts of the weak old man, which might have gone on forever, and the "single blow" with which the speaker cuts the root is itself food for thought, but what moves the speaker, and moves the reader, is the outpouring of thanks and praises from the old man, which might also have gone on forever. So little a thing is this kind deed that the gush of gratitude it earns reveals even more tellingly the misery and isolation of poor Simon Lee: though there must be passers-by from time to time who witness Simon's helplessness, they seldom stop to help him. The incident leaves a silent thought to store up in our mind, one more thought to help us hear the still, sad music of humanity.

"Simon Lee," then, seems to break off its ballad-like quality two-thirds of the way through in favor of something more lyrical and meditative in the end. By contrast, "The Thorn" integrates lyrical or psychological features with ballad-like narrative ones throughout its length by means of a distinctive and idiosyncratic narrator, a garrulous old man. It is also centered, like "Tintern Abbey," on a "spot," an old thornbush, which gathers symbolic weight as the speaker

hesitantly speculates on what went on there. The unusual eleven-line stanzas encourage dwelling for a time on spots or moments as the ballad slowly
unfolds.

> There is a thorn; it looks so old,
> In truth you'd find it hard to say,
> How it could ever have been young,
> It looks so old and grey.
> Not higher than a two-year's child,
> It stands erect this aged thorn;
> No leaves it has, no thorny points;
> It is a mass of knotted joints,
> A wretched thing forlorn.
> It stands erect, and like a stone   10
> With lichens it is overgrown.

The thorn is given contradictory human qualities: "old and grey," "A wretched
thing forlorn," but also "Not higher than a two-year's child." The lichens, however, are even more explicitly personified:

> Up from the earth these mosses creep,
> And this poor thorn they clasp it round
> So close, you'd say that they were bent
> With plain and manifest intent,
> To drag it to the ground;   20
> And all had joined in one endeavour
> To bury this poor thorn for ever.

Just what these mosses stand for is as uncertain as the symbolism of the thorn,
but it is clear that the narrator has a vivid imagination. He talks of nothing but
the thorn, and a little mound next to it, for sixty lines, before he introduces "A
woman in a scarlet cloak" (63) who often visits the thorn and moans in misery.
At that point readers might well focus on her mysterious story, and they might
well find the narrator annoyingly slow, dim, and repetitive. They might even
sympathize with the interlocutor, who makes a surprising and rather hyster-
ical appearance at stanza eight:

> "Now wherefore thus, by day and night,
> In rain, in tempest, and in snow,
> Thus to the dreary mountain-top   80
> Does this poor woman go?
> And why sits she beside the thorn
> When the blue day-light's in the sky,
> Or frosty air is keen and still,

And wherefore does she cry?—
Oh wherefore? wherefore? tell me why
Does she repeat that doleful cry?"

After his listener intervenes a second time, the narrator offers to tell "every thing I know" (105). It is nearly all second-hand knowledge, but it adds up to a plausible and pathetic tale of a young woman, Martha Ray, betrothed and pregnant but abandoned on her wedding day, and who six months later murders her baby and buries it beside the thorn. Some readers have found this a moving and mournful story, and taken Wordsworth's treatment of it as an act of social protest against the suffering of real women in Martha Ray's plight. Goethe's story of Gretchen in his play *Faust: Part One* (1808) is the most famous literary version of it, with intense and harrowing scenes of Gretchen's anguish. Yet the burden of the poem does not lie here – the story is, after all, the stuff of a thousand ballads – but on the teller and his own devotion to the thorn. It is a dramatic monologue.

No more I know, I wish I did,
And I would tell it all to you;
For what became of this poor child
There's none that ever knew:
And if a child was born or no,
There's no one that could ever tell;   160
And if 'twas born alive or dead,
There's no one knows, as I have said,
But some remember well,
That Martha Ray about this time
Would up the mountain often climb.

Wordsworth took a risk in creating this speaker, and many of his readers have been "altogether displeased" with him, as Robert Southey said he was in a review of the 1798 edition. "The author should have recollected that he who personates tiresome loquacity, becomes tiresome himself." In a note to the 1800 edition Wordsworth defended his experiment by describing the kind of speaker he thought he had created, "a Captain of a small trading vessel for example," who retires to a village and hears disturbing stories. Prone to super- stition, with an "adhesive" mind, he is the true subject of the poem, not Martha Ray. Wordsworth wanted "to shew the manner in which such men cleave to the same ideas" while conveying the passions he felt "to Readers who are not accustomed to sympathize with men feeling in that manner or using such lan- guage." With this note in mind, we might suspect that the interlocutor, who interrupts the loquacious speaker three times with unanswerable questions, represents the wrong kind of reader. By holding him up to real readers and making him as annoying as the old man, Wordsworth wards off their potential impatient disdain for the latter and invites a more sympathetic response. Whether he succeeds is certainly debatable, but the important thing is to appreciate the goal of this experiment in lyricizing the ballad.

"The Rime of the Ancient Mariner"

By far the most important ballad in *Lyrical Ballads* is Coleridge's "The Rime of the Ancyent Marinere," to give it in the original spelling. It is also by far the longest, at 658 lines. It has grown so famous, and is taught so often in the schools, that it is difficult to see it with fresh eyes. It has even redefined the word "albatross" to mean "moral burden," like the biblical "millstone." But for all its influence and quotable passages it is still not fully understood, and probably not fully understandable; it remains deeply mysterious.

Let's begin with the spelling. Coleridge wanted the ballad to seem old, a product of the Middle Ages or the early sixteenth century – the earliest days of oceanic exploration – so he archaized the spelling and some of the diction: "quoth he" (10, 14, etc.), "cauld" and "emerauld" (50, 52), "Ne shapes of men ne beasts we ken" (55), "eldritch" (234), and the like. He cannot have thought that anyone would truly believe it was that old, and the strange spelling caused complaints, so for the 1800 edition he modernized it, dropping the implicit pretense that the ballad might have been discovered in an old chest or something. Yet no matter how its words are spelled the tale does seem something out of an older time, when the South Seas and Antarctica were still unknown to Europeans and Christian allegory was a widespread narrative mode. Strange events take place – ships sail with no wind, a woman and her "fleshless pheere" (180) cast dice for the Mariner's soul, his fellow mariners die but become reanimated like zombies, sweet sounds haunt the ship, a "seraph-band" arrives, the ship suddenly sinks in the harbor – and these events are not readily subsumed under a Christian or any other allegory. They seem symbolic, but symbolic of what?

The overall pattern of the story is clear enough. As the ship enters the icebound sea, it is visited by an albatross, which the sailors hail as if "it were a Christian soul" (63) and which seems to bring "a good south wind" (69). Then, for no apparent reason, the mariner shoots the albatross with his crossbow (79–80). That ends section one, but there are six sections to follow: the ballad resembles Shakespeare's *King Lear* in that an unaccountable deed takes place in the opening moments and all the rest of the work deals with its complex train of consequences. At first the fellow sailors blame the narrator for doing "an hellish thing" (89) because the bird had brought the breeze, but then they all say it was right to kill it because it had brought the fog and mist (95–6). When the ship gets becalmed, however, and they run out of water, the mariners turn against him for good and hang the albatross about his neck (137–8).

Soon weird cosmic events take place that would seem to confirm that the killing of the albatross violated the order of nature and that the Mariner must expiate his sin, yet it is important to remember the original ambivalence of the crew about the deed, with its implication that the killing of the bird was nothing in itself and only the superstitions of the fickle crewmen made it seem a crime. It is difficult to resolve this tension, but it does seem that the natural and supernatural cosmos wheels into action in order to put the mariner-murderer through a kind of purgatory, while the other sailors die, perhaps because they were so shallow spiritually. The first thing that happens, in any case, is the arrival of another ship, sailing without a wind, on which only two figures are seen, a skeleton man and a living woman "far liker death than he" (189); they play dice, and she claims to win. The ship sails off, and all two hundred sailors but the narrator die: "And every soul, it passed me by / Like the whiz of my crossbow" (214–15).

Alone, cursed by the eyes of the dead men, the narrator cannot die. Only the water snakes accompany him. "And a million million slimy things / Lived on – and so did I" (230–1). Then, with no more explanation than that of the original killing of the bird, he finds "A spring of love gusht from my heart" and he blesses the slimy snakes, though "unaware" (276–7). With that the albatross slides off into the sea. One would think that the story has rounded to its climax at this point and only the denouement remains. The Mariner committed the crime out of lack of love for one of God's creatures, and he is released from his guilt when he comes to feel love for other ones, less lovable than the bird. That would seem to be the moral of the tale, and is so stated near the end: "He prayeth best who loveth best / All things both great and small, / For the dear God who loveth us, / He made and loveth all" (647–50).[3] But the end is not yet.

One night the sailors come to "life," that is, they rise to man the ship, which now moves without a wind. At dawn they gather round the mast and sing, or rather "Sweet sounds rose slowly through their mouths / And from their bodies passed" (341–2). After this unaccountable event the Mariner falls into a fit, during which he hears two voices discussing his case. The softer voice says, "The man hath penance done / And penance more will do" (413–14). And indeed he does, as the other sailors continue to curse him with their stares (443–6). But then a breeze comes up, and soon the ship is back in the port it set out from. Then come torchlike shapes, the seraph-men (517) who stand atop each corpse. A pilot and his boy, and a hermit, row out to the ship; at the sight of the hermit the Mariner rejoices: "He'll shrieve my soul, he'll wash away / The albatross's blood" (545–6). When the boat approaches, the ship suddenly sinks, but the Mariner is pulled out of the water. When he speaks the pilot faints, having taken him for dead, it would seem, whereupon the Mariner takes the oars and rows ashore. The hermit then blesses him and demands to know his story. In agony the Mariner tells him, and then he is released (614). But still he must retell his tale from time to time as he wanders from land to land: his purgatory continues to this very telling in our hands.

The lengthy concatenation of slenderly connected events with their uncertain symbolism has troubled many readers from the first. As an apparent apology for it Coleridge retitled the ballad in 1800 "The Ancient Mariner, A Poet's Reverie." This did not please his friend Charles Lamb. In a letter to Wordsworth about the second edition, he wrote, "I am sorry that Coleridge has christened his *Ancient Marinere*, a *Poet's Reverie*; it is as bad as Bottom the Weaver's declaration that he is not a lion, but only the scenical representation of a lion."[4] Lamb had never liked the supernatural machinery, but admitted to being "totally possessed" with the poem for days. He thought it so obvious that it was a poet's reverie, and not a traditional ballad discovered and edited by Coleridge, that the subtitle seemed as superfluous as the declarations of the "mechanicals" in Shakespeare's *Midsummer Night's Dream*. Yet it may well have been Coleridge's beliefs about ancient ballads and how they evolved that led him to prolong the penitence of the Mariner and multiply the supernatural doings. He was impressed by recent theories that the book of Genesis as well as the Homeric epics were recomposed over centuries out of ballads or similar lays and hence lack the unity of design and focus that we expect in works by a single author. *The Rime of the Ancient Mariner*, under this pretense, has elements going back to pagan times that are incompletely assimilated to the Catholic and perhaps Protestant "layers."[5] The poem is then an imitation – transparently an imitation and not a forgery – of the sort of ballad that might have evolved from something like an episode of the *Odyssey*, taking on themes from the tale of the Wandering Jew (he who scorned Christ and thus could never die but must for penance wander the earth and tell his tale), and then transferring its setting to the early days of Pacific voyaging. The problem is that no traditional ballad in English remotely resembles this one; it is obviously the work, whether "reverie" or not, of a single poet.

And so, many readers have sought its unity and meaning beneath or around the confusing literal events, mainly by following certain apparently symbolic props such as the sun, the moon, rain and drought, and fire. In an influential analysis of it in 1946 under the title "A Poem of Pure Imagination," the American poet Robert Penn Warren examined the symbolism in great detail, but his reading did not convincingly tie up all the loose ends.[6] Readers might nonetheless go through the poem a few times to see for themselves how the moon, for instance, rises, sets, and shines on certain events.

One prominent motif, which seems to be symbolic, is worth pausing over here: the role of eyes. The first description of the Mariner, by the wedding guest whom he stops, is that he has a long gray beard and a "glittering eye" (3). He fails to hold the guest with his hand, but "He holds him with his glittering eye—/ The wedding-guest stood still" (17–18). This hypnotic power suggests not only the sinister "fascination" of a serpent but the more benign if terrifying power of prophecy, as if the Mariner has had a vision that he still sees before him. The tale told by the "bright-eyed marinere" (24, 44; cf. 651) is indeed filled with visions, and even more with the power of eyes. When drought dries the throats of all the sailors so that they cannot speak, "what evil looks / Had I from old and young!" (135–6). It is these looks, it would seem, that hang the albatross around the Mariner's neck. As the sailors die a little later, "Each turned his face with a ghastly pang / And cursed me with his ee [eye]" (206–7). The Mariner closes his own eyes (240–4) but he cannot evade the stares of the men, now dead at his feet (247–8). For seven days he endures "the curse in a dead man's eye" multiplied by two hundred (252). As the Mariner goes on with his tale, the wedding guest protests against his "glittering eye" (220), "For that which comes out of thine eye doth make / My body and soul to be still" (364–5). Even the ocean, we learn, has a "great bright eye" that stares at the moon (421–2), evidently the moon's reflection. Implicit here is the old metaphor that the moon (like the sun) is an eye, and perhaps a hint that the Mariner himself is becoming a man of vision, moonstruck or lunatic from what he has seen. The dead men's "stony eyes," at least, now "in the moon did glitter" (441–2, 497), and we may guess that he caught his own glittering eye from them. If so, the Mariner is not only in the grip of a vision that conveys a saving spiritual message but is also transfixed by the stony stares aimed at him; it is as if he has seen the Medusa and is "petrified" but stays alive, in a living death, until his long penitential term is fulfilled. He can be the means of freeing others from sin, or from a certain sin, but is himself still indefinitely doomed.

The other that he chooses to save, finally, is a wedding guest, who much against his will finds himself riveted by that glittering eye.[7] He is "one of three" (2), that is, he is singled out by the Mariner, who knows to whom he needs to tell his story, or who is in need of hearing it. Despite further protests (35–6, 77–9, 216–21, 362–5) the wedding guest stays to hear it through. At the end, although the wedding festivities are still in full swing (624–7), the guest "Turned from the bride-groom's door" and walks away like one who is stunned and "of sense forlorn" (654–6). What has he learned? He is "A sadder and a wiser man" (657). What wisdom has he gained? We have no idea. And why did Coleridge make the listener a wedding guest? Weddings are gatherings of the community, while the Mariner destroyed his own community, both the community of man with "bird and beast" (646) and the community of brothers on board the ship. Sheer solitude is the most persistent penance he has undergone. Today, however, the Mariner claims he loves to go to the kirk "With a goodly company," there to pray together, "Old men, and babes, and loving friends, / And youths and maidens gay" (637–42), but he seems to distinguish that communal celebration from the wedding feast, though it too has happy maidens (627). Are we to understand that a wedding is a shallow or pagan affair? The poem has not earned that conclusion, and it seems arbitrary and even cruel of the Mariner to pass on to the guest, as it seems he does, his own curse. The guest is wiser now, but sadder too. What did he do to deserve such a blight?

Such questions have no end, and Coleridge himself seems never to have been sure what the ballad was all about. He revised it several times, most massively for an 1817 publication, where he added the marginal glosses that look like the work of an antiquarian editor who, despite moments of quiet eloquence, is not always on top of things either. I have chosen to discuss the first version of the ballad, but the 1817 version is the better known. It is well worth the effort to compare the two. For every knot the comparison loosens, another mystery seems to descend. But it is no mystery why the poem has mesmerized generations of readers.

"La Belle Dame sans Merci"

Just as mysterious, though much simpler and shorter, is Keats's "La Belle Dame sans Merci: A Ballad" (1819), and it too has haunted readers for nearly as long as Coleridge's "Rime." Part of its attraction, I think, lies in its stanza form, which departs from the standard tetrameter quatrain by reducing the fourth line to two feet:

> O what can ail thee, knight at arms,
>   Alone and palely loitering?
> The sedge has wither'd from the lake,
>   And no birds sing.

Keats makes good use of the finality or closure the short line invites: "And no birds sing," for instance, seems the more portentous for occupying its own line. Keats also archaizes his ballad, as Coleridge did, with little medieval touches, though not as intrusively. (He revised the version quoted here for publication in 1820, adding a medievalism to the first line: "Ah, what can ail thee, wretched wight.")

> O what can ail thee, knight at arms,
>   So haggard and so woe-begone?
> The squirrel's granary is full,
>   And the harvest's done.
>
> I see a lily on thy brow,
>   With anguish moist and fever dew,   10
> And on thy cheeks a fading rose
>   Fast withereth too.

The three opening stanzas are spoken by an uncharacterized persona, who seems to have happened upon this ill and miserable knight near a lake on an autumnal day; we can infer little else. The question the speaker asks the knight preempts our own about the speaker and how he came upon the knight, and we are drawn with little ado into the knight's story. There is certainly a hint that his condition – pale, haggard, woe-begone, anguished, fevered – is tied somehow to the season, now past the harvest, as the withered sedge and withering rose underscores, but how or why we cannot tell.

Without quotation marks or any other indicator the speaker now shifts, and the knight's reply takes up the rest of the poem.

> I met a lady in the meads,
>   Full beautiful, a fairy's child;
> Her hair was long, her foot was light,
>   And her eyes were wild.
>
> I made a garland for her head,
>   And bracelets too, and fragrant zone;
> She look'd at me as she did love,
>   And made sweet moan.   20
>
> I set her on my pacing steed,
>   And nothing else saw all day long,
> For sidelong would she bend, and sing
>   A fairy's song.
>
> She found me roots of relish sweet,
>   And honey wild, and manna dew,

And sure in language strange she said—
    I love thee true.

She took me to her elfin grot,
    And there she wept and sigh'd full sore,   30
And there I shut her wild wild eyes
    With kisses four.

And there she lulled me asleep
    And there I dream'd—Ah! woe betide!
The latest dream I ever dream'd
    On the cold hill side.

I saw pale kings and princes too,
    Pale warriors, death-pale were they all;
They cried—"La belle dame sans merci
    Hath thee in thrall!"   40

I saw their starv'd lips in the gloam,
    With horrid warning gaped wide,
And I awoke and found me here,
    On the cold hill side.

And this is why I sojourn here
    Alone and palely loitering,
Though the sedge is wither'd from the lake,
    And no birds sing.

The story is simple enough, and familiar from the romance and ballad traditions, but there are ambiguities and puzzles at every step. The knight seemed to know the beautiful lady is a fairy's child from the outset, so either he knew what he was getting into or he was put "in thrall" (40) from the outset as well. "She look'd at me as she did love" (19) probably means "She look'd at me as *if* she did love" (while she didn't) but it is a little doubtful. When the knight claims "And sure in language strange she said—I love thee true" (27–8) we can see he was deluded, even if in her fairy tongue she did say "I love thee true," for "sure" means "surely," a word we use when we are *not* sure. How could he be sure, speaking no elvish himself? We don't know what happened in her "grot" or cave. He closed her eyes with four kisses, no doubt, but is that Keats's discreet metonym for the sexual act, as the romance tradition would certainly lead us to expect, or is there something magical about two kisses per eye?

    If it appears that he put her to sleep we are soon told it was the other way around, as she "lulled me asleep" (33), perhaps by singing a lullaby in her strange tongue. He fell into a dream. Wasn't he in some sort of dream all along? In any case, "I saw pale kings and princes too, / Pale warriors, death-pale were they all" (37–8), and we recall with a little shiver that the speaker first notices that the knight is "palely loitering" (2). These spectral men must be the fairy lady's earlier victims, and they tell him he is now in thrall to her. Is it too late? That their mouths are open in "warning" (42) hints that the knight might awaken from his dream in time to escape, but their statement sounds definitive, and he is certainly death-pale when we meet him. Yet he is not dead. Are the others dead, or locked up in her grot, under a spell, or are they scattered about the countryside, like him, gathered together only in his dream? Is his condition different from theirs, or will he soon join them in death?

I mention all these minor mysteries not to invite research into Keats's intentions or his many sources but to show how little they matter beyond their general effect. This ballad is at home in an unspecific realm out of medieval romance, but the very absence of context gives it much of its power. We do not even know if the knight is telling the truth. There may be another story to be told, perhaps from the point of view of the lady, fairy or not, so that the version we have is just the unreliable knight's. It might all be an allegory for the consequences of passion, or sexual intercourse. We cannot say, and, as Keats's urn warns us, it might be better if we gave up the search for truths about the story and submitted to its magical beauty, its real truth, which depends in great part on its suspension in a magical world where all questions dissolve.

Chapter 9

Romantic epics and romances

"Milton! thou should'st be living at this hour," Wordsworth writes in a sonnet ("London 1802"), "England hath need of thee." She has become stagnant, self-ish, and unhappy, and Milton's spirit would raise her up again. His soul was like a star, his voice was like the sea's – pure, majestic, and free.

Milton wrote poems of every sort, including sonnets of the sort Wordsworth is writing here, as well as a great deal of prose, but he was best known, and most revered, for his epic *Paradise Lost*, that sea of majestic blank verse. Since the time of the ancients the prevalent opinion was that the epic is the highest genre, and to compose one is the highest ambition of poets, though there were a few who made fun of it. For the Roman poet Virgil the epic was the inevit-able culmination of his career, which began with little poems (*Eclogues*) and then took up a middle-sized one (*Georgics*), as stages in his preparation for a great work. His *Aeneid* became the established model of the national epic as soon as it appeared and remained so well into the nineteenth century. Milton, however, chose a biblical theme, not a national one like the founding of Rome. His immense accomplishment lent even greater prestige to the form, but left the field clear for a national English or British epic, if there was anyone worthy of entering the lists after him. There were indeed many who tried to produce one. At least two of them were friends of Wordsworth's and Coleridge's: Joseph Cottle, who wrote *Alfred* (1800), and John Thelwall, who wrote *The Hope of Albion; or, Edwin of Northumbria* (1801) – both set in Anglo-Saxon times. A closer friend, Southey, came out with several epics, set in Arabia, India, Spain, or Wales.[1] None these nor any of the others had lasting success; they are for-gotten today, perhaps because the very idea of a national epic was soon to seem quaint if not absurd. Even *Paradise Lost*, however admired, began to feel dated by the Romantic era. The Romantic efforts toward epic that we still take seriously are all *displacements* of the epic of one sort or another: toward mock-epic (Byron's *Don Juan*), toward a visionary apocalypse (Blake's *Milton* and *Jerusalem*), or toward autobiography (Wordsworth's *Prelude* and, to a degree, Blake's *Milton*). Or they are fragments, such as Keats's two *Hyperion* segments. Even the ones that are ostensibly epic may tilt toward the romance (Shelley's *Laon and Cythna*, Keats's *Endymion*), and one of them, ostensibly a romance, seems more of a meditative travelogue (Byron's *Childe Harold's Pilgrimage*).

Coleridge had long contemplated an epic on the fall of Jerusalem (destroyed by Titus in 70 CE), but, like so many of his projects, it never saw the light, though a case has been made that "Kubla Khan" is a condensed and fragmentary product of his epic plans.[2] Wordsworth, too, urged by Coleridge, hoped to write a philosophical epic called *The Recluse*, but he only finished a thousand lines or so, now known as "Home at Grasmere." He did publish *The Excursion* (1814), a kind of blank-verse philosophical dialogue in nine books, and he completed but did not publish a long autobiography in blank verse, which we know as *The Prelude* (1805). These were all installments in a grand plan for a tripartite masterwork.

Wordsworth's *The Prelude*

"How I became a poet" would seem an unpromising subject for an epic, or even a prelude to one. The traditional epic, which dealt with wars and migrations and other events of cosmic consequence, was also stringently impersonal, with just an occasional "I sing" or an invocation to the muse. In the four invocations of *Paradise Lost*, however, Milton had written at some length about himself, and these authorial intrusions may have been the germ of Wordsworth's conviction that a long poem in Miltonic blank verse would be the right vehicle for his subject, though the fact that he never published it suggests that, among other reasons, he had second thoughts about this unprecedented hybrid form.[3] It is at least a trial of strength, the prime exhibit in his own case: if he can write of his vocation in strong and memorable verse then he will confirm the vocation itself. The poem tells of his life from childhood to mid-life, with episodes as un-epical as a skating party or the offering of toasts to Milton in his rooms at Cambridge. There is a book on the books Wordsworth read. There are quite a few "spots of time," moments when an experience (usually in the natural world) turned into a vision, disturbing or exalting; together these made him feel singled out for some high mission. He describes the phantasmagoria of London. Several books are about his adventures in France during the early days of the Revolution, his alienation from his own country when it went to war with France, his pursuit of abstract moral and political theories, his despair and loss of imaginative power, and his recovery. Its overall structure, though with many digressions, follows the pattern of spiritual autobiography set by St. Augustine's *Confessions* or more recent testimonies such as John Bunyan's *Grace Abounding to the Chief of Sinners* (1666), though Wordsworth's story is not Christian, and it dwells on those events that made him a poet. The whole thing is addressed to Coleridge, which tilts it slightly toward an ode or letter.

In what ways can such a poem be called an epic? It is long, it is in blank verse, it has Miltonic touches in diction and phrasing. It opens with something like a naturalized invocation to the muse:

> Oh there is blessing in this gentle breeze,
> That blows from the green fields and from the clouds
> And from the sky; it beats against my cheek,
> And seems half conscious of the joy it gives.

Like a proper epic it enters *in medias res*, in the midst of things, as Wordsworth describes his present escape from the city and his walk toward his chosen home in the Lake District, though soon it begins again with his childhood and follows a chronological course to the end. Though it has no battle scenes like the *Iliad* and *Aeneid* (or indeed *Paradise Lost*), war is a major subject and source of grief and fear. The London books (7 and 8) resemble a descent to the underworld like those in the *Odyssey* and *Aeneid*.

If these and other features keep reminding us that the poem aspires to be an epic, Wordsworth must have been deeply committed to the belief that his subject was heroic and profound enough to risk the ridicule traditionalists might fling at it. And indeed, as he states in the "Prospectus" which concludes his preface to *The Excursion*, his subject is deeper and greater than Milton's:

> For I must tread on shadowy ground, must sink
> Deep—and, aloft ascending, breathe in worlds
> To which the heaven of heavens is but a veil.   30
> All strength—all terror, single or in bands,
> That ever was put forth in personal form;
> Jehovah—with his thunder, and the choir
> Of shouting Angels, and the empyreal thrones,
> I pass them unalarmed. Not Chaos, not
> The darkest pit of lowest Erebus,
> Nor aught of blinder vacancy—scooped out
> By help of dreams, can breed such fear and awe
> As fall upon us often when we look

> Into our Minds, into the Mind of Man,   40
> My haunt, and the main region of my Song.

Wordsworth believed at this time that "the Mind of Man" was the source of all the divine entities and machinery that populate *Paradise Lost* and Christian theology, which are but veils or allegories of the depths from which they emerge. If the human Mind in general is the greatest possible subject of a philosophical epic, then the growth of his own mind in particular is the best possible subject of a prelude to it. His subject, as we saw in Chapter 2, will be "the discipline / And consummation of the poet's mind" (*Prelude* 13.270–1). It is, he admits, a "Hard task to analyse a soul" (2.233), but the difficulty makes it the more appropriate for the high venture of an epic. In the next book he adds, "my theme has been / What passed within me." For "of my own heart / Have I been speaking, and my youthful mind." "This is in truth heroic argument" (3.173–82).

We can touch on only a few characteristics of this long poem (and of the other long poems in this chapter). It would be clear, even if we had no manuscripts from which to reconstruct a first version in two books or a later one in five, that Wordsworth's poem grew rather like his own poetic mind, with no preconceived plan beyond exploring his life and calling. As he reworked his first sections and added many more, he gave it recurring motifs, ideas, and climaxes while bringing it back round at the end to a reflection on its beginning. As M. H. Abrams has said, *The Prelude* "is an involuted poem which is about its own genesis – a prelude to itself. Its structural end is its own beginning; and its temporal beginning … is Wordsworth's entrance upon the stage of life at which it ends."[4] If it has something of a circular form, however, it also meanders like a river, as he acknowledges in an epic simile at the opening of Book 9:

> As oftentimes a river, as might seem,
> Yielding in part to old remembrances,
> Part swayed by fear to tread an onward road
> That leads direct to the devouring sea,
> Turns and will measure back his course—far back,
> Towards the very regions which he crossed
> In his first outset—so have we long time
> Made motions retrograde, in like pursuit
> Detained.

In personifying this generic river, making it masculine and ascribing memory, fear, and will to it, Wordsworth brings it closer to his subject, the rise and progress of his own imaginative power. (In describing the structure of his grand plan to a friend, Wordsworth likened *The Prelude* to a "tributary" to *The Recluse*.)[5] As he looks back in the final book he compares the power itself to a stream:

> This faculty hath been the moving soul
> Of our long labour: we have traced the stream
> From darkness, and the very place of birth
> In its blind cavern, whence is faintly heard
> The sound of waters; followed it to light
> And open day, accompanied its course
> Among the ways of Nature, afterwards
> Lost sight of it bewildered and engulphed,
> Then given it greeting as it rose once more
> With strength

> (13.171–80)

If both the faculty of imagination and the poem about it are kindred metaphorical streams, it was a real river, Wordsworth tells us, that served as his first natural teacher and muse. In what is probably the earliest passage of those later incorporated into the poem, he asks:

> Was it for this
> That one, the fairest of all rivers, loved
> To blend his murmurs with my nurse's song,
> And from his alder shades and rocky falls,
> And from his fords and shallows, sent a voice
> That flowed along my dreams? For this didst thou,
> O Derwent, travelling over the green plains
> Near my "sweet birthplace," didst thou, beauteous stream,
> Make ceaseless music through the night and day,
> Which with its steady cadence tempering
> Our human waywardness, composed my thoughts
> To more than infant softness, giving me
> Among the fretful dwellings of mankind,
> A knowledge, a dim earnest, of the calm
> Which Nature breathes among the hills and groves?

> (1.271–85)

Wordsworth not only personifies the Derwent, which flowed (and still flows) behind his childhood home in Cockermouth, but makes it a poet, a singer, like himself, and male, like himself, though with a maternal role like the nurse's. The Derwent composed songs while it "composed my thoughts" (281) he almost says, giving compositions as well as composure to him as a child. This is quintessential Wordsworth, and Romanticism generally: this tying together of the literal and metaphorical, of life and work, by endowing a river with a soul and a soul with a river.

The breeze muse that opens the poem is welcomed by the poet, who has just left "a house / Of bondage" (6–7), the city (unnamed, but presumably London), and is free to choose where to live. He asks, "what sweet stream / shall with its murmurs lull me to my rest? The earth is all before me" (13–15). He endows this happy pastoral holiday with momentous biblical resonances: the Israelites' escape from bondage in Egypt, and Adam and Eve as they depart the garden ("The world was all before them," in Milton's words). Is he serious? Can his little personal adventure (leaving London, finding a cottage) bear this epic and cosmic burden? Wordsworth seems to emulate the astonishing pride of Dante, who extends the parallels of biblical typology to include his own life, which imitates that of Christ, as he descends to hell on Good Friday. Wordsworth, as we noted, is not a Christian like Dante, Milton, or Bunyan. Indeed he reverses the Christian disparagement of "the natural man," which Paul says "receiveth not the things of the Spirit of God" (2 Corinthians 2.14); for Wordsworth, "'tis shaken off, / That burthen of my own unnatural self" (22–3). Of course, as an experience or state of mind, what Wordsworth means by "unnatural self" is not far from what Paul means by "natural man," yet by adding the negative prefix "un" Wordsworth underscores both his distance from traditional belief and his desire to invoke the ambience, the weight, the feelings that have come with it.

For the breeze and his sense of release from prison seem to bring "a gift that consecrates my joy" (40).

> For I, methought, while the sweet breath of heaven
> Was blowing on my body, felt within
> A corresponding mild creative breeze,
> A vital breeze which travelled gently on
> O'er things which it had made,
>
> (41–5)

As the Derwent gently shaped the soul of the boy, the breeze engenders its inner counterpart in the man, who has regained his harmony with nature. Yet here too there is a biblical echo: the creative breeze resembles the wind or Spirit of God that "moved upon the face of the waters" at the beginning of Genesis. Wordsworth does not flinch from his project, announced in the "Prospectus" to *The Excursion*, of retooling Christian doctrine for his own purposes. The inner breeze promises "prowess" in his chosen field, "The holy life of music and of verse" (54), his sacred calling.

If all this has a touch of the grandiose, it does not last long. After fifty-four lines in the present tense, the poem switches to the past, as Wordsworth tells how he poured out his soul in those very words while he felt "clothed in priestly robe" (61) and singled out for "holy services" (63). He walked on, then lay on the ground a while to think about where to go and what to do, then walked some more. As evening came on his soul tried again to compose poetry, "nor did she want / Eolian visitations—but the harp / Was soon defrauded" (103–5), and he ran out of creative breezes. He accepts this cheerfully enough, but I think it has a mildly self-mocking air, a bit of bathos or anticlimax after the rapturous opening.

In any case he then recounts how, settled in his home, he struggled to find a home for his scattered poetic thoughts. He produced nothing much. In a little epic catalog he names various historical themes, mostly epic in dignity, that he considered taking up, as well as "some old / Romantic tale by Milton left unsung" (179–80). His "favorite aspiration," however, is "some philosophic song" (229–30), but this proves too much for him. He labors, he procrastinates, he loses confidence. He finds something lacking in the themes, and he finds even more lacking in himself, so "That I recoil and droop, and seek repose / In indolence from vain perplexity, / Unprofitably travelling towards the grave" (267–9).

Wordsworth then asks, "Was it for this?" in the passage we have just quoted, addressed to the Derwent. We might expect him to ask the river's forgiveness, but instead he leaves the question unanswered, and turns to the story of his life. After this long preamble, then, the poem properly begins at line 305:

> Fair seed-time had my soul, and I grew up
> Fostered alike by beauty and by fear:
> Much favoured in my birth-place, and no less
> In that beloved Vale to which erelong
> We were transplanted

Here is another metaphor from the natural realm: the seed. The commonplace phrase "grew up" takes on a richer sense in this context where the soul starts out as a seed; we are reminded that the subtitle given the poem on its publication in 1850 is "Growth of a Poet's Mind." Seed and fountain, plant and river, are combined in another passage as alternative metaphors for the source of the mind:

> But who shall parcel out
> His intellect by geometric rules,
> Split like a province into round and square?
> Who knows the individual hour in which
> His habits were first sown, even as a seed,
> Who that shall point, as with a wand, and say

"This portion of the river of my mind
  Came from yon fountain"?

(2.209–16)

Though Wordsworth was to admit he was fascinated for a time by geometry, as a relief from the vexing problems of politics and morality, here he contrasts the imposition of superficial and artificial rules on the intellect with the innate mysteries of the mind. The implications for education are obvious, and he does not fail to draw them, especially with an example in Book 5 of a young prodigy of learning and accomplishment, "a child, no child, / But a dwarf man" (294–5), so stuffed with books that their contents turn metaphorically into weeds: "Rank growth of propositions overruns / The stripling's brain; the path on which he treads / Is choked with grammars" (323–5). They would seem to be nature's revenge. Mother Earth, in any case, feels bereft of this child:

Meanwhile old Granddame Earth is grieved to find
The playthings which her love designed for him
Unthought of—in their woodland beds the flowers
Weep, and the river-sides are all forlorn.

(346–9)

Wordsworth later eliminated this passage, which no doubt came to seem too much like a sentimental pastoral elegy, where nature mourns the death of a shepherd-poet (as in Milton's "Lycidas" and Shelley's "Adonais"), and substituted this: "For this unnatural growth the trainer blame, / Pity the tree" (1850 version, 5.328–9).

Wordsworth was ever grateful that his own upbringing was very different from this unnatural boy's, and when his imaginative power seemed weakened and sickened by his agonies over revolutionary France and its war with Britain (his feelings were much like those of Coleridge in "France: An Ode"), he credits "my understanding's natural growth" (10.786) for pulling him through the crisis. By the end, having completed *The Prelude*, he feels confirmed in his vocation as poet, no longer doubtful of his capacity to "speak / a lasting inspiration" to the human race (13.442–3).

The sad irony is, of course, that Wordsworth never did write the great philosophical poem that he intended, and felt guilty and embarrassed by his failure. Many readers today, moreover, feel that shortly after 1805 he ceased to write great poetry of any kind. He kept *The Prelude* in his drawer, and only on his death in 1850 was it shown to the world. A happier irony is that many of these same readers (including this one) rate *The Prelude* as the greatest long poem since *Paradise Lost*.

Blake's *Milton, a Poem in 2 Books*

One can imagine William Blake reading Wordsworth's sonnet to Milton and sputtering, "Why 'should'st be living'? He really is living at this hour. He spoke with me only yesterday!" In 1802 Blake had been at work for more than year on "an immense number of verses," as he put it in a letter the following year, which seem to have been incorporated into his first attempt at a full-scale epic, called *Milton.* The title page says "1804," but it was probably not engraved until 1809.[6] He originally engraved "in 12 Books," a signal of his intentions to emulate *Paradise Lost,* but he masked the first digit in the earliest printings. What we have is two books in forty-five plates, later expanded to fifty: a "brief epic" but dense with cosmic machinery and difficult symbolism. It is all about John Milton's return to earth in spiritual form.

Blake, that is, takes up Wordsworth's idea and carries it several steps further: he not only imagines just what Milton would encounter and accomplish in today's England, but he has Milton merge with him – "Then first I saw him in the Zenith as a falling star, / Descending perpendicular, swift as the swallow or swift; / And on my left foot falling on the tarsus, enterd there" (plate 15.47–9, E 110) – and even go through a purgation of the errors of his previous life before he is fit to join Blake and "go forth to the Great Harvest & Vintage of the Nations" (43.1, E 144). What are these errors? Too much rational Calvinist theology, too much devotion to the classics ("the silly Greek & Latin slaves of the sword," as the "Preface" says [E 95]), his support of Cromwell, his tracts on divorce. The audacity of Blake's vision is breath-taking, but, divested of its sometimes bizarre details, like the tarsus, a bone in the foot,[7] it is not unlike the sort of essay one used to see, called "What is living and what is dead in Milton" or something similar. Blake takes metaphors literally, it seems, and takes them a little further than more decorous poets: where Wordsworth likens Milton to a star, Blake likens him to a falling star, which lands on Blake's foot.

Milton begins with a cry for help in the form of a poem: "Say first! what mov'd Milton, who walkd about in Eternity / One hundred years, pondring the intricate mazes of Providence / Unhappy tho in heav'n" – no doubt the orderly and obedient heaven he had envisaged in *Paradise Lost* – "To go into the deep … What cause at length mov'd Milton to this unexampled deed [?] / A Bards prophetic Song!" (2.16–22, E 96). The Bard's song is an account of the Creation and Fall, followed by an intricate dispute and its attempted resolution among several characters, three of whom have specific agricultural tasks, to plow, to harrow, and to "turn the Mills" (4.10). These three represent the three types of creative or destructive characters (the miller is Satan, who grinds the imaginative world made by the others into rational powder), and much of the confusing story seems to reflect Blake's unhappiness during his three years at Felpham, where he felt stifled by the well-meant but trivial artistic commissions that his patron, William Hayley, found for him to grind out; at least one quarrel must have arisen between them, mediated by several friends and by Blake's wife Catherine. He must have asked himself what Milton would have done, as "the loud voic'd Bard terrify'd took refuge in Miltons bosom" (14.9). Milton learns from this song that Satan, the principle of Selfhood, is still the lord of the world, and that it is partly his own fault. *Paradise Lost* had punished Satan and his legions by confining them in hell, or at least expelling them from heaven, but from the Bard Milton hears that "it is of Divine / Mercy alone! of Free Gift and Election that we live" (13.32–3) and not of vengeance. Milton acknowledges that "I in my Selfhood am that Satan," so he descends to the land of the living, that is, to "Eternal Death" (14.30–2).

Most of Book 1 describes the progress of Milton, or of Milton's various spiritual components, variously personified, through this world, his struggles with Satan, and his entry into Blake through his left foot, as if to join in Blake's pilgrimage or "walk" of the spirit. Book 2 tells of a second descent, that of Ololon, Milton's female "emanation," who like him takes the burden of sin upon her and seeks to join her alienated mate. Just what she represents it is difficult to say, but it may be relevant to recall Milton's praise of virginity in *Comus* and elsewhere and Blake's redefinition of it in *Visions of the Daughters of Albion* (1793), where the heroine Oothoon, raped on her way to meet her lover, shakes off her defilement and proclaims that her love for him makes her pure. Milton separated from his wife, Mary, wrote a pamphlet urging the right of divorce, and disinherited his daughters. It is Ololon's mission, perhaps, to set right these deeds by reuniting with Milton – sexually as well as spiritually, if there is any difference. Near the climax of the poem Milton confronts Satan and announces that he will not annihilate him, for to do so would be to become a Satan himself, but will annihilate his own Selfhood, for "Such are the Laws of Eternity that each shall mutually / Annihilate himself for others good, as I for thee" (38.35–6). He "builds a Heaven in Hells despair," as Blake's Clod does. Satan will thus have nothing to do. At this point Albion, who represents the people of Britain, rises from his couch where he has been sleeping fitfully throughout the poem, takes a few steps, and collapses back on to it. Britain is not yet ready, it seems, but the means of rousing it are at hand. The Bard has taken refuge in Milton's bosom, Milton has entered into Blake through his left foot, then all three have joined with Los, the figure of imagination and prophecy in many of Blake's works; together they assume the task of saving Albion.

Albion's sleep of death is due in large part to the delusory grip of reason, as embodied in the empiricist and mathematical doctrines of Bacon, Locke, and

Newton. They have blotted out the light of imagination and the arts, which point the way to "Self-annihilation" and forgiveness, as taught by Jesus. The means of restoring Albion, then, as Milton proclaims to Ololon, are

> To cast off Rational Demonstration by Faith in the Saviour
> To cast off the rotten rags of Memory by Inspiration
> To cast off Bacon, Locke & Newton from Albions covering
> To take off his filthy garments, & clothe him with Imagination
> To cast aside from Poetry, all that is not Inspiration
> That it no longer shall dare to mock with the aspersion of Madness
> Cast on the Inspired, by the tame high finisher of paltry Blots,
> Indefinite, or paltry Rhymes; or paltry Harmonies.
>
> (41.3–10, E 142)

Faith in Jesus is identical to "Inspiration," for Jesus is the imagination itself. Blake defies those who have cast aspersions on him as mad and tries to prove his genuine imagination by means of this very poem. Milton's task is Blake's task too: to purge paltry indefinite blots from painting (he disliked chiaroscuro, for example, and insisted on firm outline), paltry harmonies from music (he wanted clear melody only), and paltry rhymes from poetry (though he himself rhymed in the *Songs of Innocence and of Experience*). A threefold revolution in form or style will prepare Albion's imagination for the revelation that will save him.

It is hard to suppress a snort of derision at this astonishing ambition. Britain will be brought to an imaginative paradise of selflessness and forgiveness by means of *what*? Yet it is not much more improbable than Wordsworth's plea to Milton to raise up England from her selfishness. Wordsworth said little about the regenerative power of painting and music, but he certainly announced at the end of *The Prelude* that he was ready to assume the mantle of poet and prophet. It is remarkable that these two quasi-epics, written at the same time by two poets who were unaware of each other,[8] should submit their very different poems as "masterpieces," that is, as evidence that they are masters of their craft and ready to assume the mantle of their own master, Milton, but whom they do not shrink from surpassing or correcting. *Milton* is Blake's *Prelude*. He went on to write a longer epic, *Jerusalem: The Emanation of The Giant Albion*, whereas Wordsworth abandoned *The Recluse* and offered *The Excursion* instead. Like *The Prelude*, *Milton* is arguably a greater work than the work it is a prelude to, not least for the autobiographical dimension, which reveals Blake's struggle to find his path as a poet and artist.

We should note, finally, that all the events in *Milton* – the Bard's song, the descent of Milton, his confrontation with Satan, his entry into Blake, the descent of Ololon, her encounter with Milton, and the doings of Los – these all take place simultaneously on various planes of existence and, even more remarkable, in a single moment, a moment of revelation that lights up the human psyche and the world it inhabits. *The Prelude*, too, turns around moments of revelation, most famously Wordsworth's experience during his crossing of the Simplon Pass in Switzerland, where the woods, winds, clouds, and waterfalls

> Were all like workings of one mind, the features
> Of the same face, blossoms upon one tree,
> Characters of the great apocalypse,
> The types and symbols of eternity,
> Of first, and last, and midst, and without end.

(6.568–72)

This privileging of the intense and luminous experience makes both epics examples of the lyricization of nonlyrical forms that we noted in Chapter 1. Like sonnets, they are both monuments to moments.

Romance

The romance, as we also noted in Chapter 1, is a distinctively Romantic genre, as the two words themselves attest. Even works that look as if they are epics, or aspired to be epics, tend to slide into the romance mode. Though there is no one feature that distinguishes them, a medieval setting is the most frequent and salient, if only because the romance arose during the Middle Ages. It is interesting that Keats, who alone among the Romantics set his longest narrative poems in the classical world, full of Greek gods and nymphs, nonetheless subtitled his *Endymion* (1818) *A Poetic Romance*, and his last effort to write an epic called *Hyperion* produced a fragment which is almost entirely a romance-like dream. Shelley's twelve-book *Laon and Cythna* (1818), as the names of its hero and heroine suggest, has a Greek setting, but it is not ancient Greek; as its revised title, *The Revolt of Islam*, indicates, it takes place in modern times, in Greece under Ottoman rule. It is closer to an epic in its social or political themes, yet it clearly proclaims itself a romance by its use throughout of the Spenserian stanza, indelibly associated with *The Faerie Queene*. Wordsworth had attempted a romance, not very successfully, *The White Doe of Rylstone* (written in 1807), and Coleridge had written the more impressive *Christabel* (written in 1797–1800), but left it a fragment. One of the greatest short romances of any period, of course, is Keats's *The Eve of St. Agnes* (1820), also in Spenserians; it beautifully evokes not only Spenser but Shakespeare's *Romeo and Juliet* in a mysterious near-gothic setting.

   In the remainder of this chapter I will look briefly at Walter Scott's *Marmion* (1808), which, though seldom read today, was immensely popular in its time and remained central to the Romantic canon well into the last century, as attested by the many elaborately illustrated and annotated editions still available in second-hand bookshops. (St. John Rivers gave such an edition to Jane Eyre in Charlotte Brontë's novel.) I have neglected Scott in this book so far, but a representative introduction to Romantic poetry ought to consider at least one of his romances, even though he is now much better known for his novels. Then I will take up Byron's *Childe Harold's Pilgrimage: A Romaunt* (1812, 1816, 1818), also a great success in its day, but which still fascinates many readers, though less for its romance features than for its "Byronic hero" and its meditations on exotic places and recent world-shaking events.

Scott's *Marmion: A Tale of Flodden Field*

Marmion was not the first of Scott's romances. As he explains in the "Advertisement" to its first edition, because his previous romance, *The Lay of the Last Minstrel* (1805), had been "honoured with some degree of applause" (he puts it mildly), he felt justified in attempting something similar but more ambitious, "upon a broader scale." It was not quite "an attempt at Epic composition," for that would have "exceeded his plan of a Romantic Tale." A romantic tale is what it is, in rhymed tetrameter couplets, though it is set in a context that we might call epic, the Battle of Flodden Field of 1513, a great disaster for Scotland. This context also makes the tale "historical." Scott was to go on to write historical novels, beginning with *Waverley* (1814), but this poem is historical too, not only in its evocation of the events of 1513 but also for its lovingly detailed descriptions of castles, armor, social order, and "the manners of the feudal times." The backs of most editions are burdened with long footnotes explaining who all the characters are – all but the leading characters, who are inventions. The footnotes have an antiquarian air, for Scott's success with *The Lay of the Last Minstrel* licensed his self-indulgence in displaying his research. They are part of his ongoing bid to become Scotland's historian, an ambition he was soon to achieve with his many novels. Wordsworth and Blake, we have seen, displace the national epic on to something more personal; Scott disavows the epic ambition, but through his verse romances and his prose novels together (along with his footnotes) he created something it seems fair to call an immense national epic cycle.

Marmion is also weighed down with lengthy verse "introductions" to all six cantos in the form of epistles to six different friends. They irritated the first reviewers, and they certainly slow down the poem. The first one is well more than half as long as the canto that follows, and though the subsequent cantos lengthen and the epistles shorten, all the introductions together still make up a fourth of the total poem. And they have little to do with the story. They are Scott's genial, almost pastoral reminiscences of times spent with his friends, usually rambling about the countryside hunting and talking. He disparages "this idle lay" (Intro. 4.28) with lordly nonchalance and praises his friends' talents at verse. He sometimes takes heart from them as examples or even muses for his poem; he calls on his friend Ellis, for instance, a literary scholar and translator, to inspire him: "to the bard impart / A lesson of thy magic art" (Intro. 5.161–2). But his attitude is very far from the high calling of Wordsworth and Blake as they emulate and claim to surpass Milton.

The story is about a lord named Marmion, who is a rival with Ralph de Wilton for the hand of Lady Clara de Clare. She loves De Wilton, who genuinely loves her, whereas Marmion only wants her land. With the help of his mistress, a nun (ironically named Constance) who has abjured her vows, and who wants to win Marmion's love, he forges documents that implicate De Wilton in a treasonous plot. In a joust of honor Marmion defeats De Wilton, who flees England but then returns after some years disguised as a "palmer," a monk who makes continual pilgrimages to holy shrines. Meanwhile Clara withdraws to a nunnery to avoid Marmion, though she remains a novice and could (unlike Constance) leave without breaking her vows. Constance, abandoned by Marmion, is captured by the church authorities and taken to a convent on Lindisfarne.

All this is "background": it takes place before the poem opens, and we pick it up piecemeal as the foreground story unfolds at a leisurely pace. Some of it is deliberately withheld till quite late, or is only half told, to create an air of mystery and suspense. Though veteran romance readers might well have suspicions, we do not learn the identity of the palmer, whom we meet in canto one as he agrees to guide Marmion on a diplomatic mission from King Henry of England to King James of Scotland, until canto six! During their progress north, Marmion is induced by a fantastic tale told by the host of their inn to challenge an "Elfin Warrior" (3.502) who has haunted the region. Marmion is unhorsed and about to be slain when the supernatural knight spares him. That uncanny creature, of course, turns out to be De Wilton. In the second canto a committee of abbots and abbesses sentences Constance to death by immurement – quite a gothic touch – but before she is walled up she turns over evidence that exonerates De Wilton and proves Marmion a forger and libeler. That evidence makes its way to Edinburgh just as Marmion and the palmer arrive and just as King James is making final preparations for battle with England. Clara is also there. As things get sorted out, De Wilton is vindicated, he finds Clara and pledges his love, he is ennobled again, and joins the battle on (of course) the English side. Marmion eludes capture and also joins the battle, also for the English. You would think the two would meet in battle, but they are both fighting for Henry against the rebellious if noble Scots. They both acquit themselves as heroes, but Marmion is killed, conveniently, and De Wilton emerges unscathed to claim Clara and reclaim his estates (and hers, to be sure), and they live happily ever after.

The piecemeal doling out of information, already routine in gothic novels and soon to be the central technique of mystery novels (such as those of Charles Dickens), does indeed draw the reader onward, if he or she is not deflected by the epistolary introductions. It also leads to shifting sympathies. At first we have little reason, other than a hint or two, to find fault with Marmion, who is on some sort of peace mission from his king. The mysterious palmer, of course, must have a relevant background tale, but we cannot be sure what it is for a while, and for all we know he could be an agent of evil. Even Constance gains our sympathy, as she faces her hideous and barbaric punishment without flinching and makes reparation for her collaboration in what was after all a love-driven crime. In the end Marmion, though he deserves to die for his crime, dies nobly, fighting loyally for the right cause.

Though the subtitle is *A Tale of Flodden Field*, the battle takes up only a few stanzas of the final canto. It is described mainly as it would be seen by Clara, standing near a cross on the side of a hill with a view of the entire field. It is thus more picturesque than grim, with acts of valor on both sides, though it is made clear that the Scots were beaten traumatically (King James was among the killed): the scattered survivors flee north

> To tell red Flodden's dismal tale,
> And raise the universal wail.
> Tradition, legend, tune, and song
> Shall many an age that wail prolong;
> Still from the sire the son shall hear
> Of that stern strife and carnage drear
> Of Flodden's fatal field,
> Where shivered was fair Scotland's spear
> And broken was her shield!

(6.1058–66)

The Scots certainly have Scott's sympathies, but he seems to accept that Scotland's defeat was the better outcome. James IV invaded England in the first place in part out of his obligation to the "Auld Alliance" with France. Scott makes the alliance seem a product of misplaced gallantry:

> the fair Queen of France
> Sent him a turquois ring and glove,
> And charged him, as her knight and love,
> For her to break a lance;
> And strike three strokes with Scottish brand,
> And march three miles on Southron land,
> And bid the banners of his band
> In English breezes dance.
> And thus, for France's Queen he drest
> His manly limbs in mailed vest

(5.269–78)

We have already seen, in the Scottish camp, "culverins [cannons] which France had given. / Ill-omened gift!" (4.558–9). At the time of writing, however (1807–8), France is again at war, this time not with England only but with the United Kingdom. In his first introduction Scott sings the praises of two war heroes, Horatio Nelson, commander at the decisive victory of Trafalgar, where he was killed (1805), and William Pitt, prime minister at his death in 1806. Napoleon he calls "that dragon" (Intro. 3.59). Scott was never attracted to the French Revolution, as Blake, Wordsworth, Coleridge, and so many others were, and Napoleon's conquest of most of Europe only confirmed his anti-Gallican feelings. It became part of his own war effort, then, to portray the Scots as noble but misled, and to show that, though enemies on the field, the Scots and the English have always been brothers under the skin. In his eyes even the bloody slaughter of Flodden Field, as Richard Cronin has recently argued, was "a lover's quarrel."[9] Together, in a united kingdom, where Scots are fully integrated as Britons, and honored for their courage and gallantry in their admittedly childish resistance to English domination in the past, they make one family, one nation on one island, in a struggle to the death with their real enemy across the water.

Byron's *Childe Harold's Pilgrimage: A Romaunt*

The title of *Childe Harold's Pilgrimage* would invite us to take it as a romance even without the subtitle, for "childe" (variously spelled) was used by Spenser and Shakespeare, and by Percy in his *Reliques*, to mean a young noble awaiting knighthood, while pilgrims, as the palmer in *Marmion* reminds us, were staple romance figures. And yet the subtitle, an archaic version of "romance," seems overdone, rather like the pseudo-archaic spelling of Coleridge's "Rime of the Ancyent Marinere." Surely Byron, whose public persona was witty and worldly, is mocking the medieval trappings of Coleridge and Scott, as if he is saying, "Here is a medieval romance I dug up somewhere, and if you believe that, then I'm King Arthur." He manages to keep up quasi-medieval diction and spellings for just the first few stanzas, in any case, with just a sprinkling afterward, and the point where he abandons them is about where he also abandons the pretext that his poem is a romance at all, as we shall see. Still, the romance form attracted him at first as the vehicle for a poem about a burnt-out young man who goes traveling, and even after he drops the pretext he retains the Spenserian stanza through all four cantos composed over a period of six years. It may in fact have been the Spenserian stanza that attracted him the most, with its interlocking rhymes – only three for nine lines (**ababbcbcc**) – and its long final line that tends to seal off each stanza from the others. As he states in the preface to the first two cantos, the stanza "admits of every variety," and he quotes William Beattie on the subject, whose long poem *The Minstrel, or The Progress of Genius* (1771–2), is something of a model for *Childe Harold*, not only for its Spenserians but also for its record of the wandering progress of its hero. Another precedent for Spenserians is James Thomson's *The Castle of Indolence* (1748), as Byron notes; he does not note, and may not have known, of Wordsworth's use of the stanza in several poems. His own mastery of it in *Childe Harold*, his deployment of it for "every variety" of subject and mood, inspired Shelley to use it brilliantly in *Laon and Cythna* and again in "Adonais" (1821), the elegy for Keats, who used it himself in *The Eve of St. Agnes*. The Spenserian revival, though it began in the Sensibility era, reaches its full flowering among the Romantics.

Byron may have felt the absurdity, after his initial enthusiasm, of pretending his hero is medieval when he travels not to Flodden Field in 1513 but to Saragossa, scene of terrible fighting between the Spanish and the French in 1809. Byron, or rather the narrator, who seems a lot like Byron, also loses interest in his hero altogether – "But where is Harold?" he asks (2.136), as if he had mislaid him somewhere, and again, "Where is he, the Pilgrim of my song[?]" (4.1468) – and becomes more absorbed in describing scenes in Spain, Albania, Greece, the battlefield of Waterloo, the Rhine, the Alps, Venice, Rome, and so on, and philosophizing about what he sees. The romance jacket sloughs off like a chrysalis as a different creature emerges, a kind of travelogue or loco-descriptive poem but unlike any seen before. It caused a sensation, and when the first two cantos appeared in 1812 Byron "woke to find himself famous."

The first two cantos each begin with what we might call a failed invocation to the muse which is modest, rueful, and cleverly self-assertive all at once, typical of the poem as a whole.

> Oh, thou! in Hellas deem'd of heavenly birth,
> Muse! form'd or fabled at the minstrel's will!
> Since shamed full oft by later lyres on earth,
> Mine dares not call thee from thy sacred hill:
> Yet there I've wander'd by thy vaunted rill;
> Yes! sigh'd o'er Delphi's long deserted shrine,
> Where, save that feeble fountain, all is still;
> Nor mote my shell awake the weary Nine
> To grace so plain a tale—this lowly lay of mine.

(1.10–18)

In the same spirit as Scott, who disparages his "idle lay" in the introductory epistles, Byron labels his plain tale a "lowly lay," too lowly to warrant awakening the nine Muses. This routine gesture of modesty sits beside another commonplace, the decline of poetry since the Greeks, which has two dimensions: (a) the Greeks no longer worship their gods and visit their oracles, and as a result there is no more Greek poetry, and (b) a large number of poets ("full oft") since the Greeks have nonetheless invoked the Muses in poems that only shame the Muses with the poets' mediocrity. The Muses have been awakened too often; Byron will let the weary Nine sleep. This dismissal of centuries of bad pseudo-classical verse out of concern for the poor over-invoked Muses is amusing enough, but it is all the more arch for conceding that they do not really exist, being "form'd or fabled at the minstrel's will." Then, however, Byron one-ups all these indifferent poets by letting drop that he has a better title than most to invoke the Muses after all, for he has been near their home, the sacred Mount Parnassus, and wandered by their rill, the Castalian Spring, and no doubt drunk from it, at Delphi. He tiptoes past the Muses, but he will do much in the poem that follows to awaken the ancient Greek spirit. In a final little twist, when he comes to Greece late in the canto and stands before Parnassus, he asks it, "What marvel if I thus essay to sing?" (1.617). In a note he tells us that "These stanzas were written in Castri (Delphos), at the foot of Parnassus." Yet even so he does not disturb the Muses' rest, for he will not "raise my voice, nor vainly dare to soar, / But gaze beneath thy cloudy canopy / In silent joy to think at last I look on Thee!" (1.627–9).

The second canto begins with a not quite invocation to Athena:

> Come, blue-eyed maid of heaven!—but thou, alas!
> Didst never yet one mortal song inspire—
> Goddess of Wisdom! here thy temple was,

And is, despite of war and wasting fire,
And years, that bade thy worship to expire:
But worse than steel, and flame, and ages slow,
Is the dread sceptre and dominion dire
Of men who never felt the sacred glow
That thoughts of thee and thine on polish'd breasts bestow.

(2.1–9)

It is not strictly true that Athena never inspired a song – there is a fragment
of a Homeric Hymn to Athena, for instance – but the point is a good one: the
goddess of wisdom has been neglected in song as her temple in Athens has
been allowed to fall into ruin by men who never felt wisdom's sacred glow. It
is Aphrodite who inspires most songs; wisdom cannot possibly compete with
that fickle goddess of fleeting passions. The upshot of Aphrodite's grip on us,
as the story of the Judgment of Paris reminds us, was the destruction of Troy.
Nonetheless, here is Byron, standing before the Parthenon, about which he
will have much to say. In the rest of the poem, moreover, he offers us a good
deal of wisdom: meditations on the brevity and misery of life, on the vanity
of ambition for worldly glory, the passing of great empires into ruin, and the
partial consolations of love, loyalty, courage, and wild nature.

To return to the opening of the first canto, after the "invocation" we are
offered the background to what appears to be the beginning of a long story:

Whilome in Albion's isle there dwelt a youth,
Who ne in virtue's ways did take delight;
But spent his days in riot most uncouth,
And vex'd with mirth the drowsy ear of Night.
Oh, me! in sooth he was a shameless wight,
Sore given to revel and ungodly glee;
Few earthly things found favour in his sight
Save concubines and carnal companie,
And flaunting wassailers of high and low degree.

(1.10–18)

It is easy to see why Byron soon gave up the fake medieval or Spenserian diction, but for a few stanzas he has some fun with it. Witty phrases, such as "ungodly glee" and "concubines and carnal companie," might never have enriched
the English language had he not tried to write in this half-foreign tongue. A
"whilome" or two reappear late in canto two, as Byron seems to have reminded
himself from time to time of his original pretext, but as the narrator emerges as
the central figure, absorbing into himself the traits he had assigned to Harold,
the archaisms drop away.[10] And so does any sense that we are going to hear the

romance of Childe Harold, like that of Spenser's Redcrosse Knight or Scott's Marmion. Between Harold and the narrator, however, we meet the first version of what came to be known as the "Byronic hero." He wastes his noble youth in dissipation, after which a chilling blast of misery blows upon him as he discovers "the fulness of satiety" (1.34) and wants to flee his native land. This would be just another version of the "spleen" or melancholy that was already well known in his day (we have borrowed the French word *ennui* for it, as the French have borrowed "spleen"), but Harold has an additional agony: he "sigh'd to many though he loved but one, / And that loved one, alas! could ne'er be his" (1.39–40). We are given a large hint that the one is his sister, for it would have been "pollution" for her to be embraced by him, and he "spoil'd her goodly lands to gild his waste" (1.42, 44). Sick at heart, he hides his feelings out of pride, and confides in no one, for no one was his friend; his revelry is just a momentary distraction from his woes.

And so he sets out. If this were the ordinary kind of pilgrimage, he would be traveling to some shrine or church or sacred spot, but this seems to be a pilgrimage *away* from home, not toward anywhere. At the end of a song he sings with his guitar and addresses the ship he is now aboard: "Nor care what land thou bear'st me to, / So not again to mine" (1.192–3). He has to go somewhere, of course, and he treats a few of the sights he sees as shrines (the Parthenon, Waterloo, some urns and memorial stones), so we might say he turns his negative pilgrimage into a positive one as he goes, but there is no ultimate destination. After a stay in Portugal, for instance, "Onward he flies, nor fix'd as yet the goal / Where he shall rest him on his pilgrimage" (1.328–9). In the first two stanzas of the third canto the narrator says, "I depart, / Whither I know not" (3.7–8); "for I am as a weed, / Flung from the rock on Ocean's foam, to sail / Where'er the surge may sweep, the tempest's breath prevail" (3.16–18). He is one of the "wanderers o'er Eternity / Whose bark drives on and on, and anchor'd ne'er shall be" (3.669–70). This going for going's sake may not have been unprecedented in literature, but it felt new, and Harold's gesture inspired many later characters, especially Americans, such as Ishmael in Melville's *Moby-Dick*, who can only shake off the "spleen" by taking ship (where he meets, of course, the Byronic hero Ahab), or Sal Paradise and Dean Moriarty in Kerouac's *On the Road*.

If he has no settled destination, he makes good use of the places he visits. The desolate Portuguese villa once inhabited by the writer William Beckford provides "Fresh lessons to the thinking bosom" (3.285) about the vanity and brevity of human pleasures. Traveling through the mountains, "he learn'd to moralize, / For Meditation fix'd at times on him" (3.319–20). And indeed, amidst vivid descriptions of colorful places, the poem gives a good deal of space to moralizing meditations on the vanity of honor and glory, the point-lessness and sheer misery of war (with a few heroic exceptions), the decline of human character from a more noble age in the past (especially in Portugal and Greece), and the solace and beauty of unspoiled nature. These are not new ideas; what matters is the freshness of phrasing and the way they arise from unusual locales. At several points he asks, "Where are they now?" – a com-monplace as old as Medieval Latin literature (*ubi sunt* …). "Oh, lovely Spain! renown'd, romantic land! / Where is that standard which Pelagio bore[?]" (3.387–8). "Oh! where, Dodona! is thine aged grove, / Prophetic fount, and oracle divine?" (2.469–70). More poignantly for him, as he stands before the Parthenon in canto two the narrator asks,

> Ancient of days! august Athena! where,
> Where are thy men of might? thy grand in soul?
> Gone—glimmering through the dream of things that were:
> First in the race that led to Glory's goal,
> They won, and pass'd away—is this the whole?
> A schoolboy's tale, the wonder of an hour!
>
> (2.10–15)

He dwells at such length and with such feeling on the decline of Greece under its various foreign occupations that it feels like the central theme of these two cantos, almost as if the Parthenon were the goal of his pilgrimage after all.

Byron is excellent at invective, polemic, and satirical wit, and he enlists these skills in an attack on Lord Elgin, the Scotsman who contrived to bring the bulk of the Parthenon friezes and metopes to Britain. (See Chapter 4, page 84.)

> But who, of all the plunderers of yon fane
> On high, where Pallas linger'd, loth to flee
> The latest relic of her ancient reign,—
> The last, the worst, dull spoiler, who was he?
> Blush, Caledonia! such thy son could be!
>
> (2.91–5)

Lord Elgin is "Cold as the crags upon his native coast, / His mind as barren and his heart as hard" (2.102–3). Britain, which should have protected Athena's rel-ics, "bears / The last poor plunder from a bleeding land" (2.113–14). The power of these indignant stanzas, and their explicit topicality, bring home that this poem, at least for the moment, is no longer a romance, no longer a travelogue, and no longer a meditation among ruins. It is a vehicle for whatever Byron wants to talk about, in whatever tone seems right to him, including the sort of thing he might have written for a newspaper editorial or given as a speech in the

House of Lords. By this time the reader is well advised to relax whatever expectations he or she still harbors for the shape, moral, and even the subject matter of this poem. Its rewards are no smaller for being taken piecemeal.

Byron devotes forty-five stanzas, more than a third of canto two, to Albania, which few Britons had ever visited (no doubt one of the reasons Byron chose to go there). His descriptions of customs and costumes of the fiercely proud and independent Albanians are still interesting, and would have played well to the growing British fascination with the "Orient," by which the Muslim world was meant, including North Africa and even Spain, which had been under Moorish domination for much of the Middle Ages. Among others Robert Southey had fed this appetite for things eastern with his epic-romances *Thalaba the Destroyer* (1801), set in Arabia, and *The Curse of Kehama* (1810), set in India. The year before *Childe Harold* appeared, Scott joined in with *The Vision of Don Roderick* (1811), in Spenserian stanzas; set at the time of the Moorish invasion of Spain, Don Roderick, the last Gothic king, has a vision of future events right up to Wellington's Spanish victories over the French. As Southey had been to neither Arabia nor India (though he had been to Portugal and Spain), and Scott traveled very little, we can imagine Byron taking pride in actually being present at the places he writes about and, as in the "invocation" of canto one, outdoing his rivals. In any case he rode the Orientalist craze with a vengeance upon finishing the first two parts of *Childe Harold*, with his "Turkish Tales" *The Giaour* (1813), *The Corsair* (1814), *The Bride of Abydos* (1814), and *The Siege of Corinth* (1816), all immensely popular with the public.[11]

The Albania sections also serve to show what the ancient Greeks might have been like and to contrast the independent Albanians with the downtrodden Greeks of today. Right after he presents a warlike Albanian song ("unsheathe then our chief's scimitar") Byron takes us back to Greece, where we remain until the final few stanzas, which are addressed to the nameless beloved of the opening.

> Fair Greece! sad relic of departed worth!
> Immortal, though no more; though fallen, great!
> Who now shall lead thy scatter'd children forth,
> And long accustom'd bondage uncreate?
> Not such thy sons who whilome did await,
> The hopeless warriors of a willing doom,
> In bleak Thermopylae's sepulchral strait

(2.693–9)

Readers who have seen the 2007 movie *300*, though it is a grotesque caricature of the historical facts, will appreciate the significance of Thermopylae. As

Byron was writing, the Ottoman Turks occupied much of the ancient Persian Empire, though not Persia itself, and represented the sort of oriental despotism the ancient Greeks more than once repelled. Today there is no Leonidas to lead a new Greek resistance, no Moses to lead the children of Greece out of bondage. Instead, "Nor rise thy sons, but idly rail in vain, / Trembling beneath the scourge of Turkish hand" (2.708–9). They may dream of freedom, but they "fondly sigh" for foreign arms to free them (2.717), forgetting that "Who would be free themselves must strike the blow" (2.721). Some other empire might well defeat the Ottomans, but freedom cannot be conferred on slaves. Byron then changes the scene to Istanbul at Carnival time among the Christians there, and seems for five stanzas to have abandoned his theme, but then he asks, "midst the throng in merry masquerade, / Lurk there no hearts that throb with secret pain[?]" (2.774–5). If there are such hearts, they are silent. Only ruins remain, and the beauty of the natural environment: "Thy vales of evergreen, thy hills of snow, / Proclaim thee Nature's varied favourite now" (2.803–4). And of course the written legacy, the unmatched poetry, philosophy, and history: "Long shall thine annals and immortal tongue / Fill with thy fame the youth of many a shore" (2.859–60). It is for these that "pilgrims" will come to Greece (2.856).

In canto four Byron wanders amidst an even grander set of ruins, those of ancient Rome, meditations on which had already made up a long poetic tradition. There he dwells less on the need to throw off a foreign occupier than on the sheer scale of the confused stones and rubble. The vast destruction of which they tell makes our own woes seem trivial.

> Oh Rome! my country! city of the soul!
> The orphans of the heart must turn to thee,
> Lone mother of dead empires! and control
> In their shut breasts their petty misery.

> (4.694–7)

In canto three he had likened certain ruins to human spirits – "And there they stand, as stands a lofty mind, / Worn, but unstooping to the baser crowd" (3.415–16); "By a lone wall a lonelier column rears / A grey and grief-worn aspect of old days" (3.617–18) – and earlier in canto four he had called himself "A ruin amidst ruins" (4.219), but here in overwhelming Rome, where "the very sepulchres lie tenantless" (4.708), he abandons such sentimental display. As he muses amidst the ruins of the Palatine Hill, while owls hoot in the evening, he asks "Upon such a shrine / What are our petty griefs?—let me not number mine" (4.953–4).

Rome's ruins are doubly poignant because in its prime Rome saw even older ruins as it conquered the world. Byron writes of Servius Sulpicius, who wrote a letter to Cicero describing the ruins of Greece. "That page is now before me, and on mine / *His* country's ruin added to the mass / Of perish'd states he mourn'd in their decline" (4.406–8). And Rome was the model for a thousand petty empires that have made Europe miserable. Only one man came close to Rome's power and glory, but he was "vanquish'd by himself, to his own slaves a slave" (4.801), Napoleon, "a kind / Of bastard Caesar" (4.802–3) brought low by vanity. Pondering this impressive but fleeting revival of the Roman Empire, after brooding on the disintegration of the original, Byron offers a bleak summary of what life offers: "What from this barren being do we reap? / Our sense narrow, and our reason frail, / Life short, and truth a gem which loves the deep" (4.829–31). The political world is worse than ever, as Europe is once again tyrannized by kings, "who are grown / The apes of him who humbled once the proud" (4.852–3). All of Napoleon's colossal battles accomplished nothing.

Though we noted earlier that the misery and futility of war was a commonplace – indeed it had been the theme of a good deal of British antiwar poetry in the 1790s[12] – as the war with Napoleon went on the tenor of published poetry largely shifted, partly under Scott's influence, to the celebration of martial heroism. Even in the first two cantos, however, which were published well before Napoleon's final defeat, Byron declines to join in the celebration. He appreciates heroism, and devotes a few stanzas to those who died nobly, but he never loses sight of war's enormous costs. Here he is still in Spain:

> By Heaven! it is a splendid sight to see
> (For one who hath no friends, no brother there)
> Their rival scarfs of mix'd embroidery,
> Their various arms that glitter in the air!
> What gallant war-hounds rouse them from their lair,
> And gnash their fangs, loud yelling for the prey!
> All join the chase, but few the triumph share;
> The Grave shall bear the chiefest prize away,
> And Havoc scarce for joy can number their array.

(1.432–40)

The irony of "splendid" is not very subtle, as the parenthetical second line tells us how detached we have to be to see anything splendid in a battle, while "gallant war-hounds" is wittily but bluntly sarcastic. These are presumably metaphorical hounds, "the dogs of war,"[13] who join the chase in large numbers, but only a few will triumph, really only two, the allegorical figures The Grave and Havoc, versions of Death. The Grave will win the "chiefest prize," that is, the greatest number of soldiers, while Havoc's share is beyond numbering. The superficial splendor of the scarves and glittering arms yields abruptly to the basic truth, and only Death's minions are happy in the end.

Near the beginning of canto three Byron halts at another ruin – "Stop!—for thy tread is on an Empire's dust" (3.145) – the battlefield of Waterloo. His thoughts about Napoleon here are more complex than the verdict he will deliver in canto four: "There sunk the greatest, nor the worst of men" (4.316). His thoughts about war, however, remain disillusioned. After praising the gallantry of a cousin of his who died at Waterloo, he considers the "ghastly gap" he made, like thousands of other soldiers, "in his own kind and kindred, whom to teach / Forgetfulness were mercy for their sake" (3.272–4). Glory will not revive the fallen: "though the sound of Fame / May for a moment soothe, it cannot slake / The fever of vain longing" (3.276–7). The field at Waterloo may fill up with monuments, but they will not comfort the bereaved.

Byron sometimes grants the justice of warfare if it is a defensive war on behalf of freedom, as it was when the Greeks fought the Persians and the Swiss fought the Burgundians (see 608–16). He praises tyrannicide, too: "all that most endears / Glory, is when the myrtle wreathes a sword / Such as Harmodius drew on Athens' tyrant lord" (178–80). These deserve their fame, and he would help enlarge it. But he despises the great majority of military heroes and all the emperors of history. If he could, he would obliterate them from memory, and he is happy that "Time's ungentle tide" (1.332) often does so.

Byron gave a good deal of thought to fame, especially after he acquired quite a bit of it himself, and to the role poets have played in celebrating and preserving the fame of heroes. He knew by heart (in Latin) the famous lines of Horace: "Many brave men have lived before Agamemnon, / but, unwept and unknown, they are all crushed / under eternal night / because they have no sacred poet" (*Odes* 4.9.25–8).[14] Cicero at Achilles' tomb cried, "O fortunate youth, to have found Homer as the herald of your glory!" (*Pro Archia* 24). As Byron contemplates the ruined castles of warlords on the Rhine, he asks what makes a "robber chief" a revered hero: "What want these outlaws conquerors should have, / But History's purchased page to call them great?" (3.429–30). Since poets, especially epic poets, have provided such outlaws as Agamemnon and Achilles the purchased page they needed to preserve (or indeed create) their glory, he might have felt called upon to undo some of the damage of his predecessors and reduce the stature of the bloodsoaked "great." He does not push this project as far as his friend Shelley, who wanted to obliterate the name and fame of tyrants and warriors altogether and was led into near paradoxical tangles, as we saw with the very title of "Ozymandias" in Chapter 6. Byron simply denounces the conquerors and despots, turning their fame into infamy, and he also singles out for praise a few noble souls who deserve more fame than they have. "For these are deeds which should not pass away, / And names that must not wither, though the

earth / Forgets her empires with a just decay" (2.635–7). And he praises quite
a few poets themselves.

In canto four Byron describes the home and tomb of Petrarch, whom he
names only as "Laura's lover" (4.264),

> both plain
> And venerably simple, such as raise
> A feeling more accordant with his strain
> Than if a pyramid form'd his monumental fane.

(4.276–9)

As we noted in the discussion of "Ozymandias," pyramids have been symbols
of futile vainglory since at least Horace, who proclaimed that his own fame
as a poet will outlive them. Milton asked what need Shakespeare has for a
"stary-pointing pyramid" when he lives on in "our wonder and astonishment"
("On Shakespeare").[15] After an account of Sante Croce in Florence and the
noble dead entombed within, Byron scolds "Ungrateful Florence!" for banish-
ing their greatest poet, Dante (4.505). She is now reduced to begging Ravenna
to return his bones. "What is her pyramid of precious stones" that "encrust
the bones / Of merchant-dukes?" (4.532–5). When he speaks of Torquato
Tasso, emprisoned for years by Duke Alfonso d'Este of Ferrara, Byron makes
an ironic twist on Horace's point about Agamemnon and his poet-publicist in
a brilliant set of stanzas:

> And Tasso is their glory and their shame.
> Hark to his strain and then survey his cell!
> And see how dearly earn'd Torquato's fame,
> And where Alfonso bade his poet dwell:
> The miserable despot could not quell   320
> The insulted mind he sought to quench, and blend
> With the surrounding maniacs, in the hell
> Where he had plunged it. Glory without end
> Scatter'd the clouds away—and on that name attend

> The tears and praises of all time; while thine   325
> Would rot in its oblivion—in the sink
> Of worthless dust, which from thy boasted line
> Is shaken into nothing; but the link
> Thou formest in his fortunes bids us think
> Of thy poor malice, naming thee with scorn—   330
> Alfonso! how thy ducal pageants shrink
> From thee! if in another station born,
> Scarce fit to be the slave of him thou mad'st to mourn:

> *Thou!* form'd to eat, and be despised, and die,
> Even as the beasts that perish, save that thou 335
> Hadst a more splendid trough and wider sty:
> *He!* with a glory round his furrow'd brow,
> Which emanated then, and dazzles now

To readers today (outside Italy, at any rate), for whom Tasso himself is little more than a name, the praise may seem excessive, and probably due in part to the very ill-treatment he seems to have endured – part of the cult of the suffering poet we discussed in Chapter 2 – but the abuse of Alfonso is splendid. Perhaps only a lord like Byron could so crushingly insult another lord, whether Elgin or Este; he must have longed to face them with a pistol or rapier. "Glory without end" has a religious connotation, as if heaven has replied to the "hell" of Tasso's cell; the glory around Tasso's brow is a halo. Alfonso is not even worthy of hell, it would seem, being little more than a pig with "a more splendid trough and wider sty." We would forget this disgusting beast if his name were not linked with Tasso's. Byron may have noticed as he wrote this wonderful invective that he himself was helping to keep Alfonso's name alive, rather as Shelley has preserved that of Ozymandias, and that thought may have led him to heap more abuse on him. In "The Curse of Minerva" Byron mentions one Eratostratus, the man who burnt down the Temple of Diana at Ephesus in 356 BCE, as an ancient counterpart of Lord Elgin the vandal. He seems not to have remembered that Eratostratus' motive was to become famous and that the Ephesian authorities therefore banned his name. Of course the name got out, though Byron got it wrong (it was Herostratus). Perhaps the Ephesians had a good idea, however hopeless enforcing such a ban might be, but what can you do to a name, like Alfonso d'Este, that is already known? Perhaps only what Byron does: remind his shade that it would rot in oblivion if the man he tortured were not a glorious poet.

What does Childe Harold learn on his pilgrimage? Has he changed? Surely not very much. He does not appear at all in canto four until nearly the end, at line 1468!

> But where is he, the Pilgrim of my song,
> The being who upheld it through the past?
> Methinks he cometh late and tarries long.

Indeed. Byron cannot resist a last little joke, and even resorts to quasi-medieval English again to make it (with inconsistent verb endings).

> He is no more—these breathings are his last;
> His wanderings done, his visions ebbing fast,
> And he himself as nothing

Byron did not need him in the last and longest canto and, as if he suddenly remembered his obligation to the title of his poem, he brings him up only to lay him to rest. He is mentioned again in the final stanza (with another little medieval phrase, "sandal-shoon") in a formal farewell.

Well, then, does Byron (or the narrator) learn anything or grow in spirit? Certainly canto four sounds different. There are very few archaisms besides those we have just noted. The verse is more complex in diction and syntax, and stanzas are linked together in twos and threes more tightly, not just by the argument but also by enjambment. Enjambment is the running of a clause across the stanza break, as we saw in the stanzas we have just quoted: "and on that name attend // The tears and praises of all time" (4.324–5). It is as if Byron has outgrown not only Harold but the Spenserian stanza as well, which is not well suited to this stringing out of sentences across the long alexandrine line. As for spiritual growth, we can see some signs of it amidst the repetition of war-inspired and ruin-prompted thoughts common to the first three cantos. As he visits St. Peter's in Rome, for example, its vast size and great artistic adornments prompt reflections on the power of the human mind:

> Enter: its grandeur overwhelms thee not;
> And why? it is not lessen'd; but thy mind
> Expanded by the genius of the spot,
> Has grown colossal

> (4.1387–90)

Our senses can only take it in "piecemeal" and with "gradual grasp" (4.1405, 1415), but "growing with its growth, we thus dilate / Our spirits to the size of that they contemplate" (4.1421–2). "The fountain of sublimity" (4.1429) that created the cathedral draws out a comparable fountain in our spirits as we take it in. This theory of the sublime is worthy of the Wordsworth who wrote "Tintern Abbey" and *The Prelude*. And it prepares us for Byron's great apostrophe to the ocean – "Roll on, thou deep and dark blue Ocean—roll!" (4.1603) – which dwells on the puniness of man and the brevity and inconsequence of all his works beside the vast unchangeable sea – "boundless, endless, and sublime—/ The image of Eternity—the throne / Of the Invisible" (4.1643–5). As he thinks about the ocean, on which Childe Harold had impulsively set out several years ago, Byron the narrator grasps a deep truth about the infinite being that underlies both the material world and the human spirit. It is not something that can be put into words, but it seems consoling or conciliatory, like the enlightenment of a Buddhist sage.

There are other moments of insight and reflection that extend those of the earlier cantos, but there is one passage that seems to be the moral climax of the poem, something quite unexpected and new. Throughout the poem either Harold or the poet has expressed his sorrow, his alienation from his fellow human beings, his inexpressible "Byronic" guilt. Now, late in canto four, as he sits in the Roman Colosseum, Byron turns to Time and addresses it as the comforter, the corrector, the avenger: "unto thee I lift / My hands, and eyes, and heart, and crave of thee a gift" (4.1169–70). He then calls on Nemesis, the Greek spirit of retribution, to hear his heart. He admits he may have been at fault for the nameless wound he bleeds from, and he would let it bleed freely "had it been conferr'd / With a just weapon" (4.1191–2), but "*thou* [Nemesis] shalt take / The vengeance" that he himself has not taken (4.1191–5). He will speak, however:

> But in this page a record will I seek.
> Not in the air shall these my words disperse,
> Though I be ashes; a far hour shall wreak
> The deep prophetic fulness of this verse,
> And pile on human heads the mountain of my curse!
>
> That curse shall be Forgiveness.—Have I not—
> Hear me, my mother Earth! behold it, Heaven!—
> Have I not had to wrestle with my lot?
> Have I not suffer'd things to be forgiven?   1210
> Have I not had my brain sear'd, my heart riven,
> Hopes sapp'd, name blighted, Life's life lied away?
> And only not to desperation driven,
> Because not altogether of such clay
> As rots into the souls of those whom I survey.

It is an astonishing gesture, and very theatrical. Because he first invokes Nemesis we expect a mighty Greek execration, or something like King Lear's curse of his daughters, but then we hear it is forgiveness, which should be the opposite of a curse. To forgive is certainly to forswear anything like a curse. There is a brilliant insight here: forgiveness can indeed be a kind of weapon in the spiritual arsenal of a Christian, while Gandhi and other pacifist leaders have learned to deploy nonretaliation for physical violence in a way that weakens, even humiliates, their oppressors. Byron's friend Shelley may well have been incited by this passage to imagine the chain of events whereby the mighty power Demogorgon is roused to drag down the tyrant Jupiter when Prometheus *withdraws* his curse.

Yet there is something unforgiving about this "Forgiveness." There is too much resentment, too much whining about how much he has suffered. He goes on to list "petty perfidy," "foaming calumny," and the "subtler venom" of "speechless obloquy" (4.1216–24). If he really forgives all then he should turn the page, not fill it with a record of his grievances. But he is only human, and not Christ (or Shelley's Prometheus), so he wants it both ways: the forgiveness that stings, "the late remorse of love" (4.1233). No doubt some terrible events in Byron's broken marriage lie behind these stanzas, but he nonetheless names no one and describes no particulars. His grievances are confined, though barely, within the decorum of generalities, and left mysterious, so that some readers might find his account applicable to their own lives. If they do, his example of forgiveness, though something of a hybrid force, might teach them a wise way forward.

The interest of *Childe Harold's Pilgrimage* lies in its distinct and separable sections. The war in Spain, the Albanians, Lord Elgin's pillaging, the battle of Waterloo, sublime moments in the Alps or St. Peter's, the curse of forgiveness – these accumulate in some ways, and prompt recurrent thoughts – but they do not cohere into anything very shapely. Byron was winging it, as he later improvised *Don Juan*, which might have gone on for a hundred cantos, had he lived, instead of stopping after sixteen. Of the four long poems we have considered in this chapter Byron's is least like an epic or romance in that it has no plot, and barely a protagonist. And yet it seems to have the "epic breadth" of Homer and Virgil well beyond what Wordsworth, Blake, and Scott convey. The whole of contemporary and ancient Europe is given to us through a distinctively Romantic, indeed "Byronic," sensibility.

Chapter 10

Romantic verse drama

Though comedies and tragedies were performed in several London theaters every night during the era of Romanticism, as well as in many other British cities, and audiences filled them with passionate applause or catcalls and eagerly read reviews of them in the newspapers, the prevalent view today is that the era was a low point in the history of British drama. Nothing from that time is still mounted on stage unless it is a revival by students at universities. Certain actors and actresses – Kemble, Kean, Siddons – are still remembered, but mainly for their roles in Shakespeare; the fact that they sometimes made temporary successes of new plays attests more to their skill or charisma than to the merits of the plays themselves, now forgotten.

The Romantic temperament, moreover, is often said to be antithetical to the-atrical expression or extroversion. Not for nothing was Hamlet seen as the most "Romantic" Shakespearean character: his long soliloquies, his dialogues with a ghost, and his overly articulated hesitations and dilemmas drew him to the hearts of audiences and readers and made them forget that he is in fact very active and violent. Indeed there was a tendency to prefer reading Shakespeare privately to watching his plays on stage. Charles Lamb, in an essay "On the Tragedies of Shakespeare, Considered with Reference to their Fitness for Stage-Representation" (1818), went so far as to say that Shakespeare's "absolute mastery over the heart and soul of man" has no connection with "those low tricks upon the eye and ear" an actor performs, and that "the plays of Shakespeare are less calculated for performances on a stage, than those of almost any other drama-tist whatever." If that judgment seems bizarre, it seems true of plays written by the Romantics themselves that they are best suited for reading, either silently alone or aloud among a circle of friends. Jerome McGann has recently argued that "The separation of the drama from the theatre is an index of Romanticism itself."[1] We might see this separation as a product of the "lyricization" of drama, as of the other genres, that I have discussed earlier.

Yet most of the major Romantic poets made attempts to write for the stage. Wordsworth did not at first think his play *The Borderers* (1796) suitable for public performance, but, encouraged by Coleridge, he revised it, submitted it to Covent Garden, and was rejected; he never tried another. Coleridge suffered some rejections himself, but a later play, *Remorse*, had a fairly successful run of twenty nights in 1813. Scott had no luck getting his plays staged commercially, but not for lack of effort. Keats's *Otho the Great*, a tragedy written jointly with his friend Charles Brown in 1819–20, was turned down by Covent Garden. Shelley's tragedy *The Cenci* (1819) was spurned for its themes of incest, rape, and parricide. Byron did a little better, especially after he died: *Sardanapalus* had a run of twenty-three nights in 1834, and in the same year *Manfred* was given a spectacular production. This does not amount to much. Whether the poets simply lacked the skill, or could not bring themselves to stoop to vulgar tastes, or were really lyric poets at heart, it is hard to resist the conclusion the Romantic spirit is not very theatrical.[2]

In this chapter, then, we will look at two verse dramas, or let us say two poems in dramatic form, that are central to the Romantic canon, Byron's *Manfred* (1817) and Shelley's *Prometheus Unbound* (1820). Their subtitles are revealing: Byron calls *Manfred* "A Dramatic Poem" while Shelley calls *Prometheus Unbound* "A Lyrical Drama."

Manfred

There would seem to be little reason to perform *Manfred* on the stage unless the sheer spectacle of Alpine summits, the hall of the god Arimanes, and the arrival and departure of various cosmic spirits will draw a paying audience, as apparently it did. The play has little action, and many of the speeches are either Manfred's monologues or his exchanges with spirits who seem projections of himself. The play is a gradual unfolding of Manfred's character and history, with an air of mystery – he has committed a great sin and his guilt torments him – but if the mystery holds our attention it is never fully explained. He is a nobleman of great gifts, courteous to his inferiors, but wrapt in solitude as he pursues his investigations into science and magic. Like Dr. Faustus, he acquires the power to summon all the spirits of the universe, and it is his contendings with these spirits that lend the play what dramatic power it has.

Byron denied that he knew either Marlowe's *Dr. Faustus* (1604) or Goethe's *Faust* (1808), but we know he heard some of Part I of the latter (Part II was not yet published) read aloud by Matthew Lewis, and soon Shelley was translating scenes from it. The original Faustus tale, preserved by Marlowe, has Faustus

make a pact with the devil, receiving twenty years of magical powers in pay-
ment for his immortal soul, during which he plays sophomoric tricks, inter-
feres with political affairs, discomfits the Pope, and conjures up Helen of Troy
to be his concubine. At the end, of course, he must deliver the goods, as the
devil tears him limb from limb and drags his soul to hell. Byron's Manfred has
made no such pact: as he insists when a spirit comes to take him, "my past
power / Was purchased by no compact with thy crew" (3.4.113–14) but only by
his own intellect and daring. He dies, but to die is what he wishes, and he dies
only after he banishes the last spirit. He summons up a beautiful woman, but it
is not Helen: it is the sister of his soul, Astarte, whose death of a "broken heart"
is the cause of his enormous and inexpiable guilt. Only she could forgive him
and bring him peace; no other power can offer him that.

In his superiority over the spirits Manfred resembles Goethe's hero Faust,
though Byron could not have known that Goethe planned to save Faust from
hell at the end because of his continual striving and restlessness. Goethe treats
the Christian framework of the original tale as so much allegorical furniture
to be shuffled about on behalf of a very different worldview. He himself saw in
Manfred the expression of the same "impelling principles" that governed his
own *Faust*; neither play, for instance, is remotely Christian. But the characters
of Manfred and Faust are very different from each other.

Manfred's opening soliloquy expresses the same despair that Faust feels over
the futility of knowledge: "The Tree of Knowledge is not that of Life" (1.2.12).
Philosophy and science "avail not," he has done good deeds and defeated his
foes but these acts also "avail'd not"; nothing has satisfied him "Since that all-
nameless hour" (24). It is a blunt gimmick, no doubt, to play on our curiosity
this way by making the cause of his torment "nameless" even to himself, but
at least we are duly forewarned that we will gather no more than hints about
it. It is so terrible a memory that Manfred calls on the "Spirits of earth and
air" (41) to appear so he can beg them for "Forgetfulness" (136), almost the
opposite of what Faust asks of Mephistopheles. A little later one of the spirits
assumes the shape of a beautiful woman, and when Manfred tries to embrace
her she vanishes and he falls senseless. A voice that sings over his sleeping
form tells us more of his sinful character – his "false tears" and "cold breast"
and "unfathom'd gulfs of guile" (232–42) – but we are still in the dark as to
what happened to this beautiful woman.

A good deal of this first scene, however, is given to the seven spirits of nature
that Manfred conjures up. Each has its song, which elaborates on the element it stands for, and Byron shows great skill in varying the meter and rhyme
scheme from song to song. They represent air, mountain, ocean, earth, wind,
night, and "The star which rules thy destiny" (110). These are things, except

for the last, that sometimes consoled Childe Harold, but they bring no relief to Manfred, for they cannot give oblivion to his soul, which is not a natural thing like them. In two later scenes, however, Byron softens this stern alienation from nature. As Act 3 opens Manfred feels an "Inexplicable stillness" unknown to him before, a sense of the "Kalon" (the Beautiful). In Scene 4, on the verge of his death, he lingers with the "loveliness" of the stars and moon, and remembers a similar night when he sat, like Harold, in the ruins of the Colosseum. But the main point Byron makes with the nature spirits remains firm throughout, that the human soul, or at least the soul of a lofty genius, is of a different order from nature and superior to it. Its strength, or weakness, comes entirely from within; nothing from outside, whether from nature or, as we see later when the Abbot tries to intervene, from religion, can help or harm it. Natural beauty offers at most only moments of rapt contemplation, distractions from suffering, but not its cure.

The burden of the play, then, lies more in this theme about the sovereignty or autonomy of the soul than in the solution to the mystery of Manfred's sin or the suspense over how or whether he will achieve forgetfulness. (An attempt at suicide at the summit of the Jungfrau is foiled by a well-meaning hunter in Act 1, Scene 2.) We do learn a little more about the sin. A glass of restorative wine looks like blood to Manfred, "my blood! the pure warm stream / Which ran in the veins of my fathers, and in ours / When we were in our youth, and had one heart, / And loved each other as we should not love, / And this was shed" (2.1.24–8). It sounds like incestuous love, but why was it shed? "My embrace was fatal" we learn a few moments later (87), but how? Details are tantalizingly doled out. In the next scene Manfred describes to the Witch of the Alps, another nature spirit, how much he and his sister (as we assume) looked alike and thought alike, though she was gentle and humble. "I loved her, and destroy'd her!" (2.2.117). "With thy hand?" the Witch asks. "Not with my hand, but heart – which broke her heart; / It gazed on mine, and wither'd" (117–19). When he asks Arimanes to summon Astarte's spirit he defines her as "One without a tomb" (2.4.82), another mystery, but perhaps implying that she committed suicide. This is about all we learn. It is intriguing enough, but we cannot begin to piece together a psychologically coherent story. The main point is that it is irrevocably in the past, it cannot be undone, and Manfred feels ineradicably blighted by it. It was all his doing, or the result of his character, and he has the double grief of having killed both an innocent beloved and the better part of himself. And so we are brought back to the theme of the soul's independence, to something like what the French existentialists a century later would call man's radical freedom, his transcendence of circumstance or external pressures. Man is always free, even in the face of torture, to say no.

This theme is brought out in the most theatrical if somewhat repetitive scene (2.4) set in the hall of Arimanes. This supreme spirit, the "Sovereign of Sovereigns" (23), is the Zoroastrian god Arimanes (usually spelled Ahriman today), the power of darkness and evil in that dualistic religion; Byron's stage direction describes him seated on a throne that is "a Globe of Fire." In his court has gathered an elaborate assembly of spirits, including three Destinies (from the three Fates of Greek mythology) and Nemesis. They begin by singing praises to Arimanes and professing their slavish loyalty. Then Manfred enters. A spirit cries, "Thou most rash and fatal wretch, / Bow down and worship!" and a second repeats the command; then all the spirits shout "Prostrate thyself" (29–34). Manfred calmly answers, "ye see I kneel not" and goes on to explain:

> many a night on the earth,
> On the bare ground, have I bow'd down my face,
> And strew'd my head with ashes; I have known
> The fullness of humiliation, for
> I sunk before my vain despair, and knelt
> To my own desolation.

(2.4.37–42)

He will not kneel to Arimanes but he has "knelt / To my own desolation," as if desolation were a kind of god; if so, the point seems to be that it is *his* god, himself, "my own desolation." Arimanes, whatever he represents—nature, it seems, in its destructiveness, as well as war – is an external force, and though it may kill Manfred it cannot compel his worship. When another spirit demands that he "Crouch!" Manfred's reply somewhat complicates our sense of his proud superiority: "Bid *him* bow down to that which is above him, / The overruling Infinite, the Maker / Who made him not for worship—let him kneel, / And we will kneel together" (46–9). So he acknowledges something higher than himself and Arimanes, the Creator of them both. A Christian (or Jew or Muslim) might find this a perfectly acceptable dismissal of an idol in favor of the true God. Byron, already criticized for his "Satanic" tendencies, may have thought it prudent to include a line or two like this. By the same token, when the Abbot comes to him in the next scene to try to reconcile him to the church, Byron is on safe enough ground when he has Manfred insist "I shall not choose a mortal / To be my mediator" (3.1.54–5), like a good Protestant. Yet the thrust of Manfred's stubborn assertion of self-sufficiency is not Christian, I think; it might be called Protestant atheism blended with a proud, aristocratic, pagan stoicism. For Manfred goes on to tell the Abbot that there is no power in prayer or penitence that can "exorcise / From out the unbounded spirit the quick sense / Of its own sins, wrongs, sufferance, and revenge / Upon itself" (73–6), while in the hall of Arimanes it is only the phantom of Astarte, who is a part of himself, that has any effect upon him.

I have dwelled on this theme more than on the question of what Manfred did to Astarte, or what they did together, or how she died, because the latter is so juicy a subject that it has often jostled out the former in the minds of readers and in scholarship on the play. There are scores of books about Byron's relations with his half-sister Augusta, nearly all of which recycle bits about Astarte (*Astarte*, indeed, was the title of one of them, by Byron's grandson), but they do not advance our understanding of *Manfred* one whit. Byron invited this sort of thing, it is true, both by his flamboyantly ungovernable behavior and by the hints he planted in many of his poems and plays. If *his* phantom were to be summoned and shown the gossipy books, he might feel dismay but could only (like Manfred) blame himself. In any case, we should not let our fascination with Manfred's sin, which is left studiously vague, blind us to the central theme of the soul's sovereignty over all suffering that comes upon it from outside.

Prometheus Unbound

While denying any influence from Faust or Faustus, Byron acknowledged that Prometheus was much on his mind as he wrote *Manfred*. Manfred himself, in his first encounter with the spirits, tells them

> The mind, the spirit, the Promethean spark,
> The lightning of my being, is as bright,
> Pervading, and far darting as your own,
> And shall not yield to yours, though coop'd in clay!

(1.1.154–7)

Byron had already written his poem "Prometheus," where he celebrates the great Titan, impaled on a rock and chewed by Zeus's vulture as punishment for stealing fire from Olympus and bringing it to the comfortless human race. He sees him as a symbol of man's "wretchedness, and his resistance." Like Manfred, Byron says, we can make our spirit

> equal to all woes,
> And a firm will, and a deep sense,
> Which even in torture can descry
> Its own concenter'd recompense,
> Triumphant where it dares defy,
> And making Death a Victory.

(1.1.54–9)

This stoic endurance and proud defiance Shelley also admired, but he considered it one-sided, a negative virtue. When he turned to the Prometheus myth himself he investigated a deeper question: what power can really triumph, and not just defy? What will it take to make even heroic rebelliousness no longer necessary?

Both Shelley and Byron studied the *Prometheus Bound* of Aeschylus.[3] That play begins with the chaining and impaling of Prometheus to a rock in "Scythia" by Zeus's minions. After a monologue by Prometheus complaining of his unjust punishment, a chorus of Ocean nymphs enters, and Prometheus tells them of the war between the Olympians and the Titans in which he, though a Titan, sided with the Olympians led by Zeus. But he defied Zeus's plan to obliterate the human race, and he gave it fire; for such insubordination he is tortured on the rock. Ocean appears, and offers to mediate if Prometheus will kneel to Zeus, but Prometheus proudly refuses. He recites to the chorus all his gifts to humankind. Then Io, in the form of a cow, rushes in, pursued by a gadfly, and tells how she has been punished by Zeus for refusing his overtures. Prometheus foretells her future sufferings and his own eventual release at the hands of her descendant Heracles. He also claims to know a secret, a fatal marriage Zeus will make unless he warns him off it. He predicts Zeus's downfall to the chorus, and then to Hermes, whom Zeus has sent to extract the secret. Hermes threatens Prometheus with Zeus's eagle, which will eat his liver every day, but the Titan defies all threats, and the play ends amid thunder and earthquakes. Nothing has been accomplished in this nearly actionless play except an intensification of the stalemate between two immortals.

This plot would seem to bear out Byron's view of Prometheus as a figure of unbowed but hopeless suffering, but Shelley was interested in the fact that the play was only one third of a trilogy, three plays performed together at the Athenian tragic festival, like Aeschylus' *Oresteia* trilogy, the only one that has come down to us. The other two plays of the *Prometheia* have been lost, but we know their titles and have scraps of quotations and plot summaries. Whether *Prometheus Bound* was the first play or the second, it was followed by one called *Prometheus Unbound*, in which Heracles kills the eagle and releases the Titan. Ancient commentators suggest that Prometheus struck a deal and revealed his secret – that the son of the sea nymph Thetis will be stronger than his father – just as Zeus was about to mate with her; she was then safely married off to a mortal named Peleus, and their son would be the great warrior Achilles. Shelley found this resolution dismaying, and he had no interest in simply reconstructing the lost play. He writes in his preface, "I was averse from a catastrophe so feeble as that of reconciling the Champion with the Oppressor of mankind. The moral interest of the fable, which is so powerfully sustained by the sufferings and endurance of Prometheus, would be annihilated if we could conceive of him as unsaying his high language and quailing before his successful and perfidious adversary." So Shelley set himself a higher task: to rewrite the missing play as Aeschylus ought to have written it, with the outcome reversed. The result is his masterpiece, the most ambitious expression of his philosophy and the most dazzling demonstration of his lyrical gifts.

His play begins where Aeschylus' play began (and ended), with Prometheus bound to a precipice, alone. In his preface to the play Shelley writes: "Prometheus is, as it were, the type of the highest perfection of moral and intellectual nature, impelled by the purest and the truest motives to the best and noblest ends."[4] In his opening speech he defiantly addresses the distant Jupiter (Shelley uses the Roman name for Zeus) and predicts that the hour will come that will drag the cruel king to Prometheus' feet, "which then might trample thee / If they disdained not such a prostrate slave. / Disdain? Ah no! I pity thee" (1.1.51–3). This change of heart from disdain to pity, and pity not for the human race but for his own torturer, is a decisive new element in the myth; it is the moral turning-point of the play, and it comes astonishingly early. Though the climax of the play, with its own ironic reversal, is the sudden overthrow of Jupiter in Act 3, Scene 1, all the action flows from Prometheus' initial change of mind with what in retrospect we can see as irresistible necessity. On first reading the play we might feel a suspenseful interest in what Jupiter will do, how Prometheus will respond, whether Prometheus' beloved Asia will accomplish her own mission, which side the monster Demogorgon is on, and so on, but there can be no uncertainty about the outcome. The whole of *Prometheus Unbound* is a denouement, an unknotting or unbinding of the plot that Aeschylus knitted, and if it troubles us that the unknotting should come at the beginning of the play, we should imagine we are reading the final play of a trilogy, which had knots enough in its first two parts.

Prometheus no longer hates. He now wishes to "recall" the curse he once breathed on Jupiter (1.1.59). Voices from the natural realm recite their memories of the devastating effects of the curse, because it caused a fall of nature as well as of humanity, like the sin of Adam and Eve. Prometheus demands to "hear that curse again" (131), but his mother the Earth tells him he cannot understand "the language of the dead" (138); she recounts how she rejoiced when she heard the curse that made the almighty tyrant grow pale and how mortals still preserve it as "a treasured spell" (184). When Prometheus insists, Earth tells him to summon a ghost to repeat the curse, and he calls on the Phantasm of Jupiter. Ione and Panthea, who are Oceanids and sisters of the beloved but absent Asia, begin their role as chorus, commenting on the awful shape that now appears. The Phantasm, as commanded, repeats the curse, in which Prometheus defied Jupiter to do his worst "on me and mine": "I curse thee! let a sufferer's curse / Clasp thee, his torturer, like remorse, / Till thine Infinity shall be / A robe of envenomed agony" (286–9). On hearing the curse, Prometheus says, "It doth repent me … I wish no living thing to suffer pain" (303–5). He thus completes and ratifies his change of heart.

The Earth laments, believing that Prometheus has been defeated. Mercury immediately arrives, just as Hermes arrived in *Prometheus Bound* upon hearing the prediction of Zeus's downfall. He demands to know the "secret" (1.1.371) and urges Prometheus to kneel in supplication, but Prometheus no more than Manfred will submit; Mercury threatens and tempts him to no avail, and admits he feels pity and remorse for him. Prometheus replies, "Pity the self-despising slaves of Heaven, / Not me, within whose mind sits peace serene" (429–30). The Furies then go to work. They represent spiritual or psychological torments, and they know their victim. They show Prometheus three scenes: man consumed in a feverish pursuit of knowledge, Prometheus' own gift; the gentle Christ, "Smiling on the sanguined earth; / His words outlived him, like swift poison / Withering up truth, peace and pity" at the hands of the established churches; and "a disenchanted nation," France, once a "band of linked brothers" but all too soon a land where "kindred murder kin" (542–77). These ought to make any decent soul despair, and Prometheus groans at the sights, but worse is in store. A Fury describes the condition of mortals today, where "Hypocrisy and custom make their minds / the fanes [temples] of many a worship, now outworn," those who have one virtue lack the others, "And all best things are thus confused to ill" (618–31). Prometheus replies, "Thy words are like a cloud of winged snakes; / And yet, I pity those they torture not" – those who are numb to humankind's sufferings. The astonished Fury exclaims, "Thou pitiest them? I speak no more!" and vanishes.

His newfound pity remains intact against the worst Jupiter can inflict. Indeed we come to see that what is at stake in this new and more furious struggle is less Prometheus' "secret" than his pity, for pity undermines the very basis of Jupiter's existence, and he will vanish just as abruptly as the Furies did if the factors that sustain him – hypocrisy, custom, hatred, fear, and contempt – are withdrawn or "recalled." For his part Prometheus grows stronger in his endurance and repeats his hope, or faith, that the "hour" will arrive (1.1.644). Earth now offers to cheer Prometheus by summoning the spirits of human thought as an answer to the Furies. Six of them speak individually, the first four representing rebellion against tyranny, generous self-sacrifice, wisdom of the past, and visionary poetry, while the last two report the struggle between love and "desolation" or despair. As a chorus they sing of spring's arrival after winter, and how the growth of wisdom, justice, love, and peace is a spring zephyr, the west wind. ("Ode to the West Wind" appeared in the same volume as the play.) Then they too vanish, but leave behind, as Panthea says, a musical resonance in the soul. Prometheus feels these spirits are all vain but love (808), and he turns his thoughts to Asia, now far away in an Indian vale. Dawn has come, and Panthea departs to find her.

Prometheus is absent from Act 2, which is entirely given to Asia's quest on his behalf; she plays a part a little like that of Ololon in Blake's *Milton*. In Scene 1 she is alone, expecting her sister to arrive at dawn, which she does, bearing "the delight of a remembered dream" (2.1.36), which is also "the music that I bear / Of thy most wordless converse" (52), as if she is simply the medium of love between Asia and Prometheus. Panthea reports her dream: Prometheus appeared transfigured by the shadow of love, his presence flowed into hers, and she heard Asia's name. Asia then "reads the dream" in Panthea's eyes, and sees Prometheus smiling with the hope "that we shall meet again" (124). A second dream, which Panthea had forgotten, now appears and cries, "Follow!" She recalls that she dreamt of early blossoms scattered by the north wind, each stamped with the words "O follow, follow!" (133–41). Asia remembers a similar dream. Echoes cry out, "follow!" Follow where? The Echoes sing: "In the world unknown / Sleeps a voice unspoken; / By thy step alone / Can its rest be broken, / Child of Ocean!" (190–4). They mean Demogorgon. And where is he? Asia must go "To the rents, and gulphs and chasms, / Where the Earth reposed from spasms / On the day when He and thou / Parted—to commingle now" (202–5), as if to heal the wounds that the original separation of love from Prometheus inflicted on the Earth. The journey will be a descent into a volcano.

The next two brief scenes bring the two sisters to the realm of Demogorgon.[5] A portal like a volcano's hurls up "oracular vapour" (2.3.4) like the intoxicating fumes at the oracle of Delphi, and a great change seems to be in the offing. Asia sees and hears the spring thaw unbinding the snow and thinks of Prometheus:

> Hark! the rushing snow!
> The sun-awakened avalanche! whose mass,
> Thrice sifted by the storm, had gathered there
> Flake after flake, in Heaven-defying minds
> As thought by thought is piled, till some great truth
> Is loosened, and the nations echo round,
> Shaken to their roots, as do the mountains now.

(2.3.36–42)

Scene 4 is set in the cave of Demogorgon, who is "a mighty Darkness / … / Ungazed upon and shapeless" (2.4.2–5). In a sort of reverse catechism, he instructs Asia by answering her questions with cryptic brevity, as if to draw out from her what she already knows in her own depths. Indeed the descent to Demogorgon is in part a descent into her own soul. He answers "God" to her first few questions, perhaps to suggest that "Who made X?" deserves no better reply. "I spoke but as ye speak," he explains later (112). If Asia is the embodiment of love set free by Prometheus' retraction of his curse, then one of her demands is surprising: "Utter his name—a world pining in pain / Asks but his name; curses shall drag him down" (29–30). That vengeful demand is perhaps a sign that, if Prometheus needs to reunite with love, Asia needs to reunite with wisdom, and that her dialogue in the depths is her preparation for the reunion. Demogorgon's refusal to utter the name prevents her from repeating Prometheus' original error.

Whether this is the right way to read this enigmatic scene is far from obvious, but Asia seems to gain some assurance from her interrogation. She then recites the long story of the genealogy of the gods. Under the reign of Saturn humans were happy but fainted for lack of wisdom. "Then Prometheus / Gave wisdom, which is strength" – not to mortals, as we would expect from the established myths, but "to Jupiter" (2.4.43–4). That seems to have been Prometheus' first disastrous error, more fundamental than the curse, for soon famine, toil, disease, and war fell upon the human race. Seeing their plight, Prometheus sent them hope, love, fire, speech, song, and all the arts and sciences. Now, "while / Man looks on his creation like a God, / And sees that it is glorious," someone or something "drives him on, / The wreck of his own will, the scorn of earth" (101–3). It cannot be Jupiter, she reasons, for "he trembled like a slave" when Prometheus cursed him (108). Demogorgon suggests that Jupiter is a slave to evil, but he still will not declare who or what the master is (if it is not evil itself), for "the deep truth is imageless." We might already have guessed that it is Prometheus, but Demogorgon hints that it is "Fate, Time, Occasion, Chance, and Change," or some principle underlying these, embodied perhaps in Demogorgon himself. Yet he then adds, "To these / All things are subject but eternal Love" (116–20), implying that Asia herself is at least their equal if not their superior. She asks one last question: when shall Prometheus arise? The answer: now! "Cars" (chariots) appear, one for each Hour. A charioteer with a dreadful face drives the Hour of Jupiter's eclipse, another with "dovelike eyes of hope" (160) is the Hour of Prometheus' release, and it will carry Asia and Panthea just behind the former. As they ride in their chariot toward Prometheus (Scene 5), Asia grows radiant with beauty, and she is described in terms that make her a new Aphrodite.

The climax of the drama is the overthrow of Jupiter in Act 3, Scene 1. It is interesting that Jupiter makes his only appearance in the scene of his disappearance, as if to imply that to see him clearly is to see through him. Also appearing for the only time is Thetis: she never speaks, but Jupiter quotes her anguished speech when he raped her, relishing the memory of his male pride, his "penetrating presence" (3.1.39). Like a good dramatic climax, Jupiter's overthrow comes at the moment he expects his power to be consolidated: "henceforth I am omnipotent" (3). He concedes that "The soul of man, like unextinguished fire" – Prometheus' gift – "Yet burns towards Heaven with fierce reproach and doubt / And lamentation and reluctant prayer, / Hurling up insurrection" (5–8), but now that Prometheus has withdrawn his curse Jupiter has no fears.

> Even now have I begotten a strange wonder,
> That fatal Child, the terror of the Earth,
> Who waits but till the destined Hour arrive,
> Bearing from Demogorgon's vacant throne
> The dreadful might of ever living limbs
> Which clothed that awful spirit unbeheld,
> To redescend, and trample out the spark

(3.1.18–24)

The ironies here are complex. Jupiter seems already to have learned the traditional (Aeschylean) secret of Prometheus and to have been undissuaded by it. He believes his fatal child is "mightier than either" of its parents, as he tells Thetis (44). So it becomes clear that the secret known to Prometheus, "Which may transfer the sceptre of wide Heaven" (373), has less to do with a possible child of Thetis than with "the destined Hour" (2) of the transfer, that is, that such a transfer is indeed destined. Jupiter thinks his son will act as a kind of Black Prince at his father's behest, snuffing out the last hopes of humanity. Indeed he seems to think his son has already overthrown Demogorgon himself, leaving his throne vacant and appropriating his might. Of course, what Jupiter says here is truer than he knows, for Demogorgon has left his throne and is about to arrive in place of his son. Is there a son? Jupiter believes Thetis has conceived one, but we never hear her story: perhaps the son is Jupiter's "conception" only, or "misconception."

Are we to understand, then, that Jupiter's child is really Demogorgon? He is not the son of Thetis, but he tells Jupiter, "I am thy child, as thou wert Saturn's child, / Mightier than thee" (3.1.54–5). Perhaps he is Jupiter's child in the sense that tyranny breeds the conditions of its own overthrow. Jupiter's summoning of his phantasmal "son," in any case, is parallel to Prometheus' conjuring of the Phantasm of Jupiter: Prometheus recalls the curse and thereby reveals the "real" Jupiter to be no more than a phantasm, while Jupiter learns that his existence rests on nothing more solid than a misconception. With that, Demogorgon embraces him, and both fall "down – ever, forever, down" into the "bottomless void" (81, 76).

After another brief interlude, the great reunion takes place in Scene 3, which begins with Hercules, in a cameo appearance, unbinding Prometheus and declaring that strength serves wisdom, courage, and love. The very brevity of Hercules' part, presumably a long one in the original lost play, bespeaks the negligible role of violence in a true revolution. Prometheus then announces to Asia and her sisters that he and they will withdraw to a beautiful cave "Where we will sit and talk of time and change / As the world ebbs and flows, ourselves unchanged" (3.3.23–4). Their roles in the renovation of the world are completed, and they will live on in a transcendent realm of thought and art. He asks Ione to give a "mystic shell" (71) to the Spirit of the Hour, through which he is to trumpet the good news to the world, and then return to the cave, for time will stop for the loving community; it will be perpetual spring. He then turns to Mother Earth, but before he can speak she reports a deep transformation of her plants, animals, and people, a restoration of the Garden of Eden. She also describes a cave, presumably the one Prometheus knows about, and gives it to the lovers.

The forest before the cave is the setting of Scene 4. The Spirit of the Earth steals the scene with his childlike teasing, but he describes seriously enough the transformation of a city he passed over on his way to the lovers. He has seen "Hard-featured men, or with proud, angry looks / Or cold, staid gate, or false and hollow smiles / Or the dull sneer of self-loved ignorance / Or other such foul masks" (3.4.41–4). Then there was a loud but sweet sound, from the shell of the Spirit of the Hour, "and soon / Those ugly human shapes and visages / ... / Past floating through the air ... / ... and those / From whom they past seemed mild and lovely forms / After some foul disguise had fallen" (64–70). In a moment the Spirit of the Hour returns, and his report of the transformation expands on that of the Spirit of the Earth. It is largely in negatives, but surely the most eloquent negatives Shelley ever wrote.

> None frowned, none trembled, none with eager fear
> Gazed on another's eye of cold command,
> Until the subject of a tyrant's will
> Became, worse fate, the abject of his own,
> Which spurred him, like an outspent horse, to death.
> None wrought his lips in truth-entangling lines
> Which smiled the lie his tongue disdained to speak;
> None, with firm sneer, trod out in his own heart
> The sparks of love and hope till there remained

Those bitter ashes, a soul self-consumed,
And the wretch crept a vampire among men,
Infecting all with his own hideous ill;
...
The loathsome mask has fallen, the man remains
Sceptreless, free, uncircumscribed—but man
Equal, unclassed, tribeless, and nationless,
Exempt from awe, worship, degree,—the king
Over himself; just, gentle, wise: but man
Passionless? no—yet free from guilt or pain,
Which were, for his will made, or suffered them,
Nor yet exempt, though ruling them like slaves,
From chance, and death, and mutability,
The clogs of that which else might oversoar
The loftiest star of unascended Heaven,
Pinnacled dim in the intense inane.

(3.4.137–48, 193–204)

With this stirring speech Act 3 concludes, and, as we might gather from its rhetorical climax, it ends the play as Shelley conceived it in April 1819. It was a three-act version that he sent to his publisher, more or less as we have it. The play was rounded and complete; there were no loose ends. But then Shelley decided to add another act, and what he wrote is the most sustained lyrical effusion in all his work.

Act 4 is more a pageant or a masque than an act in a drama. No more drama, in fact, is possible, for its field of action, historical or linear time, has ceased. Jupiter, the "King of Hours," is now a corpse (4.20), the "past Hours" have vanished (31), and the new Hours have no chariots (46) – they no longer race but walk or dance. The chorus of Hours sings: "Once the hungry Hours were hounds / Which chased the Day, like a bleeding deer / ... But now—oh weave the mystic measure / Of music and dance and shapes of light" (73–8). The Hours are joined by "the Spirits of the human mind" (81), whom we last met when they were consoling Prometheus in Act 1, and they all dance and sing together. Panthea and Ione serve as commentators on this display and those that follow, and some of their speeches, like most of the dialogue throughout the play, are in blank verse. All the rest are in one or another lyrical measure, with lines of varying lengths and meters and intricate rhyme schemes. The overall effect is that of a spontaneous outburst of spiritual energy. Many readers have disliked it, and have borrowed the last two words of Act 3, "intense inane," to describe it. It is Shelley at his most idealistic, in his most sustained attempt to embody his utopian vision, his sense of what it might feel like to arrive at a realm of complete social and imaginative freedom and solidarity. It draws from ancient traditions such as the music of the spheres, transformed into the music of the earth. Astounding things are seen and heard.

Panthea and Ione see two visions floating on music (4.202–3), the Spirits of the Moon and of the Earth, each elaborately and mysteriously described as infants within their respective spheres. In Earth's sphere Panthea sees "the melancholy ruins / Of cancelled cycles" (288–9), the remains of former civilizations overwhelmed by a flood, along with ancient animal forms, as if they were annihilated by a god in a passing comet who undid the work of the creator by a negative fiat: "Be not."[6] The Earth, in other words, is reborn; old Mother Earth has become, in spirit, her own child. The burden of the past is shrugged off. Not only the cycles of the past but cyclicity itself is canceled, for we are no longer caught up in the interminable tit-for-tat of injury and revenge, of vengeful Furies inflicting new vengeance-provoking crimes; instead, we have entered a new world of love and forgiveness.

There are two godlike children, a male Earth and a female Moon, and they now sing their duet. The "boundless, overflowing bursting gladness" of the Earth (4.320) penetrates the "frozen frame" of the Moon (328) as he celebrates tyranny's annihilation and love's fulfillment (350–5). This is Eros on a cosmic scale: love makes the world go round, and makes the moon go round the world. The love that transforms humans, even as a leprous child is transformed by spring waters, also governs the universe the way the sun rules the maze of planets (388–99). The Moon, "thy chrystal paramour" (463), tells how she revolves about the Earth as the Earth speeds around the Sun: "I, a most enamoured maiden / … / Maniac-like around thee move, / Gazing, an insatiate bride, / On thy form from every side" (457–72). Though Shelley knew all about Newton and the law of gravity, he reverts to the ancient doctrine that the force of "attraction" that unites all things is a kind of love, an instance of the same force that unites men and women and infuses all life.

At this point, surprisingly, Demogorgon reappears. As Asia summoned him into action in Act 2, so the song of love between Earth and Moon, particularly the Moon's "chrystal accents [which] pierce / The caverns" of the Earth (4.499–500), seems to prompt him back on to the stage. He addresses in turn the Earth, the Moon, the heavens, the elements, all living things, all meteorological forces, and man, and when he has gained their attention he gives the final speech of the play. He recapitulates in a few words the defeat of despotism by love, and praises "Gentleness, Virtue, Wisdom, and Endurance." He then intrudes a relatively realistic note: the possibility that this eternal spring might not last eternally. "And if, with infirm hand, Eternity, / Mother of many acts and hours, should free / The serpent that would clasp her with his length" – alluding to the brief final release of Satan in the Book of Revelation – "These are the spells [Gentleness, Virtue, and the others] by which to reassume / An empire o'er the disentangled Doom" (562–9). The dispiriting thought arises that we might have to do this all over again: "To suffer woes which Hope thinks in-finite; / To forgive wrongs darker than Death or Night" (570–1). Yet his point (and he ought to know) is not so much that eternity will inevitably slip back into cyclical time or that man will lapse again into violence and tyranny as that, if these things happen, we will have the means to return to Paradise. If Hope thinks the new round of woes is infinite, she will have forgotten the lesson Demogorgon is here to teach. And we, presumably, will have one ad-vantage over past generations of enslaved humanity, a handbook of hope and wisdom called *Prometheus Unbound*.

Chapter 11

Romantic satire

If this book were a survey of British Romantic poetry rather than an intro-duction to it, it would have chapters on several kinds of poetry that it has so far neglected or only glanced at. One kind we might awkwardly call the "brief narrative poem other than a ballad." It would include, for example, Blake's *The Book of Thel* (1789), *America: A Prophecy* (1793), and indeed all of his shorter "prophetic books" of the 1790s; Wordsworth's tragic stories "The Ruined Cottage," written in 1798 and incorporated into *The Excursion* in 1814, "The Brothers" (1800), and "Michael: A Pastoral Poem" (1800); Byron's "Turkish" tales, beginning with *The Giaour* (1813), as well as his disturbing apocalyptic vision "Darkness" (1816); Shelley's *Alastor* (1816), which tells of the life and death of an alienated poet; Keats's *Lamia* (1820) and *The Eve of St. Agnes* (1820), though they might be defined as brief romances; and the many poems gathered in Hemans' *Tales, and Historic Scenes, in Verse* (1819) and *Records of Woman* (1828).

Another kind is elegy. It had a broad meaning as a meditative poem on a serious theme, but even in its narrow sense as a poem of lament over the dead there are many Romantic examples, of which the greatest is Shelley's *Adonais* (1821), on the death of Keats. The genre would also include Coleridge's "On Receiving an Account that his Only Sister's Death Was Inevitable" (1791) and "Monody on the Death of Chatterton" (1794); Wordsworth's "Lucy" poems (1800), "Elegiac Stanzas" (1807) on the death of his brother, and "Extempore Effusion Upon the Death of James Hogg" (1835); Byron's "Elegy on Newstead Abbey" (1807) and "Monody on the Death of Sheridan" (1816); Hemans' "The Grave of a Poetess" (1828); Landon's "Stanzas on the Death of Mrs Hemans" (1835); and Elizabeth Barrett Browning's "L. E. L.'s Last Question" (1839), on the death of Landon.

But I shall conclude this book with a few pages on another kind, satire. Though "Romantic satire" sounds almost self-contradictory, a great deal of it was written during the period, much of it, to be sure, by non-Romantics or anti-Romantics (for the Romantics were easy to make fun of), but quite a bit by the canonical Romantic poets themselves. What defines this kind is not form but content, for witty mockery can take any form. Blake's *The Marriage of Heaven and Hell* (1790), for example, takes the form of some of the Swedish mystic Emmanuel Swedenborg's writings, with their deadpan accounts of conversations with angels. (Most of it is not in verse, however.) Wordsworth, though he expressed disdain for satire, nonetheless was capable of good satiric passages, notably in his description of London in Book 7 of *The Prelude*. Shelley's *Peter Bell the Third* (1819) is a mocking send-up of Wordsworth's unfortunate verse story *Peter Bell*, and his *Swellfoot the Tyrant* (1820), "translated from the original Doric," recasts Sophocles' tragedy *Oedipus Rex* ("Oedipus" means "Swellfoot" in Greek) to attack the leading politicians of the day. Even Keats, whom we tend to think of as earnest and sincere, made an effort at a sort of self-satire in a comic Spenserian romance called *The Jealousies* (1819), though he left it incomplete.[1] Unquestionably the greatest satirist among the Romantics, however, was Byron, and it is his greatest satire that will occupy this chapter.

Byron's *Don Juan*

The masterpiece of this master of satire is *Don Juan* (1819–24), which runs to sixteen cantos and a little more: 1,990 eight-line stanzas, or just under 16,000 lines, not counting interpolated songs in cantos three and sixteen. Satire can take any form, as we noted, and the form this one takes, obviously, is epic, an "epic satire," as Byron calls it himself (canto 14, stanza 99).

Near the end of the first canto Byron (or rather the narrator, who has a garrulous personality of his own) outlines his plan:

> My poem's epic and is meant to be
> Divided into twelve books, each book containing,
> With love and war, a heavy gale at sea,
> A list of ships and captains and kings reigning,
> New characters; the episodes are three.
> A panoramic view of hell's in training,
> After the style of Virgil and of Homer,
> So that my name of epic's no misnomer.

(1.200)

"Epic" may be the right word for it, but the plan is hardly carried out. Already at the end of the second canto he is promising "twelve or twenty-four" of them (2.216). We do get love, from the first canto onward, and a war, and a heavy gale with shipwrecks, and plenty of new characters. The "list of ships and captains and kings reigning" alludes to the "Catalog of Ships" that takes up over three hundred lines of Book 2 of Homer's *Iliad* and makes modern readers' hearts founder, but it is a playful threat and Byron never produces one. There are many more than three episodes. The "panoramic view of hell" may be a tease: there will be nothing like the descents to Hades in the *Odyssey* and the *Aeneid*, but we will be given surveys not only of a city under siege, like Troy, but also of high society in several European cities, all hells in their way.

When he reverts to this plan seven cantos later the narrator silently passes over the features he hasn't made good on:

> Reader, I have kept my word at least so far
> As the first canto promised. You have now
> Had sketches of love, tempest, travel, war,
> All very accurate, you must allow,
> And epic if plain truth should prove no bar

(8.138)

All very epic, we may agree again, but rather far from the manner of his "epic brethren gone before" (1.202), Virgil and Homer. There really is no plan, first of all, that governs the whole thing, nor could there have been one. Byron threatened in his letters to go on for a hundred cantos if he felt like it – he would certainly never have run out of material – and if he had lived his full three score and ten he might have made it to one hundred cantos at the rate he was writing. In canto twelve he makes the astonishing announcement that he is just getting warmed up: "These first twelve books are merely flourishes, / *Preludios*, trying just a string or two / Upon my lyre or making the pegs sure" (12.54). In the last completed canto the narrator tells us that his Muse is "The most sincere that ever dealt in fiction. // And as she treats all things and ne'er retreats / From anything, this epic will contain / A wilderness of the most rare conceits" (16.2–3). The clever play on "treats" and "retreats" may distract us from taking in the claim that, after 15,000 lines or so, a "wilderness" of further cantos lies ahead. It's no wonder that, a little earlier, we are promised an appendix of material he doesn't know yet, as well as an index to the whole epic, which of course never materializes (14.68).

Despite the supposed plan and his claim that he has kept his promise, the narrator confesses he follows no plan at all. "I have nothing planned" (4.5), he says. "[M]y muse is a capricious elf" (4.74). "Carelessly I sing" (8.138). "I ne'er decide what I shall say," he admits; "I never know the word which will come next" (9.41). And once they come, "I cannot stop to alter words once written" (9.77). He is an improviser, an *improvvisatore* (15.20), rather like those Byron would have known in Italy, who could turn any theme suggested by his audience into verse. He displays an aristocratic nonchalance, as if this endless epic were just something he tosses off before breakfast or when he returns from the hunt and doesn't think about afterward. Though Lord Byron had more than a touch of this aristocratic off-hand "ease," we know he did indeed "alter words once written," and he took pains about publication; the narrator or *persona* is his creation no less than the story the narrator tells.

The first target of this vast satire, then, is epic itself. Byron had certainly seen enough epics, for as we noted in Chapter 9 they were piling up in the bookshops of the day, and the most prolific epicist, Robert Southey, was one of Byron's least favorite poets. In one of his many self-conscious digressions, the narrator admits they may be tedious, and have "what our neighbors call *longueurs* / (We've not so good a word, but have the thing / In that complete perfection which ensures / An epic from Bob Southey every spring)" (3.97). *Don Juan*, in fact, is dedicated to Southey! Yet it is not exactly a mock-epic in the manner of Dryden or Pope, though Byron admired them both. There are touches of mock-epic, as in the opening words of canto three: "Hail Muse! et cetera." But the poem departs so radically from the classical conventions of Homer and Virgil that it is better described as the narrator describes it, as epic satire, a satire in epic form, and governed by a Muse that treats of everything under the sun, including epic itself. Byron's satire has been well described as "less a matter of a few sharply defined targets, programmatic investments, and systematically 'satiric' passages than of a pervasive and diffusely satiric tonality."[2] As his narrator protests, "I hope it is no crime / To laugh at all things" (7.2). The model Byron adopts is not the classical epic of Homer and Virgil, though he often invokes them, but the epic of the Renaissance Italians Boccaccio, Boiardo, Ariosto, and Tasso, not to mention poets of his own day. He was particularly taken with the *Morgante* of Luigi Pulci (1432–84), "sire of the half-serious rhyme" (4.6), who wrote a long epic with burlesque features; Byron translated a canto of it himself.

Classical epic never rhymed, and the great English epic, Milton's *Paradise Lost*, is in blank verse, but these Italian epics are in eight-line stanzas called *ottava rima*, which rhymed **abababcc**. And that brings us to a second satirical target: rhyming. Italian, like some of the other Romance languages, is easier to rhyme in than English, for English has more sounds and far fewer grammatical endings; there is only one good rhyme for "death," for example. If you are writing in *ottava rima*, you will need to find two rhymes for each of your first two end words in each stanza (and if you want "death" it will have to occupy the couplet), and if you are writing hundreds of stanzas you will need to rack your brains or scour the rhyming dictionaries if you don't want to repeat yourself constantly and create lots of *longueurs*. Byron sometimes disparaged rhymes, but he produced an endless stream of them. Quite a few of them, naturally, are imperfect, examples of "mine irregularity of chime" (15.20), and most of these are funny. Some of the best are those that torture foreign words into English: "Cadiz" rhymes with "ladies" more than once; "Lopé" (that is, Lope de Vega, the great playwright) rhymes with "copy" and "shop. He"; "Dante" rhymes with "scanty"; and so on. Most amusing, but exasperating, to today's readers, who might know some Spanish, is the name of the hero, for "Juan" cannot be pronounced like "wan" (or "whan") but must rhyme with "new one" and "true one" (1.1) or with "drew on" (2.146) and "threw on" (7.60). Those who know the ancient pronunciation of Latin will wince at stanza six of canto one, which begins "Most epic poets plunge in *medias res*," that is, "into the midst of things," in Horace's famous phrase, and then rhymes *res* with "please" and "ease." The perfect rhymes are often brilliant as well, especially the polysyllabic ones: "Plato" rhymes with "potato," "Aristotle" rhymes with "bottle," and "marriage" rhymes less often with the inevitable "carriage" than with "miscarriage." The most celebrated of these comes early on. After the narrator describes Juan's mother, Donna Inez, as a book-learned bluestocking, the narrator demands: "But—oh ye lords of ladies intellectual! / Inform us truly, have they not henpecked you all?" (1.22). Such displays of brilliance, casually tossed our way, suggest not only Byron's pleasure in coming up with them but an almost arrogant mockery of the traditions of poetry.[3]

The puns and mispronunciations are made more tolerable, and the cleverness and wit are enhanced, by the sheer speed of the poem. In this book I have recommended slow or close readings, but in this case I have to agree with the poet W. H. Auden: "Unlike most poets, [Byron] must be read very rapidly, as if the words were single frames in a movie film; stop on a word or a line and the poetry vanishes – the feeling seems superficial, the rhyme forced, the grammar all over the place – but read at the proper pace, it gives a conviction of watching the real thing."[4] Auden is alluding to a passage he quotes earlier in one of Byron's letters to his friend Hobhouse: "As to 'Don Juan,' confess, confess – you dog and be candid – that it is the sublime of *that there* sort of writing – it may be bawdy but is it not good English? It may be profligate, but is it not *life*, is it not *the thing*?" There are slow meditative moments, such as the heartachingly beautiful if slightly syrupy pages about perfect young love in canto four, just before it is destroyed, and there are many digressions by the distractable and talkative narrator, but on the whole the poem gallops along, like life itself.

However we are to pronounce his name, why is Don Juan the hero? The name inescapably calls up the famous literary character, a libertine and seducer of virgins who is dragged to hell for his sins. The earliest version seems to be the Spanish play by Tirso de Molina, *The Trickster of Seville and his Guest of Stone*, first published in 1630; his reputation grew with Molière's French play, *Don Juan and the Feast of Stone* (1665) and then Mozart's great opera *Don Giovanni*, with the Italian libretto by Da Ponte (1787).[5] Byron doubtless knew at least the latter two, but they can hardly be called sources, as his Don Juan has almost nothing in common with them beyond his birthplace, Seville. In the first canto Don Juan is more seduced than seducing, though he is willing enough, and says not one word; when his affair with an older married woman is discovered no stone guest calls on him at midnight: he is merely sent packing by his mother till the scandal dies down. In his second love affair, with Haidée, the beautiful daughter of a pirate, he is also passive at first, indeed nearly dead, as she finds him washed up on her father's island. In his third, he is the object of the desires of Gulbayez, the favorite wife of the Ottoman sultan, desires he at first resists. In his fourth, he is taken up by none other than Catherine the Great. The affairs are illicit and dangerous, but there the similarity with the original Don Juan ends. It is true that the narrator tells us that "myself, and several now in Seville, / *Saw* Juan's last elopement with the devil" (1.203), but nothing more is ever said of the traditional conclusion of the story. It is as if Byron wrote an *Achilles* about a sensitive young physician. In his choice of hero, as in so much else, we sense a cheeky teasing of our expectations, expectations he raises at the outset and then flouts, or even forgets, as other themes and adventures and satirical targets distract him from his purported subject.

It is the narrator who formally takes the blame for all this offhand and even absent-minded divagation, though it is clear that he is a handy blind behind which Byron can have his way with the story and with his readers. He seems to be a worldly nobleman, a bachelor ("I never married" 1.53), a friend of the family, very well informed, of course, but also innocent, or so he claims, of the sorts of escapades he writes about in intimate detail. At several points Byron the author seems to forget that he has created a persona who differs from himself, just as he abandons Childe Harold for long stretches in his *Pilgrimage*. In canto ten, for example, the narrator declares he is half Scottish (10.17), and discusses a literary critic named Jeffrey, who had reviewed several of Byron's works (10.11, 16). Mutable as he is, his chief defect as a storyteller, though in the end we must call it his chief glory, is his utter inability to resist digressing. Sometimes a digression is well marked as such, and then, with a little lurch, we get "Return we to our story" (1.134), or "But to the narrative" (4.113), and of course "But I digress" (5.49). Yet as early as the very opening the difference between story and digression is blurred to indistinction. Stanza one announces Don Juan as the hero. Then stanzas two, three, and four list various British and French generals and admirals who just yesterday were on everyone's lips, even Nelson, but no longer, for "There's no more to be said of Trafalgar." Then the narrator paraphrases some lines of Horace: "Brave men were living before Agamemnon / … But then they shone not on the poet's page / And so have been forgotten" (1.5). This moment of poetic self-consciousness peters out, however, as one Horace passage suggests another, the one about plunging *in medias res*, and we are off again, a digression from a digression, in which he insists he will "begin with the beginning" (1.7), precisely what he has not done, and then he begins. He describes Don Juan's mother and father with only brief asides for twenty stanzas, but when he has mentioned the strains in their marriage he digresses for two stanzas (30–1) to deny that any of them are *his* fault. When he gets to Juan's education at his mother's hands, off we go again for six delightful stanzas about the classics (40–5). And so it goes, or wanders, till stanza one hundred and ninety-nine: "This was Don Juan's earliest scrape; but whether / I shall proceed with his adventures is / Dependent on the public altogether." Then follow twenty-three stanzas about his "plan," about epic, about other poets, etc., etc., concluding with a last insult to Southey.

Even worse, or better, is the ninth canto. It begins with twenty-one stanzas ruminating on Wellington (the hero of the hour), on war, on death, and on skepticism – all in fact entirely Byron's own opinions – and then "'Tis time we should proceed with our good poem" (9.22). He tells us our hero is now on the way to St. Petersburg, but that is all it takes to launch him on a diatribe against Russia's "absolute autocrat" (9.23) for five more stanzas. Juan has with him a girl he saved from the slaughter at Ismail, and we are no sooner reminded of that fact than the narrator reflects that saving one life is a greater thing than all the fame the "twice ten hundred thousand daily scribes" can confer (9.35), and he's off again on the transience not only of fame but of civilization, a theme familiar to us from *Childe Harold*. He speculates on what future generations will think when they excavate London and find George IV. "So on I ramble, now and then narrating, / Now pondering. It is time we should narrate" (9.42). And then he narrates, for a while. But a few cantos later he confesses, "This narrative is not meant for narration" (14.7), which is true enough; indeed in the later cantos the plot itself is like a digression. It is then stupefying to come across this passing remark: "I meant to make this poem very short" (15.22). What? Well, even to stop to query it is to let go of the poem's spirit.

Digressions make at least half the poem. Readers who read for the plot had better leave *Don Juan* alone. There is plot aplenty, however, or rather a series of good episodes very slenderly connected. Don Juan, raised by his mother in total innocence of anything concerning "continuation of the species" (1.40), finds himself at age 16 in bed with the beautiful Donna Julia, whose husband arrives unannounced. Packed off to Cadiz and a long tour of Europe until the scandal subsides, Juan is shipwrecked and, after an experiment in cannibalism on board the boat, is washed up on the shore of a Greek island, owned by a pirate. The pirate's daughter, Haidée, rescues Juan and nurses him back to health; they fall in love and enjoy a beatific idyll until her father suddenly returns. Wounded in a fray, Juan is shipped off to Istanbul to be sold into slavery; Haidée dies of grief. The youngest wife of the sultan sees Juan at the slave market, sends a servant to buy him, and has him dressed as one of the harem girls. But Juan, loyal to Haidée's memory, resists Gulbeyaz' commands. Somehow (crucial steps are skipped here) he escapes the palace with one or two of the girls, and soon finds himself enlisted in the Russian army then besieging the Turkish city of Ismail. The horrors of war are horribly displayed – Byron makes up for epic poetry's long glorification of war – but Juan acquits himself with reckless bravery and wins the honor of bearing the news of victory to the Empress Catherine in St. Petersburg. She, of course, like every other woman, is smitten by his beauty and manner, and he becomes her favorite, that is, implicitly, her lover. Before long, however, he falls ill, and to restore his health (and perhaps to free herself to take a new favorite), Catherine sends him on a diplomatic mission to England, where he will remain until the end of the poem as we have it. There he attracts the interest of all the ladies, notably that of the beautiful, accomplished, virtuous, and married Lady Adeline Amundeville, who urges him to marry. But two other women are on the scene, gathered among many other guests at the old Norman Abbey the Amundevilles now inhabit: one is a cool, beautiful, pious young Aurora Raby, the other the "frolic" and irresponsible seductress the duchess Fitz-Fulke. An encounter with a ghost one night badly unsettles Juan, but the next night the ghost turns out to be the duchess, who ends up in Juan's bed. Complication enough, but we sense that a dangerous liaison is in the offing with Lady Adeline and perhaps an even more dangerous marriage with Aurora, but the poem breaks off abruptly just a few stanzas into canto seventeen.

In all this material Byron has no shortage of targets for his wit: war, the deserved evanescence of military glory, tyranny, pomposity, cant, puritan moralism, the marriage market, women's cunning, men's stupidity, blood sports, the Prince Regent, Wellington, and most literary critics, to name a few. Sometimes his wit is excoriating, worthy of Jonathan Swift, but usually it is genial and even self-deprecating. Virginia Woolf admired *Don Juan*, and thought what makes it "the most readable poem of its length ever written" is partly "the springy random haphazard galloping nature of its method."[6] "Method" seems just the wrong noun, unless it is the sort of method Polonius finds in Hamlet's madness, but the adjectives are just right. It is possible that *Don Juan* would be a better poem if it were shorter, if its narrator had stuck to his putative plan of twelve cantos and rounded out the plot, perhaps bringing the hero back to Spain instead of leaving him in England. But part of our pleasure of reading the haphazard galloping epic is our suspense over whether Byron can keep it up from canto to canto. Can he "canter gently through a hundred," as he threatens (12.55), with a pun on "canto"? Yes he can, or so it seems through sixteen at least, as his gusto and wit seldom flag, and never for long. We, however, must resist the temptation to canter any longer with him and bring this book to a close.[7]

Final thoughts

If this book were a survey, it would not only take up several other genres and themes but would spread its attention across many poems instead of concentrating on a few, as this book has done. As I suggested in the first chapter, a detailed "slow reading" or ruminating of a poem is a more valuable introduction to poetry of any period than a more distant and rapid summary, however informative it may be. If *Don Juan* is an exception and invites speedy reading, it is still interesting to stop now and then and see just how he brings off his galloping effect. Some of the other longer works I have tried to paraphrase in part, while singling out a few details for discussion, but by and large a paraphrase of a poem is helpful only to remind us of it, or to remind us to read it again. No summary can do justice to a good poem, and it might even interfere with our absorption of it, or in it, by leading us to cling to labels and concepts before fully taking it in as a sensuous and particular experience. It is also true that no analysis, no matter how long and detailed, will exhaust a good poem. A little while after writing ten thousand words on "Tintern Abbey" (in Chapter 3) I reread the poem and felt I could have written ten thousand more. My readers will be grateful that I did not, but I hope they will agree that only close or slow readings of major poems can open doors into their rich and deep interiors. Once they have thoroughly pondered a few of the great poems, they will find the others more accessible and rewarding on even a first reading.

We should remember, too, that for the Romantics poetry, especially when read aloud or chanted, was meant to be a "total" experience. It might be summed up as the "rapture" I discussed in Chapter 2, which both seizes the poet as he or she composes it and grips its reader or listener years or centuries later. Poetry arouses the emotions, but it also draws the intellect to a prolonged attentiveness or rapt thoughtfulness that expository prose seldom has the power to evoke. Echoing German Romantic theory, Coleridge writes, "The poet, described in *ideal* perfection, brings the whole soul of man into activity, with the subordination of its faculties to each other, according to their relative worth and dignity. He diffuses a tone, and spirit of unity, that blends, and (as it were) *fuses*, each into each, by that synthetic and magical power, to which we have exclusively appropriated the name of imagination."[8] In his preface to the 1802 *Lyrical Ballads*, Wordsworth celebrates the poet as one "endued with more lively sensibility, more enthusiasm and tenderness, who has a greater knowledge of human nature, and a more comprehensive soul, than are supposed to be common among mankind," and who through his or her poetry can reach mankind on these same registers of feeling and thought. Other poets lay emphasis elsewhere. For Shelley it is beauty: "Poetry turns all things to loveliness; it exalts the beauty of that which is most beautiful, and it adds beauty to that which is most deformed." For Keats it is poetry's medicinal powers: "sure a poet is a sage; / A humanist, physician to all men," while a thing of beauty brings us "health, and quiet breathing."[9] If we doubt that poetry can do all these things, we should at least be eager to find out why such gifted and intelligent poets believed it can.

Appendix

"Thou" and "thee," etc., in older English

Today we use "you" as both singular and plural, and subject and object, of the second-person pronoun. Throughout the Romantic era and even into the twentieth century, however, poets often kept the older forms:

	Singular	Plural
Subject	**thou**	**ye**
Object	**thee**	**you**

Thus three different words have given way to "you," which was originally the plural object form. Because it covers much more ground today, "you" no longer has the meaning it had in speech three hundred years ago or in poetry much more recently. It was a loss of semantic specificity, of the sort most European languages preserve (French *tu*, *te*, and *vous*, German *du*, *dir*, *dich*, *ihr*, *euch*, *Sie*, *Ihnen*, and so on). In fact we still feel the need for a singular/plural distinction, if not a subject/object distinction, so we have generated new plural forms, such as "you all" (or "y'all"), "you ones" (or "y'uns"), "you guys," "you lot," or even "youse."

"Thou" and "thee" (spelled and pronounced variously) still survive in some northern English and Scottish dialects, though they are almost extinct in North America and elsewhere. As for "ye," it survives only in "fossilized" expressions, such as "Ye gods!" and "Hear ye!" as well as in archaic churchly speech and song, such as "O ye of little faith" and "O come all ye faithful." It is *not* the "Ye" seen on fake old signs such as "Ye Olde Shoppe"; there the letter is not a Y but the old runic letter thorn (Þ) for a th sound; so it is just "The Olde Shoppe."

Here are the possessive forms:

Singular	Plural
thy, thine	**your**

It is sometimes crucial to understanding a line of poetry that you grasp the difference between singular and plural forms. Our poets are usually careful to maintain the distinctions, though occasionally they are sloppy about it, as when Keats switches between "thy" and "your" for the same addressee in "Ode on Melancholy." The rules seemed to vary a bit from dialect to dialect in spoken English, too; sometimes "ye," for instance, stands for the object, normally "you." Byron's Manfred may be speaking this dialect, though inconsistently, when he says, "I call upon ye by the written charm / Which gives me power upon you."

The second-person-singular ("thou") form of the verb ended in -**st** or -**est**. For example:

> O THOU! **meek Orb!** that stealing o'er the dale
> Cheer'st with thy modest beams the noon of night!
>
> (Robinson)

> Thou best Philosopher, who yet dost keep / Thy heritage
>
> (Wordsworth)

> Fair youth, beneath the trees, thou canst not leave / Thy song
>
> (Keats)

> Higher still and higher / From the earth thou springest
>
> (Shelley)

A few common verbs are exceptions, and take only -**t**:

> O rose thou art sick.
>
> (Blake)

> Thou shalt remain, in midst of other woe / Than ours
>
> (Keats)

> Bird thou never wert.
>
> (Shelley)

Keats disagrees with Shelley, incidentally, on the past tense of "art," at least when you address a bird:

> Thou wast not born for death, immortal Bird!

> (Keats)

Here are some full conjugations. The endings apply to both present and past tenses.

I sing, sang	we sing, sang	I love, loved	we love, loved
thou singest, sangest	ye sing, sang	thou lovest, lovedest	ye love, loved
he singeth, sangeth	they sing, sang	he loveth, lovedeth	they love, loved

I have, had	we have, had	I am, was	we are, were
thou hast, hadst	ye have, had	thou art, wert	ye are, were
he hath, had	they have, had	he is, was	they are, were
I do, did	we do, did	I go	we go
thou dost, didst	ye do, did	thou goest	ye go
he doth, did	they do, did	he goeth	they go

Poets of the Romantic period will sometimes switch back and forth between the modern and archaic verb endings when they need to add or subtract an unstressed syllable to make the meter come out right, or just to make a line sound better. In Coleridge's "The Rime of the Ancyent Marinere" (1798 version) we find these lines about the Hermit (543–4):

> He singeth loud his godly hymns
> That he makes in the wood.

The archaic endings have dominated the poem, so "singeth" is routine; without the syllable -eth the first line would not be perfect iambic tetrameter. But the second line inconsistently abandons the -eth ending and modernizes "maketh" to the one-syllable "makes." Why? Coleridge wanted a line of six syllables here, of the sort he writes throughout the poem, and "maketh" would make seven. The resulting line is a little hard to scan: one is tempted to turn it into two anapests ("That he MAKES in the WOOD") but I think it is more consistent with the prevailing meter to make it three iambs ("That HE makes IN the WOOD"), though it sounds somewhat artificial. (If Coleridge had dropped the "That" and retained the -eth ending he would have had a perfect iambic trimeter.)

Another inconsistent practice is visible in Wordsworth's sonnet "Composed upon Westminster Bridge." It begins

> Earth has not anything to shew more fair

but reverts to the archaic forms in the remainder, with "doth" in line 4 and then this line (12):

> The river glideth at his own sweet will:

Without the -eth ending this line would not glide at all. But why not use "hath" in the opening line? Probably because "Earth hath" is a bit of a tongue twister, and with another th sound four syllables later the line would sound like a lisp. And here is Byron, pretending to wonder where Childe Harold is:

> Methinks he cometh late and tarries long.

Unusual word order

English was once, according to the earliest records, a mainly verb-final language: the verb usually came at the end of the clause, especially if it was a subordinate clause. In particular English was mainly an SOV language, that is, subject–object–verb (for example, "I this poem hate"); occasionally OSV ("This poem I hate"). It is now predominantly SVO ("I hate this poem"), in those sentences that have an object.

English poetry, at least before the twentieth century, was conservative and thus preserved verb-final constructions much longer than everyday speech did; Latin, a more distinctly verb-final language, may have been an influence as well. Because of the demands of meter and rhyme, moreover, poets wanted more options in word order. So in Romantic poetry you will often find postponed verbs:

> When France in wrath her giant limbs upreared
>
> (Coleridge)

> In Xanadu did Kubla Khan / A stately pleasure dome decree
>
> (Coleridge)

> There holy silence shall her vigils keep
>
> (Robinson)

> Thus mellowed to that tender light / Which heaven to gaudy day denies.
>
> (Byron)

> The source of human thought its tribute brings
>
> (Shelley)

These passages are not difficult to parse, and when you have read a good deal of poetry from the Romantic period or earlier you hardly notice the postponed verbs.

But sometimes they can be confusing. Take this famous opening line by Wordsworth:

> A slumber did my spirit seal

We might wonder whether the slumber seals the spirit or the spirit seals the slumber. Arguments have been made for both possibilities, but it seems less of a strain semantically, and more likely syntactically, to take "slumber" as the subject, since SOV is the normal or default order. Note the function of "did": it holds the place of the verb as if it were SVO, and allows the poet to have an uninflected form (the infinitive) at the end to rhyme with "feel" – useful here since the past tenses do not rhyme ("sealed" vs. "felt"). It also provides a syllable where the meter needs it. Or one could say that "did" is the past-tense marker of the verb; hence we have StOV, where t = tense. The second Coleridge passage and the Robinson passage above are also in StOV form. (More on the function of "do" below.)

Compare these lines by Blake (from "London"):

> How the chimney-sweeper's cry
> Every black'ning church appals

What appals what? If we take SOV as the norm, then the cry appals every church, but you might make an argument for the reverse. It is hard to settle the question, but if you consider what "appal" meant in 1794 (roughly, "make pale with fear or guilt") the case for "cry" as the subject is stronger. It is also relevant to look at the next couplet, which seems exactly parallel:

> And the hapless soldier's sigh
> Runs in blood down palace walls.

In each we have a young male victim, his sound, and the sound's impact on an oppressive institution. The syntax of the latter couplet is clearer (SVO), so we may read it back on to the former.

A participle can also be postponed:

> Like a pale flower by some sad maiden cherished
>
> (Shelley)

> ... a love
> That had no need of a remoter charm
> By thought supplied
>
> (Wordsworth)

> He went like one that hath been stunned
> And is of sense forlorn
>
> (Coleridge)

An adverbial or prepositional phrase may interrupt verb and object:

> Never did sun more beautifully steep
> In his first splendour valley, rock, or hill.

(Wordsworth)

For a moment you might mistake the noun "splendour" as part of the series with "valley, rock, or hill," or as a noun used as an adjective modifying "valley."
  Often an adjective will follow the noun it modifies:

> of aspect more sublime

(Wordsworth)

> Thou from whose unseen presence the leaves dead
> Are fleeing, like ghosts from an enchanter fleeing

(Shelley)

"Dead leaves" is so common a phrase that we hardly think of it as a metaphor. By reversing the normal order Shelley defamiliarizes the phrase just enough to make us notice it and thereby take in the idea that, like ghosts, they are really dead. Note also the postponement of the participle "fleeing."
  Sometimes a noun will come between two adjectives, a habit borrowed from Milton:

> the human form divine

(Blake)

> the fretful stir / Unprofitable

(Wordsworth)

Perhaps oddest to our ears, occasionally a preposition will be postponed:

> All breathing human passion far above

(Keats)

The normal order would be: "far above all breathing human passion."

> Now like a mighty wind they raise to heaven the voice of song,
> Or like harmonious thunderings the seats of heaven among

(Blake)

The normal order would be: "among the seats of heaven."

>   Far along,
> From peak to peak, the rattling crags among,
> Leaps the live thunder.

(Byron)

[The] Helmsman on an ocean waste and wild
Sits mute and pale his mouldering helm beside.

(Coleridge)

Soft went the music the soft air along

(Keats)

Or the low rumblings earth's regions under

(Keats)

The do-forms

The "pleonastic" or superfluous use of "do" survived in poetry much longer than in everyday speech or written prose. Until about 1750 there was little felt difference between "I love thee" and "I do love thee," or between "He killed the bear" and "He did kill the bear." After about 1750 the do-forms were used for emphasis ("You may doubt it, but he did kill the bear"), and the negative particle "not" attached itself to the do-forms to become the standard form of negation of all but a few verbs, mainly the auxiliaries: "He did not kill the bear," as opposed to the older "He killed not the bear." In poetry, however, the positive do-forms remained without the emphatic sense, not only because poetry tended to be conservative in diction and syntax but also because it was too great a boon to poets to have an alternative way to deploy verbs. As Otto Jespersen writes, "it served chiefly to fill up the line and to make it possible to place the infinitive at the end as a convenient rime-word" (*Growth and Stucture of the English Language* [Garden City, NY: Doubleday, 1956], p. 219).

As a filler, however, it is semantically almost null, and can weaken a poetic line. Wordsworth gets away with it, I think, in "A slumber did my spirit seal" because everything else about the line is dense with not quite certain meanings, as well as strong alliteration. Coleridge's lines "In Xanadu did Kubla Khan / A stately pleasure dome decree" so dazzle us with exotic and euphonious names and images that we hardly care about the "did." Wordsworth's "Never did sun more beautifully steep" also succeeds, perhaps because it is striking that "steep" is governed by "sun." But these lines of Blake's seem weak:

The sun does arise
And make happy the skies;
…
Old John with white hair
Does laugh away care,

...
The sun does descend
And our sports have an end

Their justification, perhaps, is that they are meant to sound naïve and folksy. Shelley does not have that excuse in "Hymn to Intellectual Beauty," a poem at a much higher register:

Spirit of Beauty, that dost consecrate
With thine own hues all thou dost shine upon

Each "dost" here seems mere metrical filler, while the one in the first line is also a maneuver to avoid "consecratest," which would be much harder to find rhymes for (Shelley has the noun "state" and the adjective "desolate" as rhymes in the following lines). We see one of the costs of addressing Intellectual Beauty as "thou" instead of "you" – not that Shelley had much choice, as the decorum of an ode required the archaic singular (and intimate) form, as in Keats's "Thou still unravished bride of quietness."

The subjunctive mood

In English the verb has several moods (or modes): indicative, imperative, interrogative, infinitive, and subjunctive; some languages have others. The subjunctive mood is no longer used as much as it was even in the Romantic era, and much less than in Old English, but it is still normal under many circumstances.

If I **were** you ...
I wish I **were** a bird.

This form, sometimes called the contrary-to-fact conditional, is the subjunctive corresponding to the indicative **am**. It is not a past tense (though it has been miscalled the past subjunctive), and it is not a plural. Such a form often precedes (though it may also follow) a clause with the conditional **would:**

If I **were** you I **would**n't do that.
I **would**n't do that if I **were** you.

If I **were** a bird, I **would** fly to you.
I **would** fly to you if I **were** a bird.

The if-clause can be restated without the "if" by placing the verb first:

Were I a bird ...

Had you only listened to me!

This kind of subjunctive is familiar to you and should cause no confusion when you meet it in a poem, as in Shelley's lines,

> If I **were** a dead leaf thou mightest bear;
> If I **were** a swift cloud to fly with thee;
> …
> … I **would** ne'er have striven
> As thus with thee in prayer in my sore need.

But sometimes the subjunctive form of the verb replaces the **would**, as in these lines from Shelley:

> Man **were** immortal, and omnipotent,
> **Didst** thou, unknown and awful as thou art,
> Keep with thy glorious train firm state within his heart.

The first line means "Man **would be** immortal, and omnipotent …" The inversion of the subjunctive verb **didst** in the second line stands for the if-clause: "If thou didst."

From Blake:

> Then **had** America been lost, o'erwhelm'd by the Atlantic,
> And Earth **had** lost another portion of the Infinite,
> But all rush'd together in the night in wrath and raging fire.

For the two instances of **had** we say **would have**. But it is important to see, in both the Blake passage and the second Shelley passage, that the verbs are not in the past tense of the indicative mood. They do not assert that something happened, but entertain the possibility that something might have happened but didn't.

From Coleridge:

> A delight
> Comes sudden on my heart, and I am glad
> As I myself **were** there!

The last clause means "and I am as glad as I would be if I were there myself."

> … the strings of this Aeolian lute,
> Which better far **were** mute.

That means "which would be far better mute."

There are other forms of the subjunctive, sometimes misleadingly called the "present subjunctive," where the possibility of something is more likely, not contrary to fact, and sometimes hoped for or proposed.

> I move he **be** appointed secretary.
> He will be appointed if he **come** on time.

> God **bless** you.
> Long **live** the king.
> We obey the king however wicked he **be**.
> Glory **be** to God.
> **Be** it ever so humble, there's no place like home.
> We will take care of it, if need **be**.

For the second sentence today we would say "if he **comes** on time," but with the subjunctive **come** you get a slightly greater sense of doubt; this usage is probably extinct in America. But notice it is slightly more hopeful than the "past" subjunctive would be: "He **would be** appointed if he **came** on time." For the fifth sentence we would be more likely to say "however wicked he **may** be."

From Scott:

> **Part** we in friendship from your land. [i.e., **Let** us **part**]

From Wordsworth:

> If this
> **Be** but a vain belief …

> … and if this mood
> **Desert** me not …

A note on meter

Verse in the Romantic period was almost always metered, that is, it followed one or another metrical pattern such as iambic or anapestic. "Free verse" scarcely existed. Any given line might well have an irregularity, a substitute or inversion, and for good expressive or semantic reasons; without such deviations verse would sound mechanical, dull, childish, or at best merely humorous. Take the opening of Coleridge's "Frost at Midnight," which establishes the iambic pentameter that prevails throughout the poem:

> The frost performs its secret ministry,
> Unhelped by any wind. The owlet's cry
> Came loud—and hark, again! loud as before.

These lines are a perfect iambic pentameter until the second-last foot of line 3 ("loud as") which is a trochaic inversion of the iamb, and very appropriate, too, since the inversion emphasizes "loud."

> The fróst perfórms its sécret mínistrý,
> Unhélped by ány wínd. The ówlet's crý
> Came loúd—and hárk, agaín! loúd as befóre.

Much more often this trochaic inversion begins a line, as in these lines:

> Echo or mirror seeking of itself
>
> (22)
>
> Lulled me to sleep, and sleep prolonged my dreams!
>
> (35)
>
> Awed by the stern preceptor's face, mine eye
> Fixed with mock study on my swimming book
>
> (37–8)

If you give the normal or prose accent to the words you will usually bring out the meter correctly; only occasionally, as with the line from "The Rime of the Ancyent Marinere" above, will there be ambiguities that may require some sort of compromise.

Problems might sometimes arise, however, from the -ed ending of regular verbs in the past tense. In Middle English and Early Modern English the vowel in -ed was usually pronounced, adding an unstressed syllable to the verb. We say it still, as we are forced to, after –d or –t, as in "seated," "threaded," "mounted," or "handed," and we see traces of it in adjective forms such as "blessed" and "learned" ("I learned [learn'd] a great deal from the learned [learnèd] scholars"). In the Romantic era in spoken English these endings were pronounced in more or less the way they are today, but in poetry sometimes the syllables were preserved, mainly for metrical reasons. To indicate whether to sound them the usual spelling convention was (a) to omit the -e- and insert an apostrophe ("bless'd," "learn'd") if the syllable was not pronounced, and (b) to leave the -e- in if it was. The first practice was very common, and it usually seems unnecessary to us:

> Much have I travell'd in realms of gold
>
> (Keats)

We would not have been tempted to pronounce the -e- if it were printed. It is omitted because of the second rule.

We often find verbal adjectives that require the -ed to be sounded.

> The undisturbed lake has crystal space
>
> (Keats)
>
> Or hear old Triton blow his wreathed horn
>
> (Wordsworth)
>
> That thou, light-winged Dryad of the trees
>
> (Keats)

A somewhat puzzling example from "Ode on a Grecian Urn" is this:

> And, happy melodist, unwearied

I think the -ed should be made into a syllable here, turning the line into a perfect iambic pentameter. If Keats had wanted, for some reason, to truncate his line, he might have left out the -e-, as he does in five other participles (such as **unravish'd**) in the same poem. Adjectives ending in -ied, however, are seldom spelled -i'd, perhaps because the difference between -ièd and -ied seems so slight; in the same poem Keats has what must be a two-syllable **emptied**.

Here is an interesting passage from Blake, who engraved his lines on copper plate but usually followed the spelling conventions, if not those for punctuation (ignore the odd period in the first line):

> My roots are brandish'd in the heavens. my fruits in earth beneath
> Surge, foam, and labour into life, first born & first consum'd!
> Consumed and consuming!

The first two lines are "fourteeners," iambic heptameter, and the only way to get fourteen syllables is to omit, as Blake indicates, the -e- in the ending of "brandish'd" and "consum'd." That is how we would pronounce it anyway today, so the omission seems redundant, if harmless. The first line is perfectly iambic, as "heaven" was conventionally compressed into one syllable (it was often written "heav'n"). But the third line is striking. The verb is repeated, but this time its vowel must be sounded, making the line iambic and regular, one half of a fourteener.

To take a final case, Byron's "She Walks in Beauty" twice inserts the apostrophe in past tenses ("mellow'd" and "impair'd") to ensure that their lines are given eight syllables, but "heaven" is left without an apostrophe, for readers would know to make it one syllable.

Practice, however, was inconsistent, and you will sometimes have to make judgments about whether to sound the little vowel. Modern editions often put a grave accent over the **e** when it is to be sounded, as in "learnèd" or "blessèd," but mistakes are easy to make in this matter, so the best rule of thumb in doubtful cases is to try to make the meter regular by sounding the vowel or not.

Notes

1 Introduction

1 Southey is quoted in W. A. Speck, *Robert Southey: Entire Man of Letters* (New Haven, Conn.: Yale University Press, 2006), p. 94; Coleridge in *Biographia Literaria*, ed. James Engell and W. Jackson Bate (London: Routledge and Princeton University Press, 1983), vol. II, p. 51.

2 I offer this definition, with a fuller discussion of the European context, in chapter 1 of *A Very Short Introduction to Romanticism* (Oxford University Press, 2010).

3 See Frederick C. Beiser, *Schiller as Philosopher* (Oxford: Clarendon Press, 2005), especially his discussion of "On Grace and Dignity" (1793) in chapter 3. For a thorough history of the idea, see Robert E. Norton, *The Beautiful Soul: Aesthetic Morality in the Eighteenth Century* (Ithaca, New York: Cornell University Press, 1995).

4 A masterly account of the publishing business, sales of books, readership tastes, and everything connected with these is William St Clair, *The Reading Nation in the Romantic Period* (Cambridge University Press, 2004).

5 Koch is developing an idea by Paul Valéry. Kenneth Koch, *Making Your Own Days: The Pleasures of Reading and Writing Poetry* (New York: Touchstone, 1998), pp. 19–26.

6 Wain quoted by Eric Ormsby in a review in the *TLS*, May 15, 2009, p. 31.

7 An excellent anthology of "contextual" texts about the French Revolution, slavery, women, religion, science, and other subjects is Simon Bainbridge, ed., *Romanticism: A Sourcebook* (Basingstoke: Palgrave Macmillan, 2008).

8 Mark Jones, *The Lucy Poems: A Case Study in Literary Knowledge* (University of Toronto Press, 1995).

9 See David Perkins' fascinating article "How the Romantics Recited Poetry," *Studies in English Literature* 31 (1991): 655–71. You can come close to hearing the Romantic manner by listening to recordings of Alfred Lord Tennyson (1809–92) and William Butler Yeats (1865–1939) on poetryarchive.org.

2 The poet

1 Lucan, *Civil War*, trans. Susan H. Braund (Oxford University Press, 1992).

2 Two good recent accounts of the Ossian affair are Fiona Stafford, *The Sublime Savage: James Macpherson and the Poems of Ossian* (University of Edinburgh Press,

1988), and Hugh Trevor-Roper, *The Invention of Scotland* (New Haven, Conn.: Yale University Press, 2008).

3 *The Iliad of Homer*, trans. Richmond Lattimore (University of Chicago Press, 1951).

4 For a much fuller account of the eagle symbol across European poetry, see Michael Ferber, "The Eagles of Romanticism," *Literature Compass* 3–4 (2006): 846–66; see www.blackwell-compass.com

5 Letter to John Moore, quoted in Robert Crawford, *The Bard: Robert Burns* (Princeton University Press, 2009), p. 63.

6 For a now classic discussion of the breeze metaphor, see M. H. Abrams, "The Correspondent Breeze: A Romantic Metaphor," *Kenyon Review* 19 (1957): 113–30; rev. rpt. in M. H. Abrams, *The Correspondent Breeze* (New York: W. W. Norton, 1984).

7 A monody is an elegy or dirge spoken or sung in one voice, as opposed to a choral elegy.

8 An excellent study of Keats's changing views about poetic fame may be found in Aileen Ward, "'That Last Infirmity of Noble Mind': Keats and the Idea of Fame," in Donald H. Reiman, Michael C. Jaye, and Betty T. Bennett, eds., *The Evidence of the Imagination* (New York University Press, 1978).

9 Entry of August 1785, quoted in Crawford, *Bard*, p. 191.

10 Quoted in Jerome Hamilton Buckley, *The Victorian Temper* (Cambridge, Mass.: Harvard University Press, 1951), p. 68.

11 An excellent and thorough discussion of the Romantic poets' attitude to fame or immortality may be found in Andrew Bennett, *Romantic Poets and the Culture of Posterity* (Cambridge University Press, 1999).

12 A helpful brief discussion of Hemans' attitude to fame is Susan Wolfson's article, "Men, Women, and 'Fame': Teaching Felicia Hemans," in Stephen C. Behrendt and Harriet Kramer Linkin, eds., *Approaches to Teaching British Women Poets of the Romantic Period* (New York: Modern Language Association, 1997). A good account of the European-wide response to Staël's novel and its memorable heroine is the chapter "A Continent of Corinnes" in Patrick H. Vincent, *The Romantic Poetess* (Durham, New Hampshire: University of New Hampshire Press, 2004). See also Bennett, *Romantic Poets*, chapter 3.

3 "Tintern Abbey"

1 The text of the poem is taken from a facsimile of the 1798 edition and compared to that in Michael Gamer and Dahlia Porter, eds., *Lyrical Ballads: 1798 and 1800* (Peterborough, Ontario: Broadview Press, 2008).

2 "Sweet" had a broader and stronger meaning than it usually has today. For an interesting comment on the change in its meaning, and reasons for the change, see Michael Pollan, *The Botany of Desire* (New York: Random House, 2001), pp. 17–19.

3 Elsewhere Wordsworth usually uses "impress" to refer to nature's impact on the mind, but sometimes, as here, it is the reverse. From *The Excursion* 1.136–8: "deep feelings had impressed / So vividly great objects that they lay / Upon his mind like substances." Closer to his usage in "Tintern Abbey" is this from the 1805 *Prelude* 3.85–7: "all passions and all moods / Which time, and place, and season do impress / Upon the visible universe."

4 Wordsworth's account has been questioned recently by Andrew Bennett in *Wordsworth Writing* (Cambridge University Press, 2007).

5 Keats called it "Tintern Abbey" when he quoted and discussed it in a letter to John Hamilton Reynolds, May 3, 1818.

6 In a letter of 1829, quoted by Susan J. Wolfson in her helpful article "Wordsworth's Craft," in Stephen Gill, ed., *The Cambridge Companion to Wordsworth* (Cambridge University Press, 2003), p. 115. For a judicious and subtle survey of blank verse in English, see Robert B. Shaw, *Blank Verse: A Guide to its History and Use* (Athens, Ohio: Ohio University Press, 2007).

7 Quoted in Stephen Gill, *Wordsworth and the Victorians* (Oxford: Clarendon Press, 1998), p. 192.

8 "Romanticism and Classicism," in *Speculations* (1924); reprinted New York: Harcourt Brace, n.d., p. 118.

9 Discussed in Gill, *Wordsworth*, pp. 52–3.

10 It illuminates both poems to read "Tintern Abbey" beside Coleridge's "Frost at Midnight" (also 1798); Coleridge passes the torch to his infant son, who will have the "lovely shapes" of nature to teach his soul.

11 Marjorie Levinson, *Wordsworth's Great Period Poems* (Cambridge University Press, 1986), p. 25.

12 Besides Levinson's book see Jerome J. McGann, *The Romantic Ideology: A Critical Investigation* (University of Chicago Press, 1983), pp. 85–8. David Bromwich, in "The French Revolution and 'Tintern Abbey,'" (*Raritan* 10:3 [1991]: 1–23), is critical of Levinson's approach but nonetheless agrees that the abbey, the site where Wordsworth "stations himself," and his experiences in France are both "sublimated" in the poem; essay reprinted as chapter 3 of *Disowned by Memory* (Chicago University Press, 1998). Nicholas Roe, cautious about attributing veiled political allusions to the poem, nonetheless entertains one in particular, the Bourdon case, where nine royalists, some of whom Wordsworth knew, were condemned for a political assassination that did not take place; they were guillotined on July 13, 1793. See "Politics, History, and Wordsworth's Poems," in Gill, ed., *Cambridge Companion to Wordsworth*. For vigorous replies to Levinson and McGann, see M. H. Abrams, "On Political Readings of *Lyrical Ballads*," the final chapter of his *Doing Things with Texts*, ed. Michael Fischer (New York: W. W. Norton, 1989); Thomas McFarland, "The Clamour of Absence: Reading and Misreading in Wordsworthian Criticism," chapter 1 of *William Wordsworth: Intensity and Achievement* (Oxford: Clarendon Press, 1992); and Helen Vendler, "*Tintern Abbey*: Two Assaults," in Pauline Fletcher

and John Murphy, eds., *Wordsworth in Context*, (Cranbury, New Jersey: Associated Press, 1992).

13 Levinson, *Wordsworth's Great Period Poems*, p. 15.

14 Letter to John and Maria Gisborne, July 19, 1821 (*Letters*, ed. Frederick L. Jones [Oxford University Press, 1964], vol. II, p. 310).

15 Letter to Tom Moore, November 16, 1821 (*Byron's Letters and Journals*, ed. Leslie Marchand [London: John Murray, 1973–4], vol. IX, p. 64). Byron's and Shelley's letters are both quoted by Timothy Clark in *Embodying Revolution: The Figure of the Poet in Shelley* (Oxford: Clarendon Press, 1989), pp. 195–6. Victor Hugo seemed to agree: "As a person, one is sometimes a stranger to what one writes as a poet." Quoted in Graham Robb, *Victor Hugo* (New York: W. W. Norton, 1997), p. 109.

4 Romantic odes

1 The light imagery, and several other patterns of imagery, have been well explored in a classic of "New Criticism," Cleanth Brooks' *The Well Wrought Urn* (New York: Harcourt, Brace, 1947), chapter 7.

2 Stuart Curran gives an excellent brief account of the English ode (and hymn) in chapter four of his *Poetic Form and British Romanticism* (Oxford University Press, 1986). He has equally illuminating chapters on the sonnet, epic, and other forms.

3 Jonathan Culler, "Changes in the Study of the Lyric," in Chavia Hosek and Patricia Parker, eds., *Lyric Poetry: Beyond New Criticism* (Ithaca, New York: Cornell University Press, 1985), p. 39.

4 See the chapter "Romantic Apostrophe" in *The Neural Sublime* (Baltimore: Johns Hopkins University Press, 2010), pp. 58–78.

5 Jonathan Culler, "Apostrophe," in his *The Pursuit of Signs* (Ithaca, New York: Cornell University Press, 1983), p. 140.

6 The text is taken from Jack Stillinger, ed., *John Keats: The Complete Poems* (Cambridge, Mass.: Harvard University Press, 1978). It is identical but for a semicolon or two from the text in many other editions and anthologies.

7 James O'Rourke, *Keats's Odes and Contemporary Criticism* (Gainesville: University Press of Florida, 1998), p. 60.

8 See Walter Jackson Bate, *John Keats* (Cambridge, Mass.: Harvard University Press, 1963), pp. 495–8.

9 Helen Vendler, *The Odes of John Keats* (Cambridge, Mass.: Harvard University Press, 1983), p. 127.

10 Ibid., pp. 118–21.

11 Some prominent Keats scholars, in a "deconstructive" spirit, grant equal validity or probability to any or all answers to the question of who says what to whom. See, for instance, Susan Wolfson, "The Know of Not to Know It," in *Ode on a Grecian Urn: Hypercanonicity and Pedagogy*, on the Praxis Series website of *Romantic Circles*: www.rc.umd.edu/praxis/grecianurn/toc.html.

12 For a thorough canvassing of the debates of Keats's time, as well as recent readings of the ode, see chapter 2 of O'Rourke, *Keats's Odes and Contemporary Criticism.*

13 "Tercet" is the English term for the Italian *terzina*, which is a set of three lines that rhyme in various patterns with lines in preceding or following tercets, as in *terza rima*. We might want to call tercets "triplets," but "triplet" is usually reserved for a tercet with all three rhymes identical. The text is from the lightly normalized edition of Donald H. Reiman and Neil Fraistat, eds., *Shelley's Poetry and Prose*, 2nd edn. (New York: W. W. Norton, 2002). It differs at a few points in spelling and punctuation from several other texts in print.

14 Earl R. Wasserman, *Shelley: A Critical Reading* (Baltimore: Johns Hopkins Press, 1971), p. 245. On *terza rima* in Shelley's ode see also William Keach, *Shelley's Style* (New York and London: Methuen, 1984) pp. 162–5.

15 The four colors, yellow, black, pale, and red, have caused some puzzlement. Because two of them seem unlikely autumnal leaf colors, they have been taken as referring to the four races of human beings (Mongoloid, Negroid, Caucasian, and American Indian). That strikes me as arbitrary, not to mention insulting to all the races, especially to the "hectic" red one. Recently David McInnis has proposed that the colors correspond to the four "humors": yellow bile, black bile (melancholy), phlegm, and blood ("Humoral Theory as an Organizing Principle in Shelley's 'Ode to the West Wind'?," *ANQ* 20:2 [spring 2007]: 32–4). This seems less objectionable, as the imbalance of humors was long held to be the cause of disease. Byron's Manfred speaks of "a strange hectic" on Astarte's cheek, "like the unnatural red / Which Autumn plants upon the perish'd leaf" (*Manfred* 2.4.100–1).

16 There have been thousands of poems since the Greeks about the west wind of the spring (Zephyrus or Favonius), though not very many that address him (or make him female, as Shelley does); I am aware of only a few that deal with the autumnal version. See under "West wind" in Michael Ferber, *A Dictionary of Literary Symbols*, 2nd edn. (Cambridge University Press, 2007), p. 232.

5 The French Revolution

1 When he republished the poem in 1802 Coleridge changed "compel" to "persuade," a cautious move that drains the line of most of its interest.

2 See Morton D. Paley, *Apocalypse and Millennium in English Romantic Poetry* (Oxford: Clarendon Press, 1999), p. 137.

3 *The Correspondence of Robert Southey with Caroline Bowles*, ed. Edward Dowden (Dublin, 1881), p. 52, quoted in M. H. Abrams, "English Romanticism: The Spirit of the Age," in Northrop Frye, ed., *Romanticism Reconsidered* (New York: Columbia University Press, 1963), p. 31. Abrams' essay is unsurpassed in conveying the impact of the Revolution on the British Romantics, unless it is by his book *Natural Supernaturalism* (New York: W. W. Norton, 1971), which elaborates upon the essay.

4 Barbara Rooke, ed., *The Friend*, vol. II of *The Collected Works of Samuel Taylor Cole-ridge* (Princeton University Press, 1969), pp. 147–8.
5 Quoted by Abrams, "English Romanticism," p. 31.
6 The poem was not published until after her death in 1825.
7 See Abrams, *Natural Supernaturalism*, especially chapter 1, for the importance of the apocalyptic tradition to Romantic writers both English and German. A thorough and careful study of this context for the British poets, more detailed than Abrams', is Paley's *Apocalypse and Millennium*.

6 Romantic sonnets

1 Harold Bloom, *The Ringers in the Tower* (University of Chicago Press, 1971), p. 4.
2 Wordsworth wrote another sonnet about sonnets, "Nuns fret not at their Convent's narrow room" (published 1807), as did Keats, "If by dull rhymes our English must be chain'd" (written 1819). "Scorn not the Sonnet" had an impact of which Wordsworth was probably unaware. Sainte-Beuve translated it loosely into French in 1829 ("Ne ris pas des sonnets, ô critique moqueur!"), trimming Milton to one line and adding three on Ronsard, DuBellay, and his own campaign to revive the sonnet in France. The following year Pushkin read Sainte-Beuve's sonnet, found the English original, and wrote his own version ("Stern Dante did not despise the sonnet"), in which he adds a Russian poet and Wordsworth himself! So Wordsworth's sonnet was enlisted by France's leading critic and Russia's greatest poet to promote the sonnet in their own countries.
3 A good indicator of the sonnet's popularity is Paula R. Feldman's and Daniel Robinson's anthology *A Century of Sonnets: The Romantic-Era Revival* (Oxford University Press, 1999), which includes 481 sonnets by eighty-two poets from Edwards to Elizabeth Barrett Browning. See also the chapter on sonnets in Stuart Curran, *Poetic Form and British Romanticism* (Oxford University Press, 1986).
4 Quoted in Ian Jack, "Gray's *Elegy* Reconsidered," in Frederick W. Hilles and Harold Bloom, eds., *From Sensibility to Romanticism* (Oxford University Press, 1965), p. 166.
5 For interesting comments on this sonnet along different lines, see Stephen C. Behrendt, *British Women Poets and the Romantic Writing Community* (Baltimore: Johns Hopkins University Press, 2009), pp. 120–3.
6 See Charlotte Smith, "To the Moon" (1784); Helen Maria Williams, "To the Moon" (1790); Coleridge, "To the Autumnal Moon" (1796); Felicia Hemans, "To the Moon" (1808); Wordsworth, two poems "To the Moon" (both 1837).
7 The bridge Wordsworth composed upon was completed in 1750. The current bridge opened in 1862.
8 On the republican context, see Charles Molesworth, "Wordsworth's 'Westminster Bridge' Sonnet: The Republican Structure of Time and Perception," *Clio* 6:3 (1977): 261–73.

9 Some commentators have found "Great God!" a disturbing intrusion. "Whether exclamation or apostrophe, it introduces an irrelevant and unintegrated mono-theistic conception which clashes with polytheistic paganism." It seems careless, even comical. Arnold B. Fox and Martin Kallich, "Wordsworth's Sentimental Nat-uralism: Theme and Image in 'The World is Too Much with Us,'" *Wordsworth Circle* 8:4 (1977): 327–32.

10 I have never understood why Keats gives Cortez eagle eyes (in the first draft it was "wond'ring eyes"). It was Herschel who had eagle eyes, which he very much neeeded as he looked for Uranus, but the Pacific is hard to miss. What eagles tra-ditionally stare at is the sun, so perhaps Keats is suggesting that the Pacific was like another new planet.

11 In this and much of the following discussion I am drawing from my article "Percy Bysshe Shelley: 'Ozymandias,'" in Michael Hanke, ed., *Fourteen English Sonnets: Critical Essays* (Trier: Wissenschaftlicher Verlag, 2007).

12 Kelvin Everest, "'Ozymandias': The Text in Time," in his edited volume *Essays and Studies 1992: Percy Bysshe Shelley: Bicentenary Essays* (Cambridge: Brewer, 1992), p. 27.

13 Ibid., p. 42.

7 Romantic love lyrics

1 William Harmon and C. Hugh Holman, eds., *A Handbook to Literature*, 8th edn. (Upper Saddle River, New Jersey: Prentice Hall, 2000), p. 299.

2 In Frederick W. Hilles and Harold Bloom, eds., *From Sensibility to Romanticism* (Oxford University Press, 1965), pp. 527–60; reprinted in M. H. Abrams, *The Corres-pondent Breeze* (New York: W. W. Norton, 1984), pp. 76–108. For a recent comment on Abrams' genre, see Robert Koelzer, "Abrams Among the Nightingales: Revisiting the Greater Romantic Lyric," *Wordsworth Circle* 37:2 (spring 2006): 67–71.

3 I am quoting here (and will throughout this book) from Alastair Fowler's edition of *Paradise Lost* in the Longman Annotated English Poets series (London: Longman, 1968).

4 I have made a fuller argument along these lines in "In Defense of Clods," in Alexan-der Gourlay, ed., *Prophetic Character: Essays on William Blake in Honor of John E. Grant* (West Cornwall, Conn.: Locust Hill Press, 2002).

5 For the circumstances of its composition see Robert Crawford, *The Bard: Robert Burns* (Princeton University Press, 2009), pp. 343–5. "Ae Fond Kiss" is the title of a 2004 film directed by Ken Loach and the name of a website devoted to Burns.

6 Scott in *Quarterly Review* (1809), reprinted in Donald A. Low, ed., *Robert Burns: The Critical Heritage* (London: Routledge, 1974), p. 208. Seamus Heaney, "Burns's Art Speech," in Robert Crawford, ed., *Robert Burns and Cultural Authority* (University of Iowa Press, 1997), p. 228.

7 Burns meant it to be sung to "Rory Dall's Port," probably composed by James Oswald in the 1750s but atttributed to a harper of a century earlier. ("Port" is Gaelic for "tune" or "air.") There have been several more recent settings.

8 The poems are "Strange fits of passion have I known," "She dwelt among the untrodden ways," "I travelled among unknown men," "Three years she grew in sun and shower," and "A slumber did my spirit seal." Some scholars add a sixth, "Lucy Gray." Wordsworth never grouped the poems together, but in his lifetime some readers saw them as a distinct set, and they have often appeared together in anthologies. Of the six poems, four, including "Slumber," first appeared in the 1800 edition of *Lyrical Ballads*.

9 Earl Leslie Griggs, ed., *Collected Letters of Samuel Taylor Coleridge* (Oxford: Clarendon Press, 1956), vol. I, p. 479.

10 A whole book devoted to the debates over all the Lucy poems appeared over fifteen years ago: Mark Jones, *The Lucy Poems: A Case Study in Literary Knowledge* (University of Toronto Press), 1995. It does not seem to have stifled further discussion.

11 Some have argued that "spirit" is the subject of "did … seal" and thus the spirit sealed the slumber. I don't know what this might mean, but in a clause with a postponed verb it is syntactically possible. See the Appendix, p. 217.

12 Slant rhymes (or half-rhymes or off-rhymes) are near rhymes, such as "brow" and "glow" in stanza three, slightly mismatched.

13 I am tempted to say the real Byron was not the writer of these lines either; it was not the "every-day individual" we call Byron. See the Byron passage quoted in Chapter 3, page 62 above.

8 Romantic ballads

1 Letter of July 7, 1796, reprinted in *Letters*, ed. E. V. Lucas (New Haven, Conn.: Yale University Press 1935), vol. I, p. 37. William Taylor's translation (as "Ellenore") may be found in Jerome J. McGann, ed., *The New Oxford Book of Romantic Period Verse* (Oxford University Press, 1993) and (in a slightly different version, as "Lenora") in Jonathan and Jessica Wordsworth, eds., *The Penguin Book of Romantic Poetry* (Harmondsworth: Penguin, 2001). Walter Scott's version may be found in most editions of Scott's poetry, and in Michael Ferber, ed., *European Romantic Poetry* (New York: Pearson Longman, 2005).

2 In the "Advertisement" that begins the 1798 edition, the authors write: "The majority of the following poems are to be considered as experiments." At least one contemporary reviewer thought the phrase "lyrical ballads" was redundant, "for what Ballads are not *lyrical*?" For a good discussion of the title, see Zachary Leader, "*Lyrical Ballads*: the Title Revisited," in Nicola Tortt and Seamus Perry, eds., *1800: The New Lyrical Ballads* (Basingstoke: Palgrave, 2001).

3 Coleridge was later to express regret over the moral. "In a work of such pure imagination I ought not to have stopped to give reasons for things, or inculcate humanity

to beasts" (*Table Talk* I 273n7). This remark seems unhelpful and inapt to me. Does the exercise of "pure imagination" license disconnected sequences of unexplained events? Coleridge seems to be evading responsibility for his own poem. And surely it is pure theology, not pure imagination, that denies humanity to beasts.

4 Letter of February 1801, rpt. *Letters*, vol. I, p. 240.

5 For a full argument that Coleridge was up to something like this, see Jerome J. McGann, "The Meaning of The Ancient Mariner," in G. A. Rosso and Daniel P. Watkins, eds., *Spirits of Fire* (Cranbury, New Jersey: Associated University Presses, 1990).

6 *Kenyon Review* 8:3 (summer 1946): 391–427.

7 The wedding guest resembles the "gentle reader" of "Simon Lee" and the restless interlocutor of "The Thorn" as another internal audience. It is interesting to note how many poems of the 1798 *Lyrical Ballads* incorporate some such addressee, from the "Traveller!" of "Lines Left upon a Seat in a Yew-Tree" to the "dear, dear Sister" of "Tintern Abbey."

9 Romantic epics and romances

1 For more on the epics of the day, see Stuart Curran, *Poetic Form and British Romanticism* (Oxford University Press, 1986), pp. 161–3.

2 See E. S. Shaffer, *"Kubla Khan" and the Fall of Jerusalem* (Cambridge University Press, 1975).

3 See Curran, *Poetic Form*, p. 183. I owe to Curran (pp. 183–4) some of the *Prelude's* epic features I name below. I shall be discussing the 1805 version, the first completed version (in thirteen books). The 1850 version (in fourteen books), published after Wordsworth's death, incorporates revisions he made at various times, mostly minor. Scholars have recently extracted a two-part *Prelude* of 1799 and a five-book *Prelude* of 1804 from the manuscripts. The former is included in several anthologies and in Jonathan Wordsworth, M. H. Abrams, and Stephen Gill, eds., *The Prelude: 1799, 1805, 1850*, a Norton Critical Edition (New York: W. W. Norton, 1979); for the latter, see Duncan Wu, ed., *The Five-Book Prelude* (Oxford: Blackwell, 1997).

4 M. H. Abrams, *Natural Supernaturalism* (New York: W. W. Norton, 1971), p. 79. Abrams' indispensable book circles repeatedly around *The Prelude*.

5 Letter to De Quincey, March 6, 1804.

6 See David V. Erdman's note on p. 806 of his *The Complete Poetry and Prose of William Blake*, newly revised edition (Berkeley: University of California Press, 1982). This is the standard scholarly edition of the text, without the designs, of Blake's work. For the designs of those poems that were engraved (as opposed to sketched or drawn), see the six-volume *Illuminated Books* published by the Tate and Princeton University Press. *Milton* is in volume V, edited by Robert N. Essick and Joseph Viscomi (1993). It is also easy to find on the web at the William Blake Archive. Blake wrote two other poems of epic length, *Vala*, or *The Four Zoas*, left unengraved, and

Jerusalem, engraved in one hundred plates. I find *Milton* the most satisfying of the three because of its fascinating central idea, the return of Milton to earth in what amounts to an incarnation in Blake. For obvious reasons I must neglect the designs here, but readers should remember that Blake considered text and design inseparable.

7 This weird bit of symbolism, typical of Blake, has not been satisfactorily interpreted. The tarsus may allude to Saul of Tarsus, who had a conversion experience on the road to Damascus when a flash of light knocked him to the ground (Acts 22), and he soon became the leading Apostle Paul.

8 Blake later read *The Excursion* and was put off by the "Prospectus" in the Preface. See E 666–7.

9 Richard Cronin, "Walter Scott and Anti-Gallican Minstrelsy," *ELH* 66:4 (winter 1999): 863–83; quotation from p. 875. Cronin's excellent article is incorporated in his book *The Politics of Romantic Poetry* (Basingstoke and New York: Macmillan and St. Martin's Press, 2000). Another good discussion of *Marmion* and Scott's war poetry generally is in Simon Bainbridge, *British Poetry and the Revolutionary and Napoleonic Wars* (Oxford University Press, 2003).

10 You can distinguish between Harold and the narrator most of the time if you take seriously such lines as "Thus Harold deem'd" (2.271), which nominally assign to Harold many stanzas that we naturally have taken to be in the narrator's voice, but there is little point in doing so. For a careful attempt to sort out who says what, see Jerome J. McGann, *Fiery Dust* (University of Chicago Press, 1968), pp. 67–93, 301–2.

11 Studies of Romantic "Orientalism" have flourished since the appearance of Edward Said's more general study *Orientalism* (New York: Pantheon, 1978). Though that book has been severely criticized by experts in the field, its influence has been inescapable. For a brief account of Orientalism in European Romanticism, see Diego Saglia, "Orientalism," in Michael Ferber, ed., *A Companion to European Romanticism* (Oxford: Blackwell, 2005). On British Romantic Orientalism, see Mohammed Sharrafuddin, *Islam and Romantic Orientalism: Literary Encounters With the Orient* (London: I. B. Tauris, 1994); Emily A. Haddad, *Orientalist Poetics: The Islamic Middle East in Nineteenth-Century English and French Poetry* (Aldershot: Ashgate, 2002); and Peter Cochran, ed., *Byron and Orientalism* (Cambridge: Cambridge Scholars, 2006).

12 See the first three chapters of Bainbridge, cited note 9 above.

13 Byron seems to be echoing Shakespeare's line "Cry 'Havoc!' and let slip the dogs of war" in *Julius Caesar* (3.1.273).

14 Translation by David West, in *Horace: The Complete Odes and Epodes* (Oxford University Press, 1997). Jonathan Swift and Alexander Pope, among many others, translated or imitated this ode. Byron himself worked these lines into *Don Juan* 1.33–7.

15 This poetic tradition comes to a beautiful climax with Thomas Hardy's "Rome: At the Pyramid of Cestius near the Graves of Shelley and Keats" (1887).

10   Romantic verse drama

1 Jerome J. McGann, *Towards a Literature of Knowledge* (University of Chicago Press, 1989), p. 39, n. 2.
2 And yet we should remember that French Romanticism was deeply involved with the theater; the riots over Victor Hugo's tragedy *Hernani* in 1830 are only the most celebrated case.
3 Shelley was assigned the play in Greek at his first meeting with his tutor at Oxford (1810). The first English translation of it appeared in 1773, and by Shelley's day its hero had been enlisted as a symbol in the campaign to abolish the slave trade, among other causes. See Stuart Curran, "The Political Prometheus," in G. A. Rosso and Daniel P. Watkins, eds., *Spirits of Fire* (Rutherford, New Jersey: Fairleigh Dickinson University Press, 1990). In this section I am drawing in part from my book *The Poetry of Shelley* (Harmondsworth: Penguin, 1993), chapter 5.
4 There is no consensus among interpreters as to just what Shelley means, or whether the character Prometheus really fits Shelley's description. The most searching and thorough interpretation of the play remains Earl R. Wasserman, *Shelley: A Critical Reading* (Baltimore: Johns Hopkins University Press, 1971). The most fully annotated edition at the moment is in Kelvin Everest and Georffrey Matthews, eds., *The Poems of Shelley*, vol. II (London: Longman, 2000). It may soon be superseded by the relevant volume of Donald H. Reiman and Neil Fraistat, eds., *The Complete Poetry of Percy Bysshe Shelley* (Baltimore: Johns Hopkins University Press, forthcoming).
5 The name Demogorgon is not found in ancient literature. It seems to have arisen in the Middle Ages through a blunder by a scribe, who miscopied *demiourgos* as *demigorgos* or something similar. The *demiourgos* or "demiurge" is the creator of the world in Plato's *Timaeus*. Once *gorgos* got accidentally inserted into the name, it seemed to refer to the Gorgons or to the most famous Gorgon, Medusa. The segment *demi* or *demo*, which means "people," then seemed odd, so sometimes it was respelled *daemogorgon*, as if it were a cross between a daemon ("demon") and a gorgon. Boccaccio, Spenser, and Milton all name him: he has become a sovereign power dwelling beneath the earth, inferior only to the Christian god.
6 Shelley was well informed about the theories of evolution of Erasmus Darwin and others, and about scientific ideas generally (electricity, magnetism, chemistry, and astronomy, as well as biology). The classic study of this subject is Carl Grabo, *A Newton Among Poets: Shelley's Use of Science in Prometheus Unbound* (Chapel Hill: University of North Carolina Press, 1930).

11   Romantic satire

1 See Steven E. Jones, *Shelley's Satire: Violence, Exhortation, and Authority* (DeKalb: Northern Illinois University Press, 1994); Gary Dyer, *British Satire and the Politics*

of Style, 1789–1832 (Cambridge University Press, 1997); Frederick L. Beaty, *Byron the Satirist* (DeKalb: Northern Illinois University Press, 1985); Stephen M. Parrish, "Wordsworth as Satirist of His Age," in Kenneth R. Johnston and Gene W. Ruoff, eds., *The Age of William Wordsworth* (New Brunswick, New Jersey: Rutgers University Press, 1987).

2 Fredric V. Bogel, *The Difference Satire Makes: Rhetoric and Reading from Jonson to Byron* (Ithaca, New York: Cornell University Press, 2001), p. 189.

3 On Byron's rhyming see Jim Cocola, "Renunciation of Rhyme in Byron's Don Juan," *Studies in English Literature, 1500–1900* 49:4 (August 2009): 841–62.

4 W. H. Auden, "The Life of a That-There Poet," *New Yorker*, April 26, 1958, pp. 135–42.

5 For a fine account of the Don Juan legend see Ian Watt, *Myths of Modern Individualism: Faust, Don Quixote, Don Juan, Robinson Crusoe* (Cambridge University Press, 1996).

6 Virginia Woolf, *A Writer's Diary* (London: Hogarth Press, 1953), entry for August 8, 1918.

7 An excellent introduction to the poem is Anne Barton, *Byron: Don Juan* (Cambridge University Press, 1992).

8 *Biographia Literaria*, ed. James Engell and W. Jackson Bate (London: Routledge, and Princeton University Press, 1983), vol. II, pp. 15–16.

9 *The Fall of Hyperion* 189–90; *Endymion* 1.5.

Further reading

Texts

There are many anthologies large and small of British (or "English") Romantic poetry that will contain most of the shorter poems discussed in this book and some of the longer ones. For particular authors the following editions are recommended.

Barbauld

McCarthy, William and Elizabeth Kraft, eds. *Anna Laetitia Barbauld: Selected Poetry and Prose*. Peterborough, Ontario: Broadview Press, 2001.

Blake

Erdman, David V., ed. *The Complete Poetry and Prose of William Blake*, "newly revised edition." Berkeley: University of California Press, 1982. This is the standard edition, but it lacks most of the designs.

For the poetry with the designs, in accurate color, the best choice is the six-volume edition of *Blake's Illuminated Books*, under the general editorship of David Bindman, published by the William Blake Trust and Princeton University Press, 1998. The volumes include reading texts and extensive commentaries.

The best student edition is Mary Lynn Johnson and John E. Grant, eds., *Blake's Poetry and Designs*, 2nd edn. New York: W. W. Norton, 2008. The Norton Critical Edition has most of the engraved or "illuminated" texts and many designs in black and white (a few in color), with notes at the bottom and critical essays in the back.

The William Blake Archive, hosted by the University of Virginia, is a free, easily navigable, and ever-growing digital collection of Blake's visual works. www.blakearchive.org

Bürger

Bürger's poem "Lenore," translated by William Taylor of Norwich under the title "Lenora," may be found at the back of Michael Gamer and Dahlia Porter, eds., *Lyrical Ballads: 1798 and 1800*. Peterborough, Ontario: Broadview Press, 2008. A slightly altered version, under the title "Ellenore," is in Jerome J. McGann, ed., *The New Oxford Book of Romantic Period Verse*. Oxford University Press, 1993. Sir Walter Scott's translation may be found in James Reed, ed., *Sir Walter Scott: Selected Poems*. New York: Routledge (Fyfield Books), 2003. See also Michael Ferber, ed., *European Romantic Poetry*. New York: Pearson Longman, 2005.

Burns

Kinsley, James, ed. *The Poems and Songs of Robert Burns*, 2nd edn. Oxford University Press, 1971.
McGuirk, Carol, ed. *Robert Burns: Selected Poems*. Harmondsworth: Penguin, 1993. A well-edited selection.

Byron

Steffan, T. G., E. Steffan, and W. W. Pratt, eds. *Lord Byron: Don Juan*, rev. edn. Harmondsworth: Penguin, 1982.
Wolfson, Susan J. and Peter J. Manning, eds. *Lord Byron: Selected Poems*. Harmondsworth: Penguin, 1996.

Coleridge

Keach, William, ed. *Samuel Taylor Coleridge: The Complete Poems*. Harmondsworth: Penguin, 1997.

Keats

Stillinger, Jack, ed. *John Keats: The Complete Poems*. Cambridge, Mass.: Harvard University Press, 1978.

Landon

McGann, Jerome J. and Daniel Riess, eds. *Letitia Elizabeth Landon: Selected Writings*. Peterborough, Ontario: Broadview Press, 1997.

Moore

Godley, A. D., ed. *The Poetical Works of Thomas Moore.* Oxford University Press, 1929.

"Ossian" (James Macpherson)

Gaskill, Howard, ed. *The Poems of Ossian, and Related Works.* Edinburgh University Press, 1996.

Robinson

Pascoe, Judith, ed. *Mary Robinson: Selected Poems.* Peterborough, Ontario: Broadview Press, 1999.

Scott

Scott's *Marmion* may be found in James Reed, ed., *Sir Walter Scott: Selected Poems.* New York: Routledge (Fyfield Books), 2003.

Shelley

The best one-volume selection is Donald H. Reiman and Neil Fraistat, eds., *Shelley's Poetry and Prose*, 2nd edn (Norton Critical Edition). New York: W. W. Norton, 2002. Also very good is Zachary Leader and Michael O'Neill, eds., *Percy Bysshe Shelley: The Major Works* (Oxford World's Classics). Oxford University Press, 2003.

Smith

Curran, Stuart, ed. *The Poems of Charlotte Smith.* Oxford University Press, 1993.

Williams

There does not seem to be a modern edition of Helen Maria Williams' poems. Her poem "To Dr. Moore" may be found in Andrew Ashfield, ed., *Romantic Women Poets 1770–1838.* Manchester University Press, 1995. See also Neil

Fraistat and Susan S. Lanser, eds., *Letters Written in France*. Peterborough, Ontario: Broadview Press, 2001.

Wordsworth

Gamer, Michael and Dahlia Porter, eds. *Lyrical Ballads: 1798 and 1800*. Peterborough, Ontario: Broadview Press, 2008. Well annotated, with reviews and other contextual material in the back.

Gill, Stephen, ed. *William Wordsworth: The Major Works* (including *The Prelude*) (Oxford World's Classics). Oxford University Press, 2008.

Levin, Susan M., ed. *Dorothy Wordsworth* (Longman Cultural Edition). New York: Pearson Longman, 2009. Contains selections from her journals, which often prompted her brother to write a poem, as well as poems of her own.

Wordsworth, Jonathan, M. H. Abrams, and Stephen Gill, eds. *The Prelude: 1799, 1805, 1850* (Norton Critical Edition). New York: W. W. Norton, 1979. Drafts and fragments and critical essays in the back. Also good is Jonathan Wordsworth, ed., *The Prelude: The Four Texts (1798, 1799, 1805, 1850)*. Harmondsworth: Penguin, 1995.

Criticism

The Cambridge Introductions to Literature series includes titles on Coleridge and Wordsworth (see the back of this book for the full list of titles).

The Cambridge Companions to Literature series includes titles on Blake, Byron, Coleridge, Keats, Shelley, and Wordsworth, as well as on British Romantic Poetry, (British) Romanticism, and English Literature 1740–1830. The titles are all collections of essays by different scholars. Though not exactly introductions, many of the essays in them will be helpful to readers new to their subjects.

Also helpful is Duncan Wu, ed., *A Companion to Romanticism* (Oxford: Blackwell, 1998), with over fifty short essays by various scholars.

Abrams, M. H. *Natural Supernaturalism: Tradition and Revolution in Romantic Literature*. New York: W. W. Norton, 1971. A very important work, not to be missed. Centered on Wordsworth, it compares English and German Romantic themes and plots with each other and with their ultimate sources in Christian and Platonic philosophy.

Backgrounds and contexts

Bainbridge, Simon, ed. *Romanticism: A Sourcebook*. Basingstoke: Palgrave Macmillan, 2008. A collection of key documents of the Romantic period about such areas as the French Revolution, women, the slave trade, science, and religion.

Butler, Marilyn. *Romantics, Rebels, and Reactionaries: English Literature and its Background, 1760–1830*. Oxford University Press, 1982.

Ferber, Michael. *Romanticism: A Very Short Introduction*. Oxford University Press, 2010. A brief account of the Europe-wide Romantic movement in literature, philosophy, music, and painting.

Ford, Boris, ed. *The Romantic Age in Britain*. Vol. VI of *The Cambridge Cultural History*. Cambridge University Press, 1992. Sections on literature, fine arts, music, architecture, and other topics.

Gaull, Marilyn. *English Romanticism: The Human Context*. New York: W. W. Norton, 1988. Chapters on the literary marketplace, children's literature, the theater, the Gothic, painting, science, and other topics.

Moore, Jane and John Strachan. *Key Concepts in Romantic Literature*. Basingstoke: Palgrave Macmillan, 2010.

Index

Cambridge Introductions to...

Authors

Margaret Atwood Heidi Macpherson

Jane Austen Janet Todd

Samuel Beckett Ronan McDonald

Walter Benjamin David Ferris

Chekhov James N. Loehlin

J. M. Coetzee Dominic Head

Samuel Taylor Coleridge John Worthen

Joseph Conrad John Peters

Jacques Derrida Leslie Hill

Charles Dickens Jon Mee

Emily Dickinson Wendy Martin

George Eliot Nancy Henry

T. S. Eliot John Xiros Cooper

William Faulkner Theresa M. Towner

F. Scott Fitzgerald Kirk Curnutt

Michel Foucault Lisa Downing

Robert Frost Robert Faggen

Nathaniel Hawthorne Leland S. Person

Zora Neale Hurston Lovalerie King

James Joyce Eric Bulson

Thomas Mann Todd Kontje

Christopher Marlowe Tom Rutter

Gabriel Garcia Marquez Gerald Martin

Herman Melville Kevin J. Hayes

Milton Stephen B. Dobranski

George Orwell John Rodden and John Rossi

Sylvia Plath Jo Gill

Edgar Allan Poe Benjamin F. Fisher

Ezra Pound Ira Nadel

Marcel Proust Adam Watt

Jean Rhys Elaine Savory

Edward Said Conor McCarthy

Shakespeare Emma Smith

Shakespeare's Comedies Penny Gay

Shakespeare's History Plays Warren Chernaik

Shakespeare's Poetry Michael Schoenfeldt

Shakespeare's Tragedies Janette Dillon

Harriet Beecher Stowe Sarah Robbins

Mark Twain Peter Messent

Edith Wharton Pamela Knights

Walt Whitman M. Jimmie Killingsworth

Virginia Woolf Jane Goldman

William Wordsworth Emma Mason

W. B. Yeats David Holdeman

Topics

American Literary Realism Phillip Barrish

The American Short Story Martin Scofield

Anglo-Saxon Literature Hugh Magennis

Comedy Eric Weitz

Creative Writing David Morley

Early English Theatre Janette Dillon

Eighteenth-Century Poetry John Sitter

English Theatre, 1660–1900 Peter Thomson

Printed in Great Britain
by Amazon

80948660R00149